ADVANCE PRAISE

"A fantastic look at insight and creativity through a collection of ideas, quotes and theories posited by lots of well-known thinkers. Packed with entertaining industry anecdotes, many of which you probably haven't heard. Every time you dip into this book you will find something new to pique your interest."
Andy Fernandez, Bookshop and Library Manager, The Chartered Institute of Marketing

"It's the sort of book you need a seat belt for. Your Inspiratorium journey is a densely-packed world of insights, worldly wisdom and delightful detours of discovery to inspire the creative within you. Tas has a brain the size of a planet and is a true guiding star for your inspiration."
Andy Green, Director, Grow Social Capital

"A pick and mix of ideas, quotes and insightful thoughts. If you don't know the question it doesn't really matter, read it anyway. I aspire to the versatility of the fox."
Hazel Kay, Marketing and Admissions Director, ACS International Schools

"The Inspiratorium World created in this book is like a museum where the reader is a visitor and Tas is your guide. Overall, this book bursts with insightful content and imaginative expression, all with a light emotional touch. Highly recommended for anyone who works in business and communication."

Katie Zhou, Managing Director, MetaThink Strategic & Innovation Consultancy, Shanghai

"To call this a book would be too one-dimensional. It is more like a collage in a world tour of history, people, thoughts and maverick outsiders: a whirlwind of thoughts and ideas that leaves you wondering and challenging your own stereotypes."

Pieter Twine, General Manager Loyalty and MySchool at Woolworths, South Africa

"*The Inspiratorium* is an adventure for the mind and soul. It's a great study in how to meld the arts and sciences together in a way that makes magic. *The Inspiratorium* is so different from a typical business book in that, instead of giving a prescribed framework that is then regurgitated over and over again, it piques your interest in ideas and how to make new and interesting connections. Honestly, I've been waiting and looking for a book like this for a long time. Thank you for curating and pulling together such an excellent resource."

Krista Bradley, Senior Research Manager, Microsoft

"*The Inspiratorium* liberated me from process and logic and gave me permission to think freely. It pulls apart human behaviour and the need for the safety of numbers, logic and 'safe' business processes. It takes the reader from Game Of Thrones to Asterix via Black Sabbath and the Sugababes, while covering subjects from Philosophy to Neuroscience and Ancient Greek to Finnish reindeer. It's a playfully eclectic, thoughtful and intelligent provocation, teeming with humour (Coup de Grace ...French for lawnmower :)) and beautifully written to boot."
Peter Haigh, CEO, Mintel

"As inspiring as an Inspiratorium should be. Filled with provocations, prompts and great stories to stimulate how to think differently when searching for new insight, connections and possibilities. Drawing from a vast pool of unexpected sources, from movies to the classics, this is – as described – a veritable 'collide-a-scope' of ideas and stories, which inspires new ways of thinking and approaching discovery."
Bettina MacCarvill, Partner, Jump! Innovation

"In his introduction to this engaging compendium of eclectica, Tas quotes an ancient Greek poet who told us: 'A fox knows many things, but a hedgehog [just] one big thing.' As a sometime hedgehog and would be fox I found this white-knuckle dash though the arcane and the recondite both fascinating and exhilarating."
David Penn, Managing Director, Conquest Research

Published by
LID Publishing Limited
The Record Hall, Studio 204,
16-16a Baldwins Gardens,
London EC1N 7RJ, UK

524 Broadway, 11th Floor, Suite 08-120,
New York, NY 10012, US

info@lidpublishing.com
www.lidpublishing.com

A member of:

BPR
Business Publishers Roundtable

www.businesspublishersroundtable.com

© Anthony Tasgal, 2018
© LID Publishing Limited, 2018

Printed and bound by Clays Ltd
ISBN: 978-1-911498-46-9

Cover and Page design: Caroline Li

ANTHONY TASGAL

THE
INSPIRATORIUM

A SPACE FOR THE CURIOUS

LONDON   NEW YORK   SHANGHAI
MADRID   BARCELONA   BOGOTA
MEXICO CITY MONTERREY   BUENOS AIRES

CONTENTS

For Roman and Betty

INTRODUCTION

Welcome to the Inspiratorium. A place like no other. A book, an online space and (hopefully) a conceptual framework besides.

A compendium of curiosity, where ideas come to meet, grow, evolve and flourish.

A Petri dish for insight and inspiration. A space that relishes its position on the boundary of domains.

The book is crammed full of thinkers, their thoughts and their distilled wisdom, to help you develop and accelerate yours.

It is a cross-cultural, interdisciplinary cornucopia of inputs that may generate idiosyncratic and unexpected outputs in each different reader.

Be prepared to dip in and dip out freely as you set off on your journey of serendipitous connections and inspiration.

A HOME FOR FOXES, NOT HEDGEHOGS?

Let's start by taking a trip back to ancient Greece, a place we will be visiting with some degree of regularity.

Archilochus was a lyric poet of the 7th century BCE, and was considered by the ancient commentators to be worthy of being mentioned in the same breath as Hesiod and Homer. Most of his work is now lost, but some tantalizing fragments remain. One is an epigram:

———————

A fox knows many things,
but a hedgehog [just] one big thing.

———————

The 20th century philosopher Isaiah Berlin used this as the basis for an essay, largely about the Russian novelist, Lev Tolstoy. But what he built on it was more insightful and enduring: he constructed a metaphorical spectrum on which to locate great thinkers.

For Berlin, a hedgehog is the deviser and protector of "one big idea", a unique lens through which to view and understand the world; he includes the likes of Plato, Nietzsche and Proust in this category.

These days we might add Freud (whose big idea is the existence and power of the unconscious), Marx (the role and potential of class) or Darwin (the theory of evolution by natural selection). Present-day examples include Richard Dawkins (the gene-centred view of evolution), Thomas Piketty (the distribution of money) or even Malcolm Gladwell (the importance of the unconscious and of outliers).

The dream of the hedgehog is what scientists call a GUT or a TOE (for some reason, body parts loom large in the imagery of cosmologists and physicists): a 'Grand Unified Theory' or a 'Theory Of Everything'.

This was the dream of the likes of Einstein and those who sought to reconcile quantum physics and relativity.

If hedgehogs are top-down seekers of the one big idea, foxes, on the other hand, are more eclectic and less reductionist. For Berlin, this meant anyone from Aristotle to Shakespeare to James Joyce.

I like to think of this book as a space for foxes: those scrappy, eclectic hunters who thrive on working from the bottom up, building nests and thoughts from the nuances, nudges and incidental insights they find.

THINKING OUTSIDE THE FOX

Berlin's metaphor has survived and thrived in Darwinian fashion. He has many heirs who have adopted his idea.Philip E. Tetlock, Professor of Political Psychology at the University of Pennsylvania, used Berlin's hedgehog–fox spectrum to explore the success rates of experts and forecasters. The psephologist and forecaster Nate Silver also used the spectrum, with reference to Tetlock, in his book *The Signal and the Noise*. Indeed, Silver loved the idea of being a fox so much that he used it as the logo of his political blog, fivethirtyeight.com.

When discussing foxes, we ought to mention the soccer team responsible for one of the biggest sporting shocks in recent memory.

England's Leicester City Football Club has various nicknames, the Filberts and the Fossils being the best known locally. But to most they are the Foxes, based on the fact that fox hunting has a long history within Leicestershire. The club's motto is "Foxes never quit" and, at one point, the club was sponsored appropriately by a company named Fox Leisure.

A team that had come close to relegation from the English Premier League, and were 5,000-1 outsiders to win it, somehow managed the extraordinary feat of holding off big-spending football aristocrats such as Manchester City, Arsenal, Chelsea and Manchester United to win the championship in the 2015-16 season. Short of bringing Elvis and the Loch Ness monster on as substitutes, the outcome could hardly have been more unlikely.

The Foxes' feat of rampant improbability chimes poorly with the city's motto "Semper eadem" (always the same). This was also the motto of Queen Elizabeth I and, as she gave a Royal Charter to the city, Leicester presumably decided to honour her in return.

But, in these days of remorseless change and a presiding notion of adaptability and flux, it feels almost quaint that someone, somewhere, still flies the flag for stasis and inertia – or, to put a more positive spin on it (as a mainstream retailer might), reliability and reassurance.

So, this is a book for the foxes out there, those prepared for flux and the unexpected. Let's start by setting up some guidelines.

A PAEAN TO SERENDIPITY:
HOW TO EXPLORE THE INSPIRATORIUM

We've already flitted between the poles of science and art, quantum physics and epic poetry, philosophy and football. If this feels to you like the sort of material that provokes, inspires and creates new thoughts – well, read on.

But how are you meant to use (not just 'read') this book?

Here are a few ways to navigate the Inspiratorium:

- Think of it as a random-access storehouse of quotations, aphorisms, musings, vignettes and stories to peruse, reuse and absorb.
- Explore it as you might a spider's web of connections, of jumps and leaps that will take you to different places that will intrigue and inspire. It should feel challenging, quirky and eclectic, and create expanded possibilities.
- Think of it as a space based on the principles of integration and constructivism, of synthesis and collective innovation, rather than reductionism.
- Consider it as partly a mosaic of meaning, partly a mini-encyclopaedia, which doesn't just outline its topics but seeks to subvert and invent.
- Become your own DJ, mixing together a giddying symphony of quotes, utterances and epiphanies, a mash-up of hybrid samples and insightful riffs.
- Or perhaps treat it as a series of 'insight capsules' to be taken as and when needed (and don't operate any heavy machinery while doing so).

- If this doesn't feel exciting, ambitious, captivating, heartfelt, playful and fun… then this is not the place for you.
- If you want to adopt a position, brace yourself for the juxtaposition.
- Make yourself open to randomness, serendipity and spontaneity.
- Intoxication is to be encouraged; it is perfectly permissible to feel overwhelmed by layers of complexity and fidgety contradiction.
- Observe above the door the following motto: "If it ain't broke, break it." Make that leap into the unknown.

THE PATH TO INSIGHTMENT

Let me give you a brief guided tour of the Inspiratorium.

It is composed of some 300 individual items and stories. They are distributed between different rooms.

On the ground floor, you will find the plans, the keys and the guidebook for the Inspiratorium.

Having found your way around the place, you can move up to the first floor, to the Parlour Room, where you can tour a wealth of inspiration and anecdotes about words, meanings and language.

On the next floor up is the Science Lab, where the stories, heroes and learnings will have a more scientific bent. And on the third floor you will find a series of tales which cater more to the arts.

Finally, before you exit through the gift shop, you will find a concluding message to take with you as you leave.

But, in line with the philosophy of the Inspiratorium, all these stories will overlap, intermingle and (hopefully) form new links and ideas in your mind as you progress through the building.

So, let us begin.

GROUND FLOOR:
RECEPTION

0

1. THE INSIGHT ROOM

You're not thinking, you're just being logical.
– PHYSICIST, DAVID BOHM

FROM INSIGHT TO INSPIRATION

'Insight' has become something of a Holy Grail in the marketing and communications world. Over the last few years the topic of insight – how to identify it and how to implement it – has ranged from being central to every brand and research manager's agenda, to being passé or even, according to some dissenters, as dead as a doornail.

In many ways, insight has become no more than a rebranding or reframing of creativity, used to distinguish ordinary creativity from the kind that applies only to 'creatives', here defined as people with any combination of stubble, tattoos and interesting spectacles.

It is easy to think that insight just comes from trying really hard, pushing and insisting that it will come if you just...

But it is a mistaken assumption that insights are simply facts with better PR: it is not as though people just cough them up or statistics identify them as insights without assistance. Insight, it seems, reaches further and deeper than any logical recipe.

Equally, there are those who think that insight can be achieved through business as usual: that something radical, unexpected and creative will come from more of the same. Or, conversely, that insight is the result of a wondrous miracle, perhaps bestowed on lucky recipients by magic elves while we sleep.

I prefer to believe that we can prepare ourselves to generate insights, even if we are not called 'creatives' and do not work in London's Shoreditch or New York's Greenwich Village.

HERE COMES THE NIGHT-TIME

I prefer to avoid getting too bogged down in the semantics at this stage (I am only delaying – that will come soon), but I often find that thinking of insight by way of analogy is more helpful, as insight can some-times be distinguished more for what it does than what it is.

So, gather your popcorn – we're off to the movies.

M. Night Shyamalan is a movie director who burst onto the screen with *The Sixth Sense*. This carefully constructed mystery was elegantly written, acted and directed and had a quotable epigraph to go with it – "I see dead people" – spoken by the young and suit-ably creepy Haley Joel Osment. But what gave it the word-of-mouth buzz was its shock ending, which I will not reveal here to protect the sensibilities of the few people who have not seen it yet. The unexpected twist became something of a leitmotif for the director, a trick he played again in *Unbreakable* and *The Village*.

Though his career has drifted rather since, the Shyamalan effect for me is a metaphor for what makes a good insight: not so much an 'Aha!', more an 'I-didn't-see-that-coming' effect, followed by, 'Oh yes, of course! Why didn't I see that?' The director builds up a storyline only to pull the rug out from underneath the viewer's expectations.

HUMOUR: 'AHA' FROM 'HA-HA'

Analysing humour is like dissecting a frog.
Few people are interested and the frog dies.
– AMERICAN HUMORIST, E. B. WHITE

It is always awkward to try to investigate the roots of humour.

———

Two goldfish are in a tank. One says to the other "How do you drive this thing?"

———

That same moment of rug-pulling recognition that can generate insight also operates in the context of humour. The linear narrative, so beloved of the brain's interpreter module, gets its comeuppance in a way that is both surprising and rewarding.

13

One definition of humour looks at the punchline as a calculated precipitating event that triggers a restructuring – a twist, or a surprise ending, where the story of what has happened before is given a sharp jerk as the new structure is revealed.

The English comedian and writer Richard Herring explains: "Most jokes are based on surprise. They take advantage of a confusion of language, or a twist in logic, or a contradiction of some perceived truth."

The magician Teller – half of the double act Penn and Teller – puts it elegantly, when talking about the secret of a good trick:

———

It is rather like a joke. There is a logical, even if nonsensical, progression to it. When the climax of a trick is reached, there is a little explosion of shivery pleasure when what we see collides with what we know about physical reality.

———

But why do we find humour so universally appealing? I would argue that it is because comedy (satire, especially) has always reflected so much universal human truth; after all, in English we use the word 'wit' in both senses, to mean intelligence and humour.

IT'S NOT THE WINNING, IT'S THE TAKING APART

According to Sir Isaac Newton, the art of grasping connections is essentially a matter of putting different pieces together, escaping rigid compartmentalization and seeing new orders, or patterns, emerging. This is not dissimilar to the philosopher Ludwig Wittgenstein's observation that new insights emerge through rearrangements of what you already know.

Insight connects fields, forms and patterns: we often gain new insights from new arrangements, not new data. This is an observation that needs to be made forcefully to anyone who works with data, especially those who believe that quantity is everything. 'No', say Wittgenstein and Newton, arrangement, structure and point of view are what count in creating novelty of thought and implementation.

The cognitive theorist Douglas Hofstadter coined an expression for what we are effectively describing here. He called it 'JOOTSing' – Jumping Out Of The System – referring to the point when looking dubiously at what is there, then pulling back, causes something new and different to emerge.

Sometimes this is less like an 'Aha!' and more like a 'That's funny!'

The most exciting phrase to hear in science, the one that heralds new discoveries, is not "Eureka!" but "That's funny."
– SCIENCE FICTION WRITER, ISAAC ASIMOV

SOMETHING I JUST THREW TOGETHER

Another way of looking at insight is to see it as essentially concerned with making new connections, seeing things differently by throwing things together.

For that reason, the etymology of the word 'symbol' is itself significant.

It originates in the Greek word *symbolon*, with a meaning rooted in 'to throw together'.

Originally, it referred to a token or tally that could be used as a way of proving identity. The token was split or broken, the two parts were given to different individuals, and only when they were properly reunited could the parties be truly identified.

The Greeks, being almost always at war and especially with one another, were very interested in spying, messages and cryptography

The Spartans, for example, developed an early form of cipher system called the *scytale*.

This was a staff around which a strip of leather or parchment was wound; the message was written on this and then unwound, leaving what would appear to be a meaningless series of letters. Only when the receiver was equipped with a scytale of the same diameter could he decode it.

Insight works in a similar way: when we can put two parts together to reveal a whole, there is an integration, an 'Aha!' of completion.

INCUBATING INSIGHT: THE 'I'S HAVE IT

Theorists of creativity are clear about the various stages that occur before the grand dénouement that is insight.

The process of creative thinking that I am about to discuss goes back to 1926.

Graham Wallas, an English social psychologist and one of the founders of the London School of Economics, expounded the theory in a book called *The Art of Thought*.

In his four-stage system, the bookends of insight are immersion and illumination.

Stage 1, Immersion, is well known to all of us as we prepare a presentation, document or any form of analysis. We locate the domain we are seeking to understand and immerse ourselves fully in as much data and information as we can ingest. But immersion is never enough and neither is expertise. Many argue that too much expertise and experience can be a barrier to innovation, and that an attitude of failure-friendliness is supportive of innovation. Take the words of Danish physicist and architect of the Copenhagen Interpretation, Niels Bohr: "An expert is someone who has made all the mistakes that can be made in a narrow field."

Immersion in the aquatic sense was also key to Archimedes, wallowing in his bath in the 3rd century: he realized that the way to solve the problem set for him by King Hiero of Syracuse, about whether the king's crown was pure gold or not, was related to the water he displaced when he jumped in the bath – hence his

17

famous, though possibly apocryphal, cry "Eureka!" – I have found it!

Stage 3 – that of Illumination (the moment of insight) – is equally easy to define: the angelic eureka of illumination that is the final stop on the journey to creative enlightenment.

I will omit the fourth and last stage, Verification, as it tends to act merely as the rubber stamp to insight, rather than making a positive contribution. It also irritatingly destroys the elegant alliteration of all those imaginative and intuitive 'I'-words. In Wallas's original model, there was also a preliminary stage called 'intimation', which described the feeling that something important was on its way.

But where, you may ask, is Stage 2? I am coming to that.

EXPERTISE AND IMMERSION

Often, we become overly reliant on the immersion process to generate the longed-for 'blue-sky thinking'. There is a long-held love of brainstorming in the business world, especially in order to generate exactly this kind of cutting-edge thinking. But a large body of evidence suggests that brainstorms are inadequate in the pursuit of radical novelty if they rely purely on immersion (Stage 1).

All too often, I suspect, the brainstorm is devoted to data 'dumping' and 'sharing', rather than the process of creative thinking and incubation.

'Incubation' is the technical term for that crucial second stage in Wallas's theory.

This key process describes how the unconscious mind gets on with the business of heavy lifting without any conscious awareness or involvement.

Incubation is the feeling recognized by all creative thinkers (I obviously include scientists here) that there is a need to acknowledge that immersion is not enough in itself.

Here is another instance where we have to abandon any idea of a linear, causal effect between input and output.

BED, BATH, BUS AND BEYOND

Some experts in creativity theory even argue that too much prior knowledge can in fact hinder the process of generating radical new insights. This, they believe, is down to the fact that the deliberative rational processes are more likely to follow well-known paths, or ruts, in which thinking becomes entrenched and fixated. Escaping the grip of these *idées fixes*, these mental ruts, is one of the primary goals of incubation.

This oh-so-crucial Stage 2 is all too often ignored or underestimated. Incubation means allowing the immersion process to boil and bubble, before it is stirred and simmered, to permit new connections and patterns to be forged by the unconscious.

Perhaps the fact that it happens below our conscious radar is the reason why this mental meandering or 'mystery time' is so often taken for granted, minimized or dismissed by paid-up defenders of the rational, linear status quo.

But the evidence is clear: to derive new patterns, ideas and links, the unconscious must be allowed to stimulate new alliances, considerations and 'gestalts' that restructure what was obtained by immersion into something that JOOTS.

This preconscious recombination, by definition, cannot be forced by the reflective mind but needs suggestive relationships to be generated spontaneously, and so has to be given free rein in its own time and manner.

The Incubation approach to insight can best be summed up as the 'bed, bath, bus' route to insight, referring to the typical moments when the results of incubation are fed through to the conscious and the 'Aha!' bell rings, flooding us with a blissfully transcendent certainty.

When one is resting, and thinking about other things or nothing much at all, when the conscious mind is occupied with getting off a bus or taking an Archimedean bath – these seem to be the best moments to let the unconscious off the leash, to take the handbrake off those unseen constraints.

This is what I hope the Inspiratorium will do for you as you peruse and ingest its contents.

Πυθαγόρας
Pythagóras

Ἀρχιμήδης
Archimedes

COLLISIONS AND COMBINATIONS

Abrupt cross-cuts and transitions from one idea to another … the most unheard of combinations of elements, the subtlest associations of analogy.
– AMERICAN PSYCHOLOGIST, WILLIAM JAMES

Ideas rose in crowds. I felt them collide until pairs interlocked … making a stable combination.
– FRENCH MATHEMATICIAN AND THINKER, HENRI POINCARÉ

Never in the field of [the inventor's] consciousness do combinations appear that are not really useful.
– HENRI POINCARÉ

Darwin was one of many to describe this process: "I can remember the very spot on the road, whilst in my carriage, when to my joy the solution occurred to me."

This is not to deny the role of immersion, or the need for preparation (the 'prepared mind' is what fortune favours, according to the cliché.) There may even be hours of practice involved, in accordance with the oft-repeated claim that experts or geniuses need 10,000 hours of their chosen discipline to master it.

Anyone who has worked with creative people knows that very often they have no monopoly on understanding what is their deepest insight, or their greatest idea: sometimes they are too close to it and the cool view of an outsider is required. The science seems to show that another blind Darwinian process of variation and selection is involved, where a small nugget, the merest stripling of a detail, can combine with another to forge a relationship that builds a mighty and impressive edifice of originality.

This represents another nail in the coffin for linear, deliberative thinking. Most commentators agree that the actual moment of illumination tends not to appear gradually, but like an immediate burst of light without precedent, like the magician's rabbit emerging from the hat intact, where everything falls into place without any clear sense of what led up to the grand finale.

A SHOCK TO THE CISTERN

The role of art shares much of its manifesto with that of creativity and originality in general: to generate the 'shock of the new', to encourage strangeness and violate conventions. The French call it *épater la bourgeoisie* (to shock the middle class out of their complacency).

One poll that did its fair share of middle-class 'shocking' asked curators and art critics to choose what they considered to be the most influential piece of modern art of the 20th century. It wasn't Matisse's *Red Studio* (fifth) or Picasso's *Guernica* (fourth), nor was it Warhol's *Marilyn Diptych* (third) or even Picasso's *Demoiselles d'Avignon* (runner-up).

Ladies and Gentlemen, the winner was... Marcel Duchamp's *Fountain* from 1917.

Better known as the urinal that Duchamp signed and put in a gallery, it was indeed a shock to the system (or cistern) but blazed a path of ready-mades and demonstrated that art could be made from the banal.

Duchamp also prefigured much of the emerging theory about semiotics, and what is now sometimes reduced to 'engagement' and 'co-creation', not to mention conceptual art and the hegemony of the idea over the execution: "The creative act is not performed by the artist alone; the spectator brings the work in contact with the external world by deciphering and interpreting its inner qualifications and thus adds his [*sic*] contribution to the creative act."

JUXTAPOSE FOR A MOMENT

The Dada avant-garde art movement of the early 20th century and the manifestos of Surrealism and Cubism placed greater emphasis on the generation of novelty through juxtaposition.

Think of Magritte, Dalí or the comment from one of Surrealism's main mouthpieces, André Breton, who defined the movement he helped to found as "pure psychic automatism". As such, it represented a rebellion against what was seen as rather po-faced, heavy-handed and adult, in favour of spontaneity and playful childishness.

"The man that cannot visualize a horse galloping on a tomato is an idiot," wrote Breton. This playfulness helps to explain why the Surrealists themselves often had jobs in the advertising business, and why the ad and design industries remain fascinated to this day with the likes of Magritte and Dalí.

The contemporary Mexican artist Gabriel Orozco has a gorgeous way of putting this sense of art as enrichment: "Really great art regenerates the perception of reality: the reality becomes richer."

This explains in part Stalin's rather, well, Stalinist definition of artists as "engineers of the soul".

Before ending this artistic detour, let me articulate that in art, film and culture, the playful, rebellious and oblique examination of reality and search for novelty create a sense of anarchic insurgency that is all too human and, consequently, in our business world of pragmatic determinism, is all too often swept under the rug of rationality.

THE ESI FILES: COMBINATORIAL SERENDIPITY AND OPPORTUNISTIC ASSOCIATION

The secret of successful incubation is to create many opportunities to stimulate the unconscious power of linkage by applying the power of chance.

There are two concepts that I want to bring together here to show how important this issue is for insight and originality.

The first, using a term which I shall borrow from the body of insight research, is External Serendipitous Influence (ESI).

ESI stirs up the calm sea of problem-solving with some disruptive and seemingly irrelevant perturbations.

It gives dignity to the notion of 'chance': scientists give chance its due role. Chance, said the German physicist Max Born, is a more fundamental conception than causality, while Francis Crick (one of the two strands of the Double Helix) claimed it was the only real source of novelty.

DICE, DICE, BABY

In art, which we have already touched on earlier, the principle of the random or 'aleatory' (from the Latin *alea*, 'dice') is well known.

The aleatory was part of the Dada and Surrealist manifestos. More recently, the musician and theorist John Cage was a notable exponent. He used the Chinese I-Ching, originally conceived as a tool for divination, as a tool for making music by chance. For one piece, for example, Cage selected the duration, tempo and dynamics based on the I-Ching.

The painter Gerhard Richter similarly used random choices, chance and ready-mades to create his first series of Colour Chart paintings. He later introduced chance selection by numbering colours and pulling them out of a hat.

Richter said, "What interests me most about these works is that chance does it better than I can, but I have to prepare the conditions to allow randomness to do its work."

Combinatorial playfulness is also *de rigueur* to promote insight and imagination in a world where collage, montage and bricolage, riffs, cover versions, reimaginings, reboots, sampling and palimpsests are evident across most art forms.

This is the true font of inspiration and insight.

A STORY OF ENO-VATION

We cannot look at the power of guided chance without mentioning Brian Eno.

A personal introduction...

In 1972, 1 was recovering from a break-up. Not mine – 1 was far too shy, and immersed in Homer and Cicero. No, the Beatles had broken up in 1970 and all of us who were clinging on to the coat-tails of the late 60s (too young to be hippies) were desolate and aimless. The Fab Four were, even then, acknowledged to be The Greatest Band That Had Ever Lived And Probably Ever Would, and their dissolution was far more relevant to me then than that of the monasteries in mid-16th century English history. The emergence of Yoko Ono and Wings didn't seem to be quite enough in the way of consolation.

Then, in September 1972, 1 was listening to the radio and heard a track that dramatically changed my life. It was "Virginia Plain" by Roxy Music, and from the deceptively quiet start, through the glamorous lyrics and Brian Eno's fluttering synthesizers, 1 became obsessed with Bryan Ferry and Brian Eno in the way that only a teenage boy can be.

Eno, sadly, soon quit Roxy Music, giving me another break-up to recover from, which 1 did by purchasing his solo albums and following his interest in ambient music.

SAME AS IT EVER WAS

My pursuit continued as Eno began collaborating with other like-minded mavericks, such as David Bowie (Eno is on the backing vocals to "Heroes") and David Byrne (and his band Talking Heads, notably on the track "Once in a Lifetime"), as well as the film director David Lynch, before producing albums for the rather more mainstream U2 and Coldplay.

The title track of Eno's third studio album, "Another Green World", has been used as the theme music for the BBC arts programme *Arena* for over 30 years, and still is to this day.

He also created the start-up music for Windows 95 (ironically on a Mac), and has curated art exhibitions and worked on mobile apps and video games.

All this from someone who has claimed from the start to be a non-musician – another example, as we shall see, of the power of the outsider.

Then there is the *Father Ted* connection. A trivial detail is that Eno appeared as "Father Brian Eno" at the "It's Great Being a Priest!" convention, in the final episode of the Irish comedy series, "Going to America", broadcast in the UK in 1998 – an in-joke that caused me, at least, some mirth.

Most recently, Eno's eclectic progress saw him selected as Youth Affairs spokesman for the Liberal Democrats, the UK's third-largest political party.

OBLIQUE HOUSE

But beyond his musical influence and importance, Brian Eno's intellectual collaboration with the artist Peter Schmidt is especially significant.

In 1974, the two were working on Eno's second full solo album after his traumatic break with Roxy Music. During both the recording process and the writing of the lyrics, they gradually began to codify a set of working principles that they had both found useful in breaking creative gridlock.

From this, they devised a set of small prompt cards, the *Oblique Strategies: over one hundred worthwhile dilemmas* to jog their minds and jolt their patterns away from the dictates of working urgencies, the ruts of convention and, perhaps, the stresses of working with Phil Collins.

In particular, these cards offered a more tangential way of attacking problems than going at them head-on, by prompting the pair to try another approach or attitude.

Their first card read: "Honour thy error as a hidden intention."

Others included:

- What would your closest friend do?
- Are there sections? Consider transitions.
- Try faking it.

One in particular, whose remit extends beyond music, reads: "What to increase? What to reduce?"

This suggests that one of the fonts of creativity is not innovation as such, but rather the transformation of structure. Simplifying (down to an essence) is often the fastest way to explore a new direction or crystallize an existing one.

The legacy of *Oblique Strategies* remains: they were cited in Richard Linklater's 1991 movie *Slacker*, and one of the cards is referenced in REM's 1994 track "What's the Frequency, Kenneth?"

Like the aleatory approaches mentioned earlier, these cards embody the thinking of incubation and act as an external serendipitous influence system, one that deliberately invokes the fun and obliqueness of fortuitous experimentation.

Eno's *Oblique Strategies* are heartily recommended as a great tonic for those in need of unexpected direction and inspiration.

LIGHTS! ACTION! SERENDIPITY!

Some more examples of the power of combinatorial serendipity come from the film world.

Mel Brooks was asked how he came up with the idea of the film *The Producers*. His explanation shows just how novelty can be created by the juxtaposition of seemingly incompatible ideas:

I worked for a producer who wore a chicken-fat-stained homburg and a black alpaca coat. He pounced on little old ladies and would make love to them [NB *in the old-fashioned sense*]. They gave him money for his plays, and they were so grateful for his attention. Later on there were a couple of guys who

were doing flop after flop and living like kings. A press
agent told me, "God forbid they should ever get a hit,
because they'd never be able to pay off the backers!"
I coupled the producer with these two crooks and
– BANG! – there was my story.

———————

A more recent instance is *The Hunger Games* trilogy,
the wildly successful young-adult adventure series set
in a dystopian future. And by 'successful' I mean more
than 65 million sales across the trilogy and a film franchise that has been both critically lauded and equally
successful commercially, as well as making a star of
Jennifer Lawrence.

The author, Suzanne Collins, says the idea for the
concept came one evening when she was channel-
surfing between two very different genres of TV programme: one moment she was watching a reality
show competition, the next war coverage. "I was tired,
and the lines began to blur
in this very unsettling way."

From this fortuitous
collision, emerged the seed
of something special.

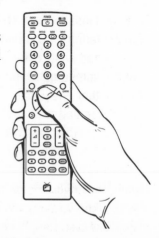

HORSES WITH ANTENNAE

Inspiration requires not just the unconscious, serendipity and chance; it needs constantly topping up.

In the words of screenwriter Charlie Kaufman:

————————

Allow yourself time, let things brew.
You're thinking about it, whether you realize it or not.
Letting the unconscious take over brings in freedom
and surprise and removes judgment.

————————

Kaufman uses the same language as Mel Brooks did, when he talks about how he came up with the idea(s) for *Being John Malkovich*, his breakthrough 1999 screenplay for Spike Jonze's movie, about which it is almost impossible not to use the word 'quirky'.

————————

Mmmm, I just wrote it. The germs were, I had this idea
that someone finds a portal into someone's head, and
then I had another idea that somebody has a story
about someone having an affair with a co-worker.
And neither one was going anywhere in my head, so
I just decided to see what happened if I combined
them. And then I just wrote it.

————————

Finally, the English writer Michael Morpurgo, now probably best known as the writer of the novel, and then stage play, *War Horse*, says: "The prerequisite for me is to keep my well of ideas full. This means living as full and varied a life as possible, to have my antennae out all the time."

So Brooks, Kaufman and Morpurgo are all unanimous in showing the enormous creative potential in seeking out unexpected combinations.

LEGO OF CONVENTIONS

Here is yet more proof that in order to succeed with new ideas and create meaning, there is no substitute for exposure to the widest variety of stimuli. It is highly likely that these will cross-pollinate under the natural force of incubation.

At a more playful level, serendipity is cited in many cases by the makers of 'brick films' using Lego bricks.

"Lego makes it a lot easier to throw things together," said veteran brick-film maker Chris Salt, who admitted that a moment of serendipity enabled him to make his big break:

One day at work someone brought a digital camera in that had some stop motion software on it and they were playing around with desktop toys and things. That caught my imagination and I just happened to have a box of old Lego from my parents' house lying around."

Now YouTube is bursting with amateur brick films, from movie 'homages' (*Star Wars*, *The Matrix*, *Indiana Jones* and *Shaun of the Dead*) to topical football moments (painfully, I recall the film that lovingly recreating Germany's 4-1 victory over England in the 2010 World Cup).

And, to top that, the Lego movies are now fast becoming a significant film franchise in themselves.

AN APOLOGY: ON PUNNING

Humour, wit and punning are a natural home for the making of connections. In this spirit, I wish to mount a vigorous defence of the pun, the exuberant form of wordplay that depends on multiple meanings of words, or on words that sound alike.

Plato's telling of his mentor Socrates' last days is the crux of *The Apologia*, which differs from the modern sense of 'apology' in one crucial sense: namely that this isn't an expression of regret. The original Greek meaning is rooted in the notion of defence and explanation, rather than admission of error and/or guilt.

Dryden went as far as saying that "A pun is the lowest and most grovelling form of wit." This is a most inexcusable slur on what I consider to be the King of the Linguistic Jungle, and something I wish to rectify here

– hence my Apologia for the pun.

As someone who has been known to favour this form of communication on very rare occasions, and having established that insight and pattern are key to creating meaning, I feel it is time both to launch a defence of the habit and to provide a cultural analysis of its history.

A pun is language on vacation.
– AMERICAN WRITER, CHRISTOPHER MORLEY
(CITED IN DAVID CRYSTAL, *LANGUAGE PLAY*)

This for me captures the essence of the poor, mistreated thing. A pun is an acceptable use of language, but one which has been subjected to a spin, a twist, a creative reframing in order to add another level of meaning to the dialogue. It can refer to other events, other cultures; it can be a form of jesting; a declaration of humour and intellect (remember that 'wit' itself shares both these meanings).

These days, when so much of the buzz across the 'Whole Wired World' is about networks, creativity and interrelatedness, what better symbol is there of the ability of the human mind to forge connections, engage creativity and transcend disparity than the humble pun?

Think, for instance, of the Danish Meister-Punner, musician and raconteur, Victor Borge. It is, surely, a very special brain that can take a seemingly innocuous expression and then, by sequentially adding 'one', create "Any two five eleven-nis?" ('Anyone for tennis?')

The pun is, indeed, mightier than the sword.

Socrates

A TURING POINT

And although it is usually portrayed as a jocular kind of beast, the pun can also be tender, thoughtful and sensitive.

What comes to mind for me here is the play *Breaking the Code* by Hugh Whitemore, based on the biography of Alan Turing, *Enigma*, written by Andrew Hodges.

Turing was a pioneer in mathematical logic who virtually founded computer science single-handedly in the 1930s, giving his name to the 'Turing machine' (an 'abstract machine' which exists only as a theoretical model) and to a test to identify the success of candidates for Artificial Intelligence. He later played a major role in the Allies' code-breaking effort in WWII, with many historians suggesting that his work helped shorten the war significantly.

Hodges's title plays on Turing's role in cracking the German 'Enigma' code at the cryptography unit at Bletchley Park, northwest of London. This story was also dramatized in Robert Harris's book *Enigma*, and more recently adapted for the silver screen in *The Imitation Game*.

But the book's title, *Breaking The Code*, also explicitly refers to Turing's homosexuality, which – despite his extraordinary efforts behind the scenes in the war effort – led to his persecution and eventual suicide after being hounded in the climate of postwar paranoia. The title of the stage version reflects even more deeply the emphasis on Turing's life as a hero-turned-misfit.

Only in 2013 was he posthumously pardoned.

WHO'S A-FREUD OF A PUN?

The dream has been used as a medium for interpreting puns for millennia. From the Egyptians who built many temples to Serapis, god of Dreams, to the *Oneirocritica* ('Interpretation of Dreams') of the late Roman writer Artemidorus, many have thought that dreams are in fact unconscious puns, concealing deeper meanings.

My own preferred Classical-military-pun story revolves around the English general Sir Charles Napier. Having served with distinction in the Napoleonic Wars, in 1841 he went to India, where he undertook the conquest of the (then) Indian province of Sind.

In the days of the short telegraph note, he could write back of his success in capturing Sind, using a single word of Latin: "Peccavi". For those not versed in Latin, let me explain that this is the first person singular of the perfect indicative of the verb *pecco*, 'I sin' (this has evolved into *pécher* in French and leaves an English footprint in the adjective *impeccable*, meaning 'beyond sin' or 'perfect).

So what Napier declared was "I have Sin(ne)d" – wonderful brevity, delicious wit and a clever means of displaying breeding and education.

JEU DE MOTS

The French call certain words *faux amis* (false friends): those that sound as though they mean something recognizable, but actually deceive you. So, *parent* can mean any relative, not just a parent; *pièce* can mean anything from a room to a play or a coin; and, ironically, *décevoir* means to disappoint (not to deceive). Sorry.

Just to confuse matters further (or add texture, depending on your viewpoint), language evolution creates different subspecies of language which, like Darwin's finches, evolve differently when separated by geographical distance. Take Cajun, a dialect of French used by locals in parts of Louisiana. It takes its name from the Acadians from Canada, French settlers who settled in the area now known as Nova Scotia in the 1600s before being exiled in the mid-18th century by the British. Over the next 30 years, several thousand of the exiled Acadians made their way to south Louisiana.

The Cajun website for Louisiana State University (available at http://www.lsu.edu/hss/french/undergrad-uate_program/cajun_french/faux_amis_cadiens.php) points out some of the errors you can make when trying to speak Cajun French. For instance, all Franco-phones know that *essence* (itself a *faux ami* for the English, being essentially different from what it appears) is French for 'petrol' (in the sense of gasoline). But in Cajun it means 'perfume' (the linkage of cars and sensuality seems to run deep across cultures).

Perhaps it is fitting to leave the last word with the French themselves. The pun is translated into French as *jeu de mots*, that is 'a game of or with words'. The very playfulness at the heart of the pun is appreciated by some people, it seems.

Then there is what I consider the meta-pun, the pun about punning.

Sadly, I can't recall where I heard this but I do think it rather special:

And finally, there was the person who sent ten different puns to his friends, with the hope that at least one of the puns would make them smile.
No pun in ten did.

So, can we please issue a lasting amnesty for those who pun: they are merely seeking to make new connections in the pursuit of insight.

WHEN INSIGHTS COME... [YES! YES! YES!]

Insight shows us things in a way we haven't seen; it forces a rethink and reappraisal.

We can all experience that tingle, that emotional jolt of surprise and shock that accompanies the 'Aha!' of revelation and recognition.

Alison Gopnik is a professor of psychology and affiliate professor of philosophy at University of California Berkeley, where she runs the Cognitive Development Lab. She specializes in the study of children's learning and development, and the broader philosophical and epistemological issues it raises.

I will spare you the details of 'the phenomenology of the theory formation system' here, but her insight is as elegant as it is mighty. A simple analogy: in the same way that we have a sex drive designed to help us reproduce and propagate our genes and engage in an evolutionarily beneficial activity (reproduction), we have a theory or explanatory drive that provokes our curiosity to find a suitable explanation.

Specifically, in what can only be called her seminal 1998 paper "Explanation as Orgasm", she drew a very particular analogy: that explanation is to cognition as orgasm is to reproduction.

Gopnik's hypothesis emphasized the link between the satisfaction of an orgasm as a reward for and spur to more sex, and the satisfaction of finding a good explanation as a spur to further exploration. So, curiosity gives us a 'hmm', while the 'agreeable feeling' (as it is rather quaintly described in some quarters) comes with the 'Aha!' The learning, the discovery, the insight becomes worthwhile (at the very least). Or, in science speak, explanation is the 'phenomenological mark of the fulfilment of an evolutionarily determined drive'.

But again, here we find an example where the arrow of causality may be misdirected. From an evolutionary perspective, the reason we reach orgasms and explanations is precisely to ensure that we go on making babies and more explanations.

So that's why finding things out, solving puzzles, developing theories... just feels good.

Anyone else need a lie down?

HOW QUAINT

We just referred to the word 'quaint', a word often used to mean twee, or delicate, old-fashioned, charming or picturesque – and now we have also dipped our wick (yes, I know) into matters sexual.

So let's continue with both these themes.

The word 'quaint' has a less than delicate heritage if we dig a bit further down into the etymological undergrowth.

Its first meaning, which seems antediluvian now, was actually 'cunning' or 'clever', from the Old French *cointe*. In this we can see its Latin roots showing: from the past participle, *cognitus*, of the verb *cognoscere* (to know), familiar to us in 'cognitive', 'cognition' and 'incognito' (see, for example, the wondrous book of that name by the annoyingly handsome neuroscientist and author, David Eagleman) – not to mention 'recognize', 'reconnaissance' and 'to acquaint'.

By the mid-14th century, it evolved into something like 'strange and clever', so it is still a while before our modern understanding of the term heaves into view.

Around the end of the 18th century, the meaning of 'old-fashioned but charming' is attested (as linguists say).

But – parental advisory – at some point the word was punned against, and its meanings crossed with another, more notorious term, obliquely (quaintly?) referred to from the 18th century as 'the monosyllable'.

In Middle English, that word was also being spelled 'queinte' or 'queynte'.

So, Geoffrey Chaucer, for example, in *The Canterbury Tales* (late 14th century) writes in 'The Miller's Tale', where Nicholas takes the direct route to seeking Alison's sexual favours:

———————

And privily he caught her by the queynte
And said "Ywis [surely], unless I have my will,
For dearest love of thee, leman [my love], I spill [die]."

———————

The word occurs too in 'The Wife of Bath's Tale' as one of a number of terms she deploys to describe the organ, as well as 'bele chose' (beautiful thing) and 'Chamber of Venus'. (I suspect this is one Harry Potter title we won't be seeing in the near future.)

[*And "spill" adds yet another layer of double entendre*]

COUNTRY MATTERS

As we may already know, Shakespeare had much pun-fun with the monosyllable (the C-word), but his play of choice was on 'country matters' in *Hamlet* and *Twelfth Night*. Even by the late 19th century the C-word was acceptable enough to be used in Sir Richard Burton's privately printed translation (no, not *that* Richard Burton) of *The Arabian Nights*.

Devotees of English topography will also tell you that the word was once a common feature in medieval English towns and villages.

Specifically, 'Gropec*nt Lane' was often found as a street name. At the time, many streets were named after the economic activity associated with them, so for areas where prostitutes plied their trade, this label thrived from at least 1230. And it existed in the Cheapside area of London at least until 1720, where various spellings were in use but Gropecount (*sic*) Lane was listed on the map, alongside two other streets: Bordhawelane (namely, 'bordello') and Puppekirty ('pokeskirt') Lane.

As tastes and tolerance changed, the name was excised or bowdlerized to Grope or (occasionally) Grape Lane. In Shrewsbury, county town of Shropshire, Grope Lane still exists as a faint testimony to its quaint history.

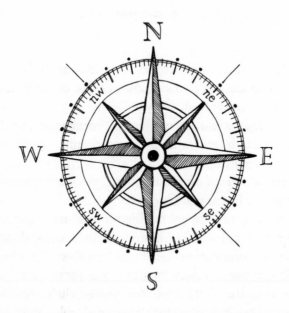

INSIGHTFUL EXAMPLE:
A MATTER OF LIFE AND DEATH

To encourage you to search out insightment, to find the explanatory orgasm, here are a few samples of insights that I have come across over the years.

I was doing some work with a pharmaceutical research company and I observed some doctors talking about what their work, their responsibilities, their hopes and frustrations were; I was also given copious documentation. In one of the reports I read, there was a verbatim (or direct quote) from a doctor:

It's either coffin or glory.

And there you have it: an entire world of analysis, feeling, experience and observation in one concentrated capsule of insight.

If insight acts as a compression mechanism, pause a moment to reflect on what can be unzipped from those six words.

The life of a doctor since the time of Hippocrates and his oath is about life and survival.

Doctors therefore find themselves making decisions that constantly place them in a quasi-divine situation (often, other healthcare professionals complain that doctors think they are gods, for this reason).

But at the sharp end, this doctor elucidates the binary opposition in a rational and yet deeply emotional sense too. There is no grey area – doctors either win

43

and achieve glory, victory, plaudits and approbation

... or it's the coffin.

A brutal simplicity perhaps, but one that clarifies, reduces and brings the meaning to the surface.

So, what do all these examples have in common?

They reveal that an insight feels good, because it has the explanatory power that Alison Gopnik characterizes so suggestively.

Seeing something new, seeing things afresh, opening up new vistas and possibilities culminating in a 'Yes! Yes! Yes!' moment can indeed bring some of the more bodily pleasures into play.

We tend to think that new ideas can be squeezed out by force of repetition, or sheer will, but incubation isn't like that: we need to be more playful, less scarred by the fear of failure and bunker mentality that leads to the relentless reiteration of the mundane that many of us have to tolerate in our work lives or in the personal sphere, where we may feel creatively undernourished.

INSIGHTMENT: AN INSIGHT RECIPE

I have used the word 'Insightment' for this process as it combines a number of features:

- It reeks of the verb 'to incite'. Often rather distractingly followed by 'a riot', this verb still carries within it the idea of provocation and direct action, elements that are so crucial to the discovery and implementation of insight. We should be able to conjure up images of flames being fanned, actions being triggered, the dormant being roused and the meek provoked.

- But it also reminds us of the sense of excitement that we should feel when a true insight emerges like the sword from the stone. Like any creative revelation, there should be an accompanying mood or emotion – of awe, of surprise, of wonderment – before the knee-jerk response of rational validation and verification kicks in.

So, my easy-to-prepare recipe for insight is as follows:

1. Three parts understanding: the immersion and preparation that fuels the engine and provides the raw material for linkage and association.
2. One part undetected news: trying to ensure that something new, some unprecedented angle or frame, can be introduced.

Then leave it to simmer in your subconscious. Read, think of other activities, let the incubation do its work and the ingredients fuse and blend.

3. Surprise: the final taste of insight can only be achieved if there is a surprise, or a shock of recognition that accompanies the discovery.
4. Actionability: much of the literature on the implications of insight has rightly emphasized that an insight without applicability is just an interesting observation. To be an insight it must have immediate relevance and commercial actionability. There is a difference between having an insight (or any good idea) and doing something with it.

LOSE THE JARGON

A short list of *verboten* terms follows. These are expressions that seem to work against insightment because they disguise, or indeed belie, the reality they purport to describe. Too often they condone and legitimise sloppy thinking, which obstructs innovation.

QSR

This stands for Quick Service Restaurant, which was chosen to avoid some of the less than flattering associations of 'fast food'. 'QSC and V' is a phrase that was seared and branded into my memory from when I used to work as an ad agency strategist in that market: 'quality, service, cleanliness and value'. This also goes to show that someone got the geolocation of cleanliness wrong, or that godliness didn't make the final cut. I remember feeling rather alarmed by this phrase as it seemed to have several shortcomings:

- In many cases, they are not necessarily all that quick, except in relation to traditional eat-in restaurants.
- Service is arguably not as relevant a factor for such establishments today as it was when Ray Kroc first built McDonald's into what it is.
- The biggest issue I had as a Brit (and I was also speaking for the UK consumer) was applying the word 'restaurant' to these brands. The culture and meaning surrounding the word was far more sedate, upmarket and special, and I always felt that 'restaurant' indicated a common self-delusion for this sector. It also

seemed indicative of a tendency among some brands and brand owners to aspiration-inflation: if we call ourselves 'restaurants' we will be able to compete on the same terms as the Michelin-starred establishments.

Too often, the very definition of the brand or sector in question becomes an accepted truth, an assumption that becomes ingrained and can only be shifted by a 60-degree boil wash. Those who realized that QSR was erroneous and misleading did start using expressions like 'casual dining', but even this phrase still fell foul of the euphemistic tendency. 'Dining' again has a semiotic undercurrent that is at odds with how the sector is seen in the UK.

CAR JARGON (CARGON?) AND MORE

The car sector used to have a bizarre way of defining its composition, from small and light (?) to medium and large. Despite the huge number of car launches and the fact that many of them have played on their boundary-crossing qualities – such as Ford's C-Max, S-Max and indeed Fusion, which boasts of 'the advantages of a robust larger car, combined with a compact car's road handling' – these sector definitions also impede insight as they simply don't reflect consumer reality.

The American term, 'full size' is equally perplexing to the onlooker.

CREDIT CARD

To me, this term feels both antiquated and closed in its opportunity for association. Cards are now so much more complicated, and compete with so many other products and services, that it becomes a barrier that chokes innovation. And don't even get me started on terms like 'revolve' as a synonym for credit, rather than 'charge card', referring to the ability to 'revolve' your money rather than having to pay it off at the end of each month. If you are trying to gain insight and 'disentrench', then losing dependence on terms like these (or, at the very least, burrowing into their roots) is key.

YELLOW FATS

Before it's time for my medication, let me just mention 'yellow fats'. Again, my objection is based to some extent on bitter experience: when I worked for what was then called the Butter Council, the manufacturers' unappetizing definition of butter, margarine and other spreads was 'yellow fats'.

Henry Ford

BLEND IT LIKE BECKHAM

And now a sort demonstration and exercise for you to try at home. It will help rid you of safe preconceptions and assumptions. I call it 'sector blending'.

This exercise works as follows:

1. Work out the conventions of market/person/ group A. What are its assumptions? How does it describe or distinguish itself?
2. Do the same for a different market/person/ group. This must be chosen to be as self-evidently different from A.
3. Now for the creative bit: to view sector A through the lens of sector B and vice versa, thereby deliberately forcing you to reconsider how you see a market, person or group, and how it is currently perceived.

As a not-entirely-serious demonstration of how this works in the marketing and branding world, here are a few examples of new brands and companies that have emerged during sector-blending workshops: see back for answers.

1. The search engine that will find you the yummiest chocolate dessert.
2. The Korean car manufacturer which has just announced the launch of an internet-enabled model that also doubles as a retailer of good-value, flat-pack furniture.
3. An operating system built in Scotland (and thus

served deep-fried in batter), which also sells pensions and investment products. Its graphic user interface features Bill Gates in a hood and billowing cape.

4. An adult ice cream and laundry detergent that builds on our fascination with body parts and live autopsies, on top of our desire for moral and physical hygiene.

5. The new perfume that is emitted as you pass posters or billboards.

IF IT AIN'T BROKE…

…then break it.

There are many times when we need to experience the liberation and awe of being able to tear apart a definition and blow it up to see what happens when we try to rebuild from the bottom up.

Graham Linehan, the Irish comedy writer – creator of *Father Ted* and more recently *The IT Crowd*, and co-writer of *Motherland* – talks about this when 're-imagining' a much-loved classic, *The Ladykillers*, which he adapted for the London stage in 2011:

———

In adapting – often but not always – you must first plant dynamite around the ground floor of the original. After the detonation, you keep what's still standing and bid farewell to the rest.

———

As a thought experiment, when you have that presentation or think-piece to prepare, or a new client to impress: take out your hammer, and chip, smash and rebuild your way to insightment and inspiration.

SPACE AND PLACE FOR INCUBATION

If we want to keep our antennae out, as the British writer Michael Morpurgo suggested, we can think about the sort of company and culture we want to nurture in order to make it happen.

Some places are renowned for their attitude to breeding creativity. Take the HQ (or campus) of Pixar, for example, in Emeryville, California. They have explicitly renounced the grey cubicle approach and created an environment which feeds the imagination and storytelling faculties that are a hallmark of their output. This includes individually furnished cubicles, one of which is a garden shed; an atrium vast enough to encourage random meetings of all staff; a swimming pool and volleyball court; a cereal bar (that's a location, not a food item); and scooters as the favoured mode of transport.

No wonder they tend to come top in various 'coolest office to work at' polls.

MILITANTLY ENFORCE DIVERSITY

Here is what I recommend to help foster an insightful culture. Through the levers of culture and personal precedent, the more diversity that can be established, the better.

One organization I worked with set up 'Diversity Days', where once a quarter each person is allowed a day off to do something they have always wanted – the condition being that they each report back, so that the individual and the collective can seek to learn how the experience has brought new thinking to them.

In accordance with incubation theory, of course, much of what has actually been learned will not be accessible to the individual's consciousness, but that is precisely the point – and there will be others to gain the benefit.

A PUD FOLDER

Stephen Jay Gould was a palaeontologist, scientific popularizer and controversialist, often finding himself at war with British biologist Richard Dawkins. In one of his many books, his eighth collection of essays, "Leonardo's Mountain of Clams and The Diet of Worms", he talks about the importance of exploring "previously unapplied detail" (PUD).

This may well be a formal way of doing something you're already doing, but in honour of Gould I have long kept a PUD folder on my person and/or on my portable communication devices of choice.

In the days of hovercraft and Vesta instant dishes, this was created in the form of a paper-based medium such as a notepad, to jot down anything random that I found to be interesting or amusing. Then when we all went binary, a PUD folder could be created on computers or other devices to the same end.

A cursory glance at the folder every so often can give a new spring to thought processes and consciously – as well as unconsciously – set various mental hares scampering around enthusiastically.

A PUD folder should have a gadfly role too, and I hope the Inspiratorium should act as one large, evolving PUD folder.

THE IDEAS ORPHANAGE

A key organizational requirement can be to bolster the culture of innovation beyond a redecoration, new eating areas and rooms that look like small fields.

Taking the concept of the PUD to the collective level, every good company should maximize its use of each individual's PUD folder by building a space on the company server that acts as a collective zone for nurturing ESIs (external serendipitous influences).

I call this space the Ideas Orphanage.

It can be used for any or all of these ends:

- For people to generate and test hypotheses.
- To act as a collective catalogue and resource that embeds the 'we-think' ethic of connect, create, contribute and collaborate, popularized by Charles Leadbeater in 2010. It helps incorporate a more informal café culture that is discursive, playful and uncorporate.
- To allow people to wander and see whether their mental wandering can collide with other people's to generate genuine insight.
- To create a 'metaphorest', where useful, intriguing and recyclable metaphors can be stored and

viewed and relinked by different people working on different projects for different clients.

In fact, you could even call it a giant incubation machine.

These days most companies already have intranets
which have the capacity to act as proto-ideas orphan-
ages. But I think that branding it in this way and
allowing people to use it in more of a bottom-up,
systems-oriented manner often needs some benign
behavioural-economics-style nudging from above.

And the fact is that it takes time to institute, it
requires buy-in across the organization, and it can be
something that takes time away from urgent matters
like the 10 a.m. conference call or the fifth edit of the
debrief. But, as with all cultural change, if the outcome
justifies the input, and the sense of achievement at
all levels merits the input, then it will feel like a good
thing and not just another Taylorist imposition.

So, if we want to work in cultures that breed
insight, that incubate ideas, these short-term behavioural changes have to be accommodated for the
greater good.

MY BOOK CLUB

Book clubs are now big news. The numbers of these
are hard to verify, but 50,000 in the UK and 500,000 in
the US are some rough estimates.

Over the years, I have been running a book club
and the premise is quite simple. Attendees have to
read the book (or a section, if they are too busy) and
then we discuss.

The only rule I impose is in the selection: NO BUSI-NESS BOOKS. Too often business books tend to be very narrow, technical and outdated by the time they are published. 'Look, another book on social media.'

Participants are instead encouraged to choose books that are about ideas, about people, about culture, and which are designed to provoke new 'outside-in' thinking.

We then discuss the ideas and issues and afterwards, working outside-in, apply this thinking to specific issues of concern.

Read a book that is not your 'usual' reading and see how it might challenge your thinking and keep the echo-chamber effect at bay.

Oh, and rather than book clubs, shouldn't they be called 'chapters'?

AND SO...

- Following on from our observations about 'wandering and wondering', we must all maximize serendipity. So, sign up and become a member of the Opportunistic Association. Assume the juxta-position (a bit like zumba but without the lycra).

- Pursue the wise words of Irish writer Colm Tóibín and stay in your mental pyjamas all day. Be susceptible, porous and open to new ideas. Your unconscious will love you for it.

- Remember that the process of generation and variation is blind. Best not to go looking for a solution but let it come unbidden.

- Think of insight as compression + incubation.

- If you are going to have, set up, be part of or lead a brainstorm or workshop, acknowledge that for all of the pragmatics and logistics of jetting in the yellow fats team from Geneva and the R&D guys from Dallas, the feel of the session needs to be more conducive to something that will be genuinely incubatory and combinatorial.

- Small details can lead to unexpectedly radical outcomes, so be alert to small signals in the noise.

- Create a PUD folder to store any previously unapplied details and do not be ashamed of what goes in there. Consult frequently, especially without reason. Use them as Oblique Strategies.

- Find someone – or even better, be someone – who can create an Ideas Orphanage within your company. They'll thank you for it. Then use it and enjoy it. They'll thank you for it.
- Do this all with an ABC: ambition, bravery and challenge.

2. A ROOMFUL OF SURPRISES

Our next room is the home of the unexpected and the startling. It provides many examples of why surprise is such an underestimated part of our creative repertoire and why we need to give in to its power a little more willingly.

> The definition of surprise: being an actor on *Game of Thrones* and finding your character survives the series.
> — **ANTHONY TASGAL**

DARWIN TO EKMAN

Following in the footsteps of Charles Darwin, psychologist Paul Ekman proposed that there are six universally recognizable human emotions, as evidenced by facial expressions: happiness, sadness, fear, anger, disgust and surprise.

There are some disputes about whether there is a seventh – contempt – and the extent to which they are universally hardwired, rather than culturally coded.

Emotions are designed to ensure that our genes survive and thrive. Among many insights, Darwin showed that our emotions are both immensely powerful and beyond our conscious control. Hence, we often find ourselves seized by and overwhelmed by them (talking about the sense of joy, awe and oneness, the French thinker and mystic Romain Rolland used the term *sensation océanique* – oceanic feeling). They act as emergency overrides to jolt our conscious selves into paying attention to, or behaving in accordance with, new information that is of relevance to our long-term evolutionary benefit.

Surprise is a messenger from our interests, warning us of something that needs our attention. That is why being surprised can be so disturbing and awkward: the sense that we have been involuntarily knocked off course.

In terms of how our minds process surprise, it works at the level of 'unexpected information = surprise'.

Heuristics – the system of shortcuts our brain creates to maximize its efficiency by repeating previously efficient behaviour – means that we expect the world to follow certain paths; but when it does, we tend to get bored.

Roger Schank, the distinguished American theorist of Artificial Intelligence, explains it like this:

What makes something worth knowing is organized
around the concept of expectation failure. Scripts are
interesting not when they work but when they fail.
When the waiter doesn't come over with the food,
you have to figure out why; when the food is bad
or the food is extraordinarily good, you want to figure
out why. You learn something when things don't
turn out the way you expected.

Tiffany Watt Smith, a cultural historian, Research
fellow at Queen Mary University London and author
of *The Book of Human Emotions*, puts it beautifully:

Darwin ... showed us that our emotions don't
entirely belong to us. And that though we might fondly
imagine ourselves to be the drivers of our bodies,
we are more like passengers, along for a ride.

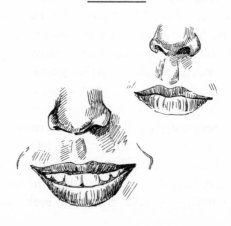

THE MOST POWERFUL EMOTION OF THEM ALL?

There is a strong argument that surprise is the most powerful emotion of them all.

The evolutionary origins of our emotions' influence make eminent sense. Natural selection designed our emotions to be the executioners of evolution, so their only goal is to help us (our species, tribes) to survive and thrive so genes can be passed on. Emotions are not especially driven by long and slow calculations of probability. If that stick-looking thing in front of us might be a snake, emotion kicks in immediately and sends a message to the body, and that message is 'Run!'

Four of the big six emotions – happiness, sadness, fear, anger, surprise and disgust – are negative and their survival benefit is clear: to warn and ward; to instil fear and anger when it is evolutionarily beneficial for our genes, to signal disgust at potentially lethal foodstuffs. But where does that leave the positive emotions?

The psychologist Barbara Fredrickson wrote a famous paper called, "What Good Are Positive Emotions?" She noted that the burgeoning research into emotions had concentrated on negative emotions, and had tended to under-explore emotions that left a pleasant feeling, such as joy, interest, contentment and love.

Her paper posited a clear distinction: negative emotions have a narrowing or shrinking effect; they are there precisely to ensure that the individual can eliminate unnecessary distractions and fix on the urgent issue at hand (avoid bear, find food, seek out mate) and work out the optimum strategy (the so-called "four Fs": flee, fight, feed or ... mate).

Fredrickson's theory of 'broaden and build' suggests that positive emotions make us more playful, more curious, more creative, more sociable and more reflective.

These 'broadening' emotions widen our perspective and thus allow us to build up our physical, mental, emotional and social resources when the going is good. In the language that is most at home in these sorts of articles and journals, they 'expand our attentional focus'. Fredrickson's thesis highlights ways in which they act as broadening agents: they broaden the scope of attention, the scope of cognition and the scope of action, as well as building physical, intellectual and social resources.

LIE TO ME?

Pioneering American psychologist Paul Ekman garnered more mainstream recognition for his work on the emotions after the Fox Network began broadcasting the drama series *Lie to Me*, featuring Tim Roth as Dr Cal Lightman, the world's leading deception expert, a scientist who studies facial expressions and involuntary body language to discover not only if you are lying but why. And clearly based on Ekman.

In his 2006 book, *Unmasking the Face*, written with Wallace Friesen, Ekman describes the surprise brow and its distinctive role in demonstrating surprise. The look is one where the eyebrows appear curved – and high.

We may be unaware of this expression but, when the brow rises, it extends our field of vision and, at the same time, our jaw drops and we are left speechless and halting: the imperative is for us to react – to this – now.

These very clear and distinctive facial expressions may have a secondary, social benefit, of serving to alert others to the unexpected event.

ANOMALY SEER

Why do so many people watch hockey for the fights, or car races for the crashes? Why are epic fails – especially from live TV broadcasts – so popular on YouTube? It's the surprise, the unexpected, the anomaly that viewers are looking for.

The value of surprise as an emotion, and the reason it is underestimated in so many ways, is that we are predisposed by evolutionary forces to be alert to news that is likely to be evolutionarily significant. For example, so much of what we take for granted only breaches awareness when sensory inputs violate expectations. Awareness is irrelevant as long as there is nothing to concern it.

Only when something extraneous and unexpected occurs that breaches expectations does conscious awareness get alerted.

Screenwriter Charlie Kaufman's *Anomalisa*, funded by the Kickstarter corporation, was the stand-out film of 2016.

Existentially profound, creepily hypnotic, skin-crawlingly unsettling and unforgettably inventive in its stop-motion alienation-animation, it was another intensely weird but compellingly humane and compassionate Kaufman riff on the fragile hell of identity, anonymity and a culture of bland and stultified consumption. And it features a version of "Girls Just Want to Have Fun" like no other.

The protagonist is Michael Stone, voiced by Blackpool's David Thewlis, a middle-aged British ex-pat who makes his living as a customer service guru and speaker, but for a motivational speaker he is pretty demotivated. On one level, this could be just another of the umpteen Hollywood stories of the midlife crises of the privileged middle-aged male.

But then he checks in at the Hotel Fregoli in Cincinnati – an allusion to the Fregoli delusion, the belief that everyone except you is the same one person in some sort of disguise (echoes of Kaufman's 1999 writing debut, *Being John Malkovich*).

In the film, this means that all the voices for all the characters – male and female – are voiced by one actor (Tom Noonan), apart from Lisa (Jennifer Jason Leigh), the sales rep whom Michael meets and engages in an affair.

She is, therefore the anomaly, the salient one – hence 'Anomalisa'. There is even a stop-motion puppet sex scene (nothing like as ludicrous as *Team America*, but in fact surprisingly fond).

So, to find inspiration, it's sometimes necessary to look for anomalies and actively break down conventions, something for which Charlie Kaufman has a well-honed instinct.

KAUFMAN-A-BUNGA

Charlie Kaufman is especially fond of word play and working with delusions: see his directorial debut from 2008, *Synecdoche, New York*. This is a play on Schenectady, a county in New York State, but also an allusion to the rhetorical trope of the part standing for the whole ('head' of cattle, 'crown' for king, 'wheels' for car, 'England' for the perennially disappointing football team).

To add mental illness to mental illness, Philip Seymour Hoffman's character is called Caden Cotard – the Cotard delusion, also known as 'walking corpse syndrome', being the belief that one is already dead.

There is a subtle moment when Cotard checks the address list at an apartment building: one of the names he sees is Capgras, referring to another mental disorder, where the sufferer believes someone close to them has been replaced by an impostor. As postmodernistically self-referential as *Malkovich*, blurring fiction and reality, this is another of Kaufman's cinematic essays on identity and the despairing search for an authentic self.

Across Kaufman's work, you can point to influences such as Jorge Luis Borges, the Argentine writer with a fondness for libraries, labyrinths and memory, whose 'Library of Babel' prefigured the arrival of Google and was an inspiration to everyone from Umberto Eco to Terry Pratchett.

Kaufman wins his place in the Pantheon as Inspirator General. His work is never less than vaultingly ambitious and conceptual, eclectic, quirky, profound and haunting; yet it is never less than touchingly humane.

But at another level, *Anomalisa* can be seen as the story of the consciousness, of System 1 and System 2 (as defined by Daniel Kahneman in his book *Thinking, Fast and Slow*), of our perceptual and attentional systems and the role of attention.

Anomalisa is about how the two systems work and how one of them is alert to changes which could affect our lives and the performance of our genes.

A TURNING POINT: PERIPETEIA

Surprise is a key component of the art of storytelling, and storytelling is hard-wired into our brains.

Peripeteia is the rhetorical term for a sudden change in a story which results in a (usually) negative reversal of circumstances. It is the turning point, the place in which the protagonist's fortunes change from good to bad.

It can also be translated as 'reversal of fortune', which is the title of a 1990 film (based on his 1985 novel of the same name) written by high-profile law professor Alan Dershowitz, who was also part of the defence team in the O. J. Simpson case. In 1984 Dershowitz defended British socialite Claus von Bülow, who stood accused of killing his wife Sunny. In the film, Jeremy Irons and Glenn Close play the couple and Ron Silver plays Dershowitz (who had a cameo role in the film as a judge). Irons won the Academy Award for the role.

Peripeteia comes from the Greek preposition *peri* (meaning 'around', as in 'periscope') and the root *peptein*, meaning 'to fall', and detectable in the word 'symptom', but separate from 'peptic'.

According to Aristotle, peripeteia is the most potent element of plot in tragedy.

It is a form of surprise for the audience but is also meant to feel like a consequence of a character's previous actions or mistakes.

It is designed to cause fear and pity in the audience, upon witnessing the tragic twist of fate that abruptly ruins the life of the protagonist.

Peripeteia provides a point of shock and dismay in a complex plot, often ironically weaving previous actions with their present effects. Peripeteia imbues the tragic plot with surprise and emotional complexity and is something we need to cherish in the search for freshness and inspiration.

RECOGNIZING THE TRUTH

Peripeteia is one part of the equation; the other half is called *anagnorisis*. This is recognition or discovery of the truth: both the fact and the emotional response that accompanies it.

Take the story of Oedipus, the locus classicus or gold standard for Aristotle and perhaps still the best-known example of peripeteia.

The play starts with Oedipus the hero having saved the people of Thebes from the Sphinx; but the Thebans are now struck by a mysterious plague. Creon, Oedipus's brother-in-law, reports that the plague will only be lifted when the killer of the former King Laius is brought to justice.

Jocasta, Laius's widow and Oedipus's new bride, had been told by an oracle that her husband would one day be killed by her son; so she abandons Oedipus, having pinioned his feet (*Oedipus* means 'swollen foot', and echoes remain in the medical term for swelling, *oedema* or *edema*). Laius, she believes, was killed by a band of robbers.

As the pieces start to coalesce, Oedipus's certainty that he is the son of Polybus of Corinth is shaken by a messenger announcing Polybus's death and revealing that Oedipus was not really his son. This becomes the peripeteia, the point at which the hero realizes his tragic flaw or error (*hamartia* is the Aristotelian term).

For Oedipus that flaw is stubbornness in the face of truth, the soothing belief that ignorance is bliss.

The full anagnorisis, or recognition of the shocking truth, comes when Oedipus tracks down the shepherd who had long ago given the messenger an abandoned baby, who was then adopted by King Polybus.

Threatened with death, the shepherd reveals the gruesome truth that (spoiler alert) the baby was none other than the son of Laius and Jocasta. Despite what he thinks have been his best intentions, Oedipus discovers that he is his father's killer and the cause of the plague, and has been in an incestuous relationship with his mother.

The reversal of fortune takes place when he – and we – realize the backstory of the king: that the young Oedipus was the one who killed the old King Laius in an argument at a crossroads, and that he had subsequently married the King's wife, Jocasta, his own mother. The truth drives Jocasta to kill herself, and Oedipus to blind himself using pins from her gown, mirroring the blindness of the prophet (the 'seer', ironically) Teiresias.

The reversal is so mighty because Oedipus is a genuine hero to the people of Thebes, has committed no obvious sin and has sought to find out the truth. Ironies abound: he has solved the riddle of the Sphinx but cannot solve his own; oracles and seers tell him the truth but he cannot face it; sight and blindness is a motif throughout.

One final Greek term can be invoked with Oedipus: that of *hubris*, an overweening arrogance.

The story has been retold again and again over the 2,400 years since Sophocles wrote *Oidipous Tyrannos* (the Greek equivalent of the Latinized *Oedipus Rex*).

OEDIPUS WRECKS

On the subject of Oedipus, Woody Allen created one of the three segments that make up the 1989 film anthology *New York Stories*, called 'Oedipus Wrecks'.

Displaying some typically 'Woody' motifs – magic, a box, extensive use of psychiatry – his character, Sheldon, finds that his interfering mother has disappeared during a magic act. Sheldon confronts the magician and the theatre manager, but she is nowhere to be found.

The dumbfounded magician generously suggests: "If anything happens to your mother, I'll get you two free tickets to any show we do."

His mother only reappears later, looming over the New York sky like can omniscient deity. It is only when Sheldon falls for his psychic that his mother returns to earth.

You don't have to go the full Freudian hog, or even submit to Tom Lehrer's spoof song "Oedipus Rex", to realize the terrible power of the Oedipus story and what it tells us about the search for truth, fate and free will, and whether knowledge is always a good thing.

Oedipus Rex is perhaps the world's first detective story – the moral: that we don't always discover what we think or expect, especially about ourselves.

It is an inexorably logical psychological thriller, a political exposé, an inevitable journey of self-discovery with hints of horror that remains timeless and universal.

SPOILER ALERT ALERT

Someone who knows about peripeteia is John Yorke, former controller of BBC Drama Production, founder of the BBC Writers Academy and director of Company Pictures.

His CV covers the TV series *Hustle*, *Spooks*, *Casualty* and *Holby City* alongside *Wolf Hall*, *Life on Mars*, *Shameless* as well as the long-running soap EastEnders.

He talks of the importance of peripeteia as subversion of expectation, the tool that catapults the protagonist into the opposite of their current state; screenwriters such as Christopher Vogler also use the terms 'inciting incidents' and 'explosions of opposition'.

One of the stock areas for the double act that is peripeteia and anagnorisis is the 'twist' or surprise ending.

INTERLUDE

Here are a few twists to ponder on, from movies and TV: unexpected yet inevitable. A profusion of Spoiler Alerts. Answers again can be found on p356.

- "You maniacs! You blew it up! Ah, damn you! God damn you all to hell!" (Great anagnorisis from Charlton Heston).
- Kevin Costner was the spy all along.
- The Verbal Kint revelation.
- Malcolm Crowe's shocking realization.
- Who is Tyler Durden? But we don't talk about it, except about the Pixies' "Where is My Mind?"
- Nicole Kidman, Christopher Eccleston and their two children.
- Gwyneth Paltrow's head in a box (no, not a meal solution).
- Residents of a 19th century commune.
- Two rival magicians in 19th century London (double twist – and David Bowie).
- Leonardo di Caprio investigates a disappearance at a hospital for the criminally insane.
- Dutch film (remade in US) with the protagonist buried alive (Kiefer Sutherland in the US version).
- Dorothy has a bad dream.
- Two people on the Starship *Avalon*.
- Tim Robbins as a traumatized Vietnam war veteran finds out that his postwar life isn't what he believes it to be.
- 1955 French film: corpse in bathtub.
- Keira Knightley and James McAvoy don't actually get together at the end.

- A Nobel Prize-winning mathematician has imaginary friends.
- 1953 Vincent Price horror.
- Edward Woodward, Christopher Lee, 1973.
- Dil isn't who Stephen Rea thought.
- Second Charlton Heston appearance where he discovers the secret of a processed food.
- The main character dies a third of the way through the movie.
- A 6-foot rabbit named Frank.

KNOWING TOO MUCH

One of the insights tucked away in this exploration of surprise concerns our use and dissemination of information.

Anyone who communicates or shares information may need to come a little closer.

Here's the thing: too much information, too much exposition in storytelling terms, can be detrimental to its impact.

The brain cannot absorb, compute, process or respond to streams of unmediated data. And that is why information has to be framed in terms of a story.

So, we should always be seeking to make our communication (letter, interview, presentation, website) memorable and enduring. We know that our long-term memories seem to be the ones which have a deep emotional anchor: that emotion can be positive (a happy time, pride, success, love) or negative (shame, failure, embarrassment, that time on the pier when you were 15).

But the key to creating something emotionally memorable is to ensure that it conveys meaning: as distinct from data, facts, information and material that I lump together as 'messaging' (or 'stuff I am telling you that I really think you need to listen to, whether you do or not').

The bigger point is this, and it is emphasized by all great storytelling theorists: too much information, too much narration kills participation, numbs emotion and leaves the audience with nothing to give, nothing to feel. Just because you (the messenger or the story-teller) have a lot to say does not mean that you have to share it all. Use it sparingly, make the audience work, make them share, make them active participants in the story. Explanation is the enemy of drama and story.

THE ONLY WAY IS UP

Andrew Stanton knows a thing or two about storytelling.

As a *grand fromage* at Pixar, he was involved in writing and/or directing *Ratatouille*, *WALL-E*, and *Up* – as well as co-writing all the *Toy Story* series, including the episode which is still 'fourth-coming' at the time of writing – an extraordinary run of era-defining movies.

In a 2006 lecture he said: "You often hear the term 'You should have something to say in a story,' but that doesn't always mean a message. It means truth, some value that you yourself as a storyteller believe in…"

Stanton argues that the audience wants to work for their meal, but that they just don't want to know that they are doing that. The job of the storyteller (and of any communicator) is to hide that from them.

While we remain with great storytellers, let us spend a moment with Jed Mercurio, the screenwriter best known for the Sky medical series *Critical* and the riveting BBC police corruption drama *Line of Duty*, which has entranced TV viewers over four series.

"If you disguise exposition with 'emotional overlay' it's rendered undetectable," he says.

So, it is precisely the absence of a full deck – the refusal to provide all the answers and fill in all the boxes – that creates anticipation and emotional involvement. It is no trick of etymology that 'deduct' and 'deduce' are so closely related: taking things out means the brain has to puzzle and think, and in so doing becomes emotionally implicated in the process.

Neuroscience has also opened up the door to explaining the significance of surprise and uncertainty. The brain treats new or surprising information as a special kind of reward. Other evidence confirms the role of the neurotransmitter dopamine in processing novelty.

As far as the limits of surprise can be established, we appear to need a mix of familiar and unfamiliar to find satisfaction: the pleasure comes from the contrast between expectation and surprise. The same principle holds for gripping passages in books and films: too much surprise that feels illogical, and we feel frustrated and disappointed.

THE MAYA PRINCIPLE

This way of thinking has a parallel in the world of design: the MAYA principle.

Raymond Loewy is often considered the father of industrial design, bringing innovation and style to an era obsessed with efficiency. A *New York Times Book Review* critic once commented, "Mr. Loewy has indeed changed the shape of the modern world," and *Cosmopolitan* magazine remarked in 1950 that "Loewy has probably affected the daily life of more Americans than any man of his time."

His work included designing logos for Air Force One, Shell Oil, the US Postal Service and Greyhound buses, as well as landmark designs for the Coca Cola bottle, the Lucky Strike cigarette pack, the 1947 Studebaker Starlight Coupé, not to mention the 1961 Studebaker Avanti, the 1947 line of Hallicrafter radio receivers and the 1929 Gestetner duplicating machine.

Streamlining was his hallmark; he called it "beauty through function and simplification".

Loewy was a theorist too, and formulated his 'MAYA' (Most Advanced Yet Acceptable) principle, which is where he comes into our story.

He felt strongly that product designs are bounded by functional constraints of materials and logic on the one hand, but also by social expectations on the other.

In psychological terms, he appreciated that human behaviour and attitudes swing between two poles: the safe and familiar, and the novel and original; between fear and curiosity, neophilia and neophobia, the reassuring comfort of the present and the thrill of an uncharted future.

He believed that:

––––––––––

The adult public's taste is not necessarily
ready to accept the logical solutions to their
requirements if the solution implies too vast
a departure from what they have been
conditioned into accepting as the norm.

––––––––––

MAYA was about a universal human truth, though
expressed in the realm of design. Give people what is
most advanced, but only insofar as they are willing to
accept it – 'optimal newness' in the words of Harvard
professor Karim Lakhani.

To sell something surprising, Loewy recommended,
make it familiar; and to sell something familiar, make
it surprising.

MERE EXPOSURE

Robert Zajonc (rhymes with 'science' – no, really) was a Polish-American social psychologist, whose work in uncovering the 'mere exposure effect' is grounds enough for his place in the scientific pantheon.

His work in the 1970s and 1980s did much to herald the ushering of emotions back into the mainstream of cognitive science, but his argument showing that preferences could be formed on the sole basis of familiarity – just by being exposed to something – was and remains groundbreaking.

In one of his typically ingenious experiments, subjects were shown some visual patterns on a screen, so briefly that they could not be registered consciously. After being asked to sort them, the subjects could not tell which they had seen. But (and here's the thing) when pressed to indicate which of a selection of patterns they preferred, they indicated the ones they had been exposed to subliminally.

But to add strangeness to strangeness, when Zajonc's team asked their guinea pigs why they preferred those particular patterns, they would offer a whole range of ostensibly sensible reasons.

This led him to suggest that we have a precognitive mechanism that ensures that caution is the default response in encounters with novel or unknown stimuli – which might be harmful, after all – until familiarity renders them acceptable and safe.

All this suggested to Zajonc that our brains can process things which then influence us without our conscious awareness (or permission).

THE SPLIT BRAIN

Neuroscientist and Professor of Psychology at University of California, Santa Barbara, Michael Gazzaniga is a major force in the field of cognitive neuroscience and reckons that the brain has a system which he calls the 'interpreter'.

Gazzaniga's early work with Roger Sperry into split-brain patients (where the two hemispheres of the brain are surgically separated from each other – a drastic treatment for severe epilepsy – and each is unable to communicate with the other) was later repeated more broadly. Gazzaniga theorized that the left brain has an 'interpreter' module or neural network. This attempts to assemble disparate inputs and experiences into something resembling a coherent whole. It will go out of its way to construct a story (often an outlandish one) to explain what the right hemisphere has seen or experienced without the left hemisphere's knowledge.

The developed human left hemisphere excels at inferences, constantly searching for patterns that can 'make sense' of what is going on, bringing order out of chaos, and giving us answers to 'why?' questions by discovering causes behind phenomena.

Gazzaniga calls this our 'interpreter module,' because it continually explains the world using the inputs it has from the current cognitive state and cues from the surroundings. This ability to articulate stories that explains what is going on is described by Gazzaniga as a 'phase shift' between humans and other animals.

So, we have to be aware that we will often find ourselves led by our interpreter module to explain and justify things rationally that are prompted emotionally and preconsciously.

The surprise room should teach us, therefore, that this most crucial yet under-valued emotion, designed by evolution to demand our attention, should be cherished more than is normally the case. Seek out ways to startle and be startled, and to create that shock of recognition.

3. THE FAIL ROOM

In this room we learn to value the creative inspiration that lies behind failure and error, to understand why being lost and abandoning didactic certainty can create the sort of serendipitous originality we seek. So be prepared for everything from French festivals to US sitcoms, to the economist Vilfredo Pareto and 'fruitful errors' that laugh in the face of sterile truth.

STAYING FOOLISH

Stay foolish.
— **STEVE JOBS, 2005**

The difference between the amoeba and Einstein is that, although both make use of the method of trial and error or elimination, the amoeba dislikes erring while Einstein is intrigued by it: he consciously searches for his errors in the hope of learning by their discovery and elimination.
— **KARL POPPER, QUOTED IN *THE CEREBRAL CODE* BY WILLIAM CALVIN.**

Making mistakes. Being wrong. Taking risks.

It's funny how these three all seem to be interlinked and suffer from terrible PR. No-one likes to be wrong, to fail, to have the finger pointed at them. We see any sign of fallibility as deeply threatening to our sense of self, our personal narrative and our belief in our personal omniscience.

Or maybe that's just me.

One of the central truths of the human condition is that cognitive dissonance rules. We don't like anything that conflicts with the central edifice of our beliefs and identity, and we go out of our way to screen or ignore any such incongruent material.

As far back as the 4th century CE, St Augustine said, "Fallor ergo sum" (I am wrong; therefore I am), prefiguring Descartes by over a thousand years.

Error has always been our species' dirty little secret.

We should reinstate error to its rightful place, not just within the business world but also the ordinary lives we all lead. If we do so, we are more likely to generate fruitful and innovative ideas that will evade the stringent scrutiny of those whose view of error and failure is punitive, and lead happier, more balanced lives.

THE FRENCH FESTIVAL OF ERROR

This festival, which took place in 2010 at the École Normale Supérieure in Paris, looked at the concept of error and invited people to challenge the *idée reçue* (received idea) that error is a negative concept. It was designed by a group of French academics and employed a mixture of workshops and lectures to appeal to a generation of French schoolchildren, who – according to many French commentators – are stuffed with and stifled by an educational diet that smothers creativity and independent thinking.

A report by a BBC radio correspondent in Paris at the time bemoaned the "focus on the absorption, and then reproduction, of a standard corpus of knowledge" rather than the pleasures of independent learning.

The correspondent (also speaking as a parent) bemoaned the extent of prescriptive, repetitive learning. Other specialists and intellectuals (France being one of the rare cultures where declaring oneself an intellectual is not an invitation to aggravated assault) concur in claiming that their system is creating a generation of children lacking in creativity, flexibility of thought and self-confidence.

Now, listening to complaints of a school system that is too dependent on results and league tables, and always giving the right answer, may seem familiar to those attuned to the British educational system.

Tonally, the French Festival of Errors has got it about right. Rather than being didactically dull, they have gone for an approach which is, to quote the poster, "interactif et ludique" (interactive and playful).

In fact, for wordsmiths and Francophones, the French title of the festival is 'Détrompez-Vous!', which is a clever play on words meaning something like 'Unmistake yourself'.

This is not just an academic exercise; it is worth digging a bit deeper into the history of error.

ERROR: A BRIEF HISTORY

Back to etymology. The root of the word 'error' – and of the verb 'to err' – is the Latin *errare*, meaning 'to wander'.

Funny, isn't it, how we seem to have lost that sense of the word (though 'erratic' and 'aberration' remind us in English) when we look at error so critically.

The business guru Tom Peters is typically forth-right about how the dominant business model needs to amend its attitude to failure.

In *The Pursuit of Wow!* (1994) he openly attacked bosses who did not understand or support the idea of failure as part and parcel of the business of business. In so doing he quoted Kevin Kelly, founder of *Wired* magazine, on his prognosis of neo-biological culture, *Out of Control* (also 1994).

"Honour error," said Kelly, who made the added point that evolution, seen in this way, can be defined as "systematic error management".

This powerful metaphor suggests that we must all act more within the model of biology rather than physics – a model in which organisms are renowned for complex adaptive behaviour rather than linear and predictable progression.

ERROR IN SCIENCE AND THE SCIENCE OF ERROR

In another of his essay collections, The Panda's Thumb" [1980], the late Stephen Jay Gould mused on the treatment of the poet Goethe, who, although revered for his literary prowess, also carried out much serious work in anatomy, botany, geology and optics, but to little critical acclaim.

With his customary wisdom and breadth of view, Gould concluded that although Goethe's botanical thinking on leaves was flawed in many ways, it opened up new paths for progressive exploration. As an outsider, moreover, Gould applauds Goethe for refusing to accept the narrowness of vision which his contemporaries accepted as the norm. In this essay, Gould also quotes the Italian economist Vilfredo Pareto (author of the Pareto principle or '80/20 rule'):

Give me a fruitful error any time, full of seeds bursting with its own corrections.
You can keep your sterile truth for yourself.

Darwin himself made a pronouncement on the virtue of fostering idle speculation and false hypotheses:

False facts are highly injurious to the progress of science for they often endure long; but false hypotheses do little harm as everyone takes

a salutary pleasure in proving their falseness;
and when this is done, one path toward error
is closed and the road to truth is often at
the same time opened.

———————

The economist William S. Jevons put it well more than a century ago:

———————

It would be an error to suppose that the great
discoverer seizes at once upon the truth or has
any unerring method of divining it. In all probability
the errors of the great mind exceed in number those
of the less vigorous one. Fertility of imagination
and abundance of guesses at truth are among
the first requisites of discovery.

———————

What makes us different as a species is that we can carry out our trial and errors without any great loss.

Philosopher Karl Popper once said that "Our hypotheses die in our place," and the accumulated wisdom of our results is absorbed and retained in our cultures, histories and recording mechanisms.

Trial and error is part of learning and thus integral to human psychology, and recent advances in evolutionary psychology have done nothing to diminish its relevance. The very process of Darwinian evolution thrives on errors in the copying of the genetic code. Mutations, or errors in DNA, sometimes lead to extinction, but more often provide that spark of novelty and complexity. Evolution, according to Darwin, was a series of successful mistakes.

Creativity, in natural selection, has error written through it.

FAILURE: THE AMERICAN WAY

Few TV series have inspired as much personal devotion in the watching and left such a void at their demise as has *Parks and Recreation* (2009-2015).

This was a warm series, lovingly populated with memorable characters, often blindingly funny but never far from the central premise of small town team-work and cooperation (it was created by the people who brought us the American version of *The Office*).

The team that run the Parks and Recreation depart-ment in the small town of Pawnee, Indiana – Leslie Knope (played by co-writer Amy Poehler), Ben Wyatt, Ron Swanson, April and Andy, Ann and Chris and the rest – are more human (or humane) and less self-de-luded than many of the characters in the American (or UK) *Office* and other sitcoms; the tone of poignancy and humour is far removed from some of the more bitter comedy that has come into vogue (by the likes of Ricky Gervais, Larry David, Jimmy Carr and Louis C. K.).

In the two-part series finale, we witness the char-acters' futures, and in the case of Tom Haverford (Aziz Ansari), his latest business venture has ended catastroph-ically. He is bankrupt, but as we fast-forward further into the future, we see that he has learned from his mistakes.

He is on a podium launching his new book, *Failure: An American Success Story*. This (of course with oodles of dramatic irony) is followed up by *Failure to Fail: Failure 2.0.*

Conclusion: failure can breed success, even beyond the world of sitcoms.

ERROR AND ADAPTATION IN ART

Charlie Kaufman, the writer, producer and director whom we met in the Surprise room, knows a thing or two about creativity. He wrote *Being John Malkovich*, *Human Nature*, *Adaptation* and *Eternal Sunshine of The Spotless Mind*, as well as writing and directing *Synecdoche, New York*, surely the dream title for a fan of classical rhetoric.

In a recent speech at BAFTA, the organization that supports the British TV, film and games industry and is famed for its annual awards ceremony, he started by accepting that he was no expert at speaking at this type of event and invited audience support for watching him fumble. This, he suggested, gives us all an opportunity to recognize our common humanity and vulnerability: this is sometimes known as the "pratfall effect".

He came back to this theme later:

Do not worry about failure. Failure is a badge of honour. It means you risked failure. And if you don't risk failure you're never going to do anything that's different than what you've already done, or what somebody else has done.

Someone else who knew about success and failure was the late TV producer Stephen J. Cannell, who was responsible, among other output, for *The Rockford Files*, the James Garner series broadcast in the mid to late 1970s. He then conceived and wrote most of the episodes for *The A-Team*.

"All hits are basically mistakes," Cannell remarked. "Everyone starts out desperately trying to make a hit, but some people are just more mistake-prone than others. I happened to be fairly mistake-prone. Of the 40 shows I made, I'd say 10 were hits, which is a pretty good average."

FUCKUP NIGHTS

Doing largely what you'd expect from the label, Fuckup Nights was started by five friends from Mexico who had had enough of symposia and events celebrating largely idealized success stories in the business world and beyond.

So they conceived the idea of Fuckup Nights.

At each event, three to five speakers discuss their failures. Each is given only 7 minutes and is allowed to use a maximum of 10 images (note: simplification and storytelling in action – see previous chapter). After the talks there is always a lively Q&A.

Their philosophy – which seems to have struck a chord, as there are now some 100 cities hosting Fuckup Nights – is that by focusing on failure and the negative we can all learn more about what makes a success.

Apart from just trying to do things differently, it therapeutically legitimizes failure and error and reinforces the belief that failure is part of life, part of growing and learning rather than a taboo to be shunned publicly and privately.

FAILURE IN THE HOUSE

The TV series *House* already holds a number of records. The medical-detective story of the grumpy medical genius with more than a punning hint of Holmes about him was the most-watched TV programme in 2008 and garnered several Emmys and Golden Globes. Its star, Hugh Laurie, became the highest-paid and most watched actor on television.

Part of the fascination of *House* was the way it exploded the myth of hospital consultants as infallible and omniscient masters of all they survey.

According to Dr Lisa Sanders of the Yale School of Medicine, one of the show's medical advisers:

What *House* shows is that on the way to being right, we're often wrong. And that is something doctors have never been able to talk about. Incompetence isn't interesting. What's interesting is when really smart doctors get things wrong.

Another cultural example is from Ira Glass, producer of *This American Life*, the iconic weekly hour-long radio programme which has been broadcasting on over 500 stations throughout the United States since 1995. It is also often the most popular podcast in the US.

Here is how Glass expresses his belief in being wrong:

―――――

I don't go looking for stories with the idea of wrongness in my head, no. But the fact is, a lot of great stories hinge on people being wrong. ... The collision of reality against expectation is what makes it work.

―――――

In an interview for the online magazine, "Slate", Glass also explained what it was like working at the satirical magazine *The Onion*, and the demand to generate its legendarily witty headlines:

―――――

Every Monday they have to come up with like 17 or 18 headlines, and to do that, they generate 600 headlines per week. I feel like that's why it's good: because they are willing to be wrong 583 times to be right 17.

―――――

GETTING LOST

For many, the most thrillingly wandering series of the last decade was *Lost*. Immersed in its own mythology over six series aired between 2005 and 2010, it featured a smoke monster, a group called the Others, a wayward polar bear, philosophical references to the likes of John Locke and Jeremy Bentham, the mysterious 'numbers' and multi-layered timeframes. It was complex, kaleidoscopic and immensely well-received and adored, at least by those who stuck with it.

It made stars of many of its characters, but no-one became more stellar as a result of *Lost* than one of its co-creators, J. J. Abrams, who went on to write and direct *Star Trek* and *Star Wars* movies.

Here is how *Lost*'s other co-creator, Damon Lindelof, described it:

———————

Lost was like a journey from LA to NY: we knew the beginning and we knew the end, but the middle was tricky. We didn't know how much gas we had, or whether the car would make it.

———————

ERROR AND CERTAINTY

Error is, at root, about straying, and generally straying from the truth. Admitting to error jeopardizes our sense of certainty and authority and goes against the evolutionarily powerful drive to place certainty above doubt and denial.

Mistakes, as Karen Schultz puts it in her book *Being Wrong*, should be legitimized as part of our evolutionary brilliance, rather than being demonized as the regrettable by-products of a separate and deplorable process.

Membership to the 'Club of Self-Evident Truth' leads to the worst excesses of 'groupthink', from the Cuban missile crisis of 1962 to the *Columbia* shuttle disaster of 2003. It challenges our belief that we are good, trustworthy, intelligent and in control and provides a temporary disruption to the service of self – 'normal service will be resumed as soon as possible'.

The artist Robert Rauschenberg, who became one of the later exponents of Pop Art and a fan of the sort of *objets trouvés* (found objects) that Marcel Duchamp had pioneered, said:

Screwing things up is a virtue. Being correct is never the point. I have an almost fanatically correct assistant, and by the time she re-spells my words and corrects my punctuation, I can't read what I wrote. Being right can stop all the momentum of a very interesting idea.

THE BUSINESS OF ERROR

Many business commentators are finally beginning to stress the need to accept failure as part of the drive for innovation, be it with new products or new communication ideas.

Risk is only one step away from invention: nothing ventured, nothing gained.

Examples of inventive error abound in the business world.

For instance, the drug Viagra was first developed to combat high blood pressure.

The person who conceived the original European multipurpose vehicle (MPV) or sport utility vehicle (SUV) was an engineer at French carmaker Peugeot. Peugeot rejected the idea ("A car? – that's like a van?"), so he took it to the rival firm Renault, who created the Espace. It became a ground-breaking success, selling over 900,000 units after its launch in 1984.

It also became the spearhead of a whole new approach to the car market: acknowledging that children were important factors in car purchasing and so should be a key consideration when choosing a car. Anyone with kids and an MPV/SUV will vouch for how much kids (too) appreciate the high seating position, the feeling of space on long journeys and the play value and stress reduction that entails.

A CONSTRUCTIVE THEORY OF ERROR

The world of business – from new product development to research, to advertisement testing, to measurement and prediction or trend forecasting – is still relentlessly positivist. Targets to be set, targets to be met.

The way we introduce people to the theory and practice of marketing has unhealthy parallels with our school system, and it is quite shocking that this mindset of certainty, dogmatic Stepford-like thinking and the stigmatization of error is allowed to go largely unchallenged.

As the American writer Ambrose Bierce said, "Being positive is being mistaken at the top of one's voice."

There is also an unhealthy veneration for experts.

Let me be clear that I am not in favour of having callow ignoramuses in charge of major decisions. Neither do I endorse the wholesale rubbishing of experts that one particular British politician engaged in before the Brexit vote in June 2016. But there is plenty of research evidence to suggest that relying on experts who know a lot about a little can place restraints on innovation.

There is an Italian expression which sums it up succinctly: *Impara l'arte, e mettila da parte*, which roughly translates as 'Learn your skill, then set it aside'.

In terms of how we approach the business application of error, let's make sure that we legitimize, and even encourage, fruitful error, so that we can learn from mistakes in a way that generates genuine innovation and eliminates the fear of the unknown.

If we follow this approach, we are less likely to create homogeneous markets with wallpaper communications that our target audiences are liable to ignore or dismiss, and more likely to breed a spirit of independent thinking.

FURTHER AND WIDER...

Here are a few thoughts to ponder:

- Sometimes the "I/we don't know" response is not necessarily a bad thing. How often, when we are presenting, thinking or answering questions, do we openly acknowledge our uncertainty, and openly posit alternative (conflicting) hypotheses and scenarios? Let's accept more hypothesis-generation and an acceptance that some will fall by the wayside.

- What I have elsewhere termed 'insightment' depends on the universal emotion of surprise and the sense of the unfamiliar. We need to surprise ourselves more often, without care for the safety net, or for the comforting consensus of groupthink.

- This also ties in with the thesis of economist John Kay's book *Obliquity*: that things we actively seek, like success or happiness, may best be sought indirectly, and that often we have to go back in order to go forward. Maybe doing new research isn't the answer; it may well be more profitable and surprising to go back and look at what we already have through new eyes.

- As an antidote to relentless introspection, may I recommend a little more 'wandering'?

As Tolkien said (and he knew a thing or two about the imaginative impulse), "Not all those who wander are lost."

- We should be thinking of human beings first, rather than (for instance) 'financial transaction agents'.

- Let us not forget the realization that those who answer market research questions are unreliable witnesses. We are inherent confabulators, our left-brain primed to legitimize what is going on in the right brain, whether we know (or like) it or not. In isolation, asking people questions just perpetuates the vicious circle of 'same questions, same answers, same solutions'.

- Admitting mistakes takes us back to being children; mistakes should be more playful. Work itself should be more playful, or what the French refer to as *ludique*.

- In fact, our spirit should be one of 'combinatorial playfulness', mixing different sources, strategies, ideas and outlooks. There will be plenty of time later to bring the evaluative aspect of Daniel Kahneman's rational System 2 into the proceedings.

- In the words of that noted philosopher, Bryan Ferry: "Learn from your mistakes is my only advice and 'stay cool' is still the main rule."

So, let us begin the campaign to Bring Back Error. And let us all wander wider and further...

4. THE OUTSIDE ROOM

It is hardly possible to overrate the value
of placing human beings in contact with
persons dissimilar to themselves, and with
modes of thought and action unlike those
with which they are familiar.

– JOHN STUART MILL

One aspect of wandering is being outside, crossing boundaries and actively going beyond what is internally safe and comfortable.

To build insight and thoughtfulness, to seek new patterns and sources of meaning, we must actively seek out external ideas from new domains.

But one more criterion needs to be in place.

And that is the need to be an Outsider.

THE CREATIVE CAPITAL OF FLORIDA

Let's start with Florida. The US has a creation myth based on the dream that any outsider can 'make it' in their country. After all, if you make it there, you can make it anywhere.

Diversity, hybridity and the emergence of a more cosmopolitan pluralism have often been cited as the foundations of US economic growth and innovation.

Professor Richard Florida's theory of 'creative capital' suggests that the success of cities depends on their pursuit of the three 'T's: technology, talent and tolerance. He emphasizes the role of immigration as a cornerstone of US economic success and an economic driver.

Work by Ronald S. Burt, Professor of Sociology and Strategy at the University of Chicago Booth, also highlighted the importance of not relying on inside information. His paper, published by the University of Chicago, "The Social Origin of Good Ideas" (2002), used archival and experimental data within a large US electronics company to demonstrate how good ideas emerge within companies. He concluded that most arise from bridging gaps between departments. The risk – now often seen with the internet – is that ideas that remain among insiders just create a self-propagating echo-chamber effect where groupthink takes over and a homogeneous lowest-common-denominator process becomes the norm.

Burt's experiment showed that it is the diversity and incongruity across clusters rather than within (the 'surprise', if you like) that gives outsiders' ideas more appeal to managers. This view sees creativity as akin to an import–export business.

One of Burt's phrases also resonates with our general thread: "People who live at the intersection of social worlds are at higher risk of having good ideas."

The 'risk' of becoming dedicated 'insiders' is that we fall prey to what business theorist Chris Argyris termed 'skilled incompetence', which means getting wrapped in defensive routines and allowing confirmation bias to rule our decision-making.

A STORY OF RUSSIA, BERLIN AND NEW YORK

Israel Baline was just part of the Jewish exodus from Russia to the New World in the wake of the pogroms in the latter part of the 19th century.

His rags-to-riches trajectory and self-reinvention saw him change his name, and as Irving Berlin he would write thousands of songs, from "Alexander's Ragtime Band" in 1911 to "What'll I Do?" "Blue Skies" and "Puttin' on the Ritz".

Now Berlin was not the only great songwriter of his generation, but what distinguished him was his ability to mine the collective unconscious of his adopted country.

If it is true that America is not a place but an idea, then Irving Berlin did more than anyone to create the soundtrack for that idea. He gave the United States its definitive Easter song ("Easter Parade"), created the soundtrack for a war with a patriotic anthem ("God Bless America") and the tune that more than any other summarized the world of US entertainment, "There's No Business Like Show Business."

But perhaps his greatest cultural legacy was the enduringly seasonal "White Christmas," generally acknowledged as the biggest-selling single of all time with some 500-odd cover versions.

The tune, originally something of a throwaway, became a massive hit for Bing Crosby, once it had been recorded in the film *Holiday Inn* in 1942. Now it has become part of the quintessential Christmas experience of melancholic nostalgia – an almost Victorian-Utopian idyll seen from an immigrant and Anglophile perspective to rival that of the more UK-based image of Charles Dickens' *A Christmas Carol*. It is even said that it created the concept of snowfall at Christmas being a bettable option, now that part of the seasonal anticipation concerns the probability of snow falling on a particular day.

So: a story of the Outsider who not only reinvented himself but refined how the mainstream defined itself.

Given the hot-button contemporary discussion of the role of the outsider-immigrant, we can look at Lin-Manuel Miranda's world-beating musical "Hamilton", the story of one of the American Founding Fathers. The song "Yorktown" features the line "immigrants – we get the job done".

IMAGINATION OF THE OUTSIDER

The broader perspective that embraces Irving Berlin as the Outsider is the concept of Hollywood and the movies as being dependent on the experiences and imaginations of a group of Ashkenazi (that is, Eastern European) Jewish émigrés, who originated from a small area with Warsaw as its epicentre, to become the founding moguls of the movie industry.

These were men like Adolph Zukor (the force behind Paramount Pictures), Carl Laemmle (Universal), Louis B. Mayer (MGM), Harry Cohn (Columbia), William Fox (what would soon be Twentieth Century Fox) and the founders of the Warner Brothers Studio. Others who helped shape this cultural and commercial landscape included Marcus Loew, who built the chain of cinemas that took his name, and youthful producer and so-called 'Boy Wonder' Irving Thalberg.

Individually, collectively and culturally they escaped much of their own history and created, in a spirit of idealized escapism, much of the mythology that is now considered to embody the authentic American dream.

HOW TO BE AN OUTSIDER: BE NAÏVE

What are the key ingredients to becoming an outsider, or at least creating the outsider mentality?

Naivety (or naïveté, depending on your mother tongue) has always had a lingering sense of pejorative condescension. "Oh, how naïve of you to think that..." (just add a patronizing sneer).

Yet beneath the surface is a history of tension. Related to 'innate', 'nature', 'natural' and cognate to 'native', *naïve* implies 'natural' or 'artless' and is opposed to the artificial, the faux and the fake (terms which have recently enjoyed renewed currency).

It is the sense of 'just born' or even 'rustic' that gives rise to the critical spirit, as in that other putdown, "Were you born yesterday?"

The naïf as a noun has a literary tradition: the naïf, such as Voltaire's Candide, is the outsider in a state of personal flux and searching for 'actualization'. Naïve art (sometimes called 'primitive art', though with some diplomacy issues) emphasizes a more informal, almost childlike method to technique and approach.

But this natural, part-formed, uncritical spirit is something that should be prized by outsiders if we are to try and create meaning and insight. The need for cognitive diversity and the over-reliance on (narrow) expertise is a hindrance to genuine new thinking in all its forms. There is a strong body of evidence, from the likes of Professor Philip Tetlock, whom we discussed earlier, that the accuracy of experts in all fields is disconcertingly mythical.

A NON-LINEAR OUTSIDER

One example of the naïve outsider who succeeded is Michael Ventris.

Born in 1922, he became supremely adept at languages, and also developed a fascination with the tablets containing the so-called 'Linear B' script, discovered in 1900 by the famous archaeologist Sir Arthur Evans at the supposed palace of King Minos at Knossos on the island of Crete.

Knossos dated from 1700 BCE, was cited in Homer (late 8th or early 7th century BCE) and was the legendary home of the labyrinth with its Minotaur, designed by Daedalus and his son Icarus. This was where Ariadne, daughter of Minos, fell in love with Theseus and helped him escape by giving him a ball of golden thread.

Progress in deciphering the script had been hampered by Evans' own strongly held assumption that the language was Cretan (and Cretan only) and not Greek, and his belief that as the discoverer he should be entitled to be right about its origins.

Despite the onset of World War II, and while pursuing a career as an architect, Ventris remained obsessed with deciphering the script, though very conscious of his lack of academic expertise in the field. He gave up his career to devote himself to the decipherment, all the while bottling up many of his feelings (his mother had committed suicide) in a stereotypically 'English' manner. As a talented amateur, he sent questionnaires out to experts in the field, many of whom responded.

Later, in 1952, the astonishing realization dawned on him that the tablets were in fact a form of Greek that predated Homer by some 500 years; this indicated that Cretan civilization at this time was linked to that of Mycenaean Greece.

This caused a sea-change in the prevailing view of ancient Greek. It was a stunning discovery, which would be taken further after Ventris's death by the Classical scholar John Chadwick.

The Outsider had triumphed.

TABLETS OF STONE?

Sadly, Ventris's success was short-lived. Once he had cracked that problem, he could not fit into the academic role that might have been expected of him.

Four years after his success, his car smashed into a stationary lorry and he died immediately. The verdict at the time was a sad accident, but suicide was not ruled out, given that he had suffered from depression like his mother.

The moral here is that Ventris confronted the orthodoxy, as defined by Evans, that Linear B could not be Greek; his amateur status and naivety gave him permission to crack the code in a way that was liberated from the consensus, and in so doing he smashed a variety of fiercely held beliefs.

Though he was never a trained classicist and never even went to university, he did have the advantage of approaching things from a different point of view. As an architect, he brought a visual, codifying approach to the interpretation of the words and symbols.

Even his architecture betrayed his idiosyncratic approach: he designed and built a house in Hampstead, London, radically laid out so the children were on the ground floor and the adults above.

THE SENSE OF VERSATILITY

One aspect that characterizes the Outsider, in our definition, is the sense of versatility.

Bart Kosko, author of *Fuzzy Thinking*, has quite a portfolio: as well as holding degrees in Electrical Engineering and Law from the University of Southern California, he is a thriller writer. One of his core writing beliefs is that commas are dispensable, as they keep the reader waiting too long to get to the verb.

We could also point to all-round renaissance polymath Sir Jonathan Miller, whose multitudinously diverse talents have ranged across theatre and opera, but who is also an author, medical doctor, neuropsychologist, television presenter, satirist, secular thinker and sculptor.

Star of the *Cambridge Footlights* revue, which conquered the United States, and co-writer of *Beyond the Fringe*, alongside Peter Cook and Dudley Moore and playwright Alan Bennett, Miller is now as happy welding and creating collages as directing the English National Opera.

He also has an interesting angle on creating art, based on the serendipity we have been championing throughout *The Inspiratorium*:

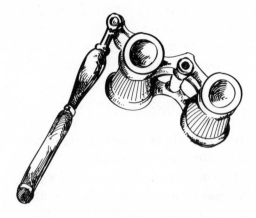

———

I'm interested in the overlooked and the negligible.
That's where some of the most interesting
breakthroughs in art and science come from.
Until Freud, nobody thought about the significance
of slips of the tongue. And now we think: how stupid
not to have thought of that before. I make no grand
claims for my work, but it seems to me to come from a
similar noticing of the negligible.

———

OH, BROTHER...

There are many books now on applying the mythologies and theologies of the classical civilizations to modern life.

There have been frequent modern reimaginings. The Coen brothers' movie *Oh Brother, Where Art Thou?* acknowledges its debt to Homer's *Odyssey*; the second series of HBO vampire series *True Blood* owes much to the story of Dionysus and the maenads; and the writer of the BBC's hit drama *Doctor Foster* has acknowledged the influence of the Medea story.

Much of current neuroscience is based on the polarity between rationality and emotion, a spectrum that Greek theatregoers would recognize in Euripides' play *The Bacchae*, setting up the spirit of rational correctness, within the character of Pentheus, against the wild, hedonistic impulses of the god Dionysus. Pentheus' fate was to be torn to pieces by Bacchus' followers, the maenads, in a possessed trance. This dichotomy is sometimes depicted as a battle between Apollo and Dionysus.

But, leaving aside the pantheon of Greek gods, Proteus is perhaps the Greek character (along with the wandering Odysseus) who most typifies our modern age: the sea-god who can change shape at will.

The sense of versatility sometimes means that we need old ways to show us thinking that we like to think is cutting-edge and modern.

GENRE-HOPPING PROTEANS

Success increasingly comes from outsiders unafraid to vault barriers and hop across genres.

Take a couple of present-day Proteans: the film-makers Nick Broomfield and Michael Winterbottom.

Winterbottom, whose big break came with his adaptation of Thomas Hardy's *Jude the Obscure*, straddles so many different characters and styles that the concept of *auteur* seems wholly inappropriate for him – from the pseudo-documentary *Welcome to Sarajevo* to the social realism of *Wonderland*, from the free-wheeling analysis of 1990s music- and drug-fuelled 'Madchester' (*sic*) to the futuristic sci-fi mystery of *Code 46*.

With *9 Songs* he made the most sexually explicit movie to be released with a certificate in the UK, which he followed with an adaptation of the 1759 satirical novel by Laurence Sterne, *The Life and Opinions of Tristram Shandy, Gentleman*, which revelled – like the book – in all sorts of postmodern and meta-textual shenanigans. Next came a documentary, *The Road to Guantanamo Bay*, a docu-drama about three British Muslims.

Most recently he has directed an ultra-violent period piece based on Jim Thompson's noir novel, *The Killer Inside Me*, and a quasi-travel-cooking-mockumentary comedy series, *The Trip*, with British comedians Steve Coogan and Rob Brydon travelling round the Lake District – and, in later series, Italy and Spain – enjoying a semi-fictionalized narrative to boot.

A GONZO PROTEAN

Another, very different protean outsider is the English filmmaker Nick Broomfield.

He pioneered a particular methodology for documentary filmmaking and in so doing blazed a trail of what we could call Heisenbergian documentary makers who forgo dispassionate observation to become intrinsically wrapped up in the subject they are exploring, by analogy with Heisenberg's Observer Effect that an observer influences what is being observed.

Since then, we have seen this approach adopted by the likes of Michael Moore, Morgan Spurlock and, in the UK, Louis Theroux and Jon Ronson.

Some of this is clearly channelling the 'gonzo' approach of American journalist, author and countercultural maverick Hunter S. Thompson, where the hero's quest becomes a part of the narrative, but Broomfield has a very specific naïve and shambolic British sensibility.

His works include *The Leader*, *His Driver* and *The Driver's Wife*, featuring Broomfield's doomed attempt to set up an interview with South African apartheid leader Eugène Terre'Blanche; *Tracking Down Maggie*, a series of doomed attempts to track down former Prime Minister Margaret Thatcher; and, most recently, *Sarah Palin: You Betcha!*, a failed attempt to interview the most famous daughter of Wasilla, Alaska.

As Broomfield himself put it: "You have to find a structure that is a portrait by omission. I think sometimes people reveal more about themselves by the questions they won't answer. I work that way and I've done lots of subjects that are off-limits."

New ways of asking questions, however doomed, are the signature of the Outsider.

A PROFESSIONAL ALIEN

This approach to extracting insight and meaning to create something both entertaining and informative has been gathering pace for a while and jibes nicely with the insightment process we discussed earlier.

In the same way, research is more likely to bring back something instructive, inspirational and insightful if the researchers adopt a more Heisenbergian approach and accept that their role is not to spectate from the outside but to catalyse from the inside.

The best auto-ethnographer and professional alien is perhaps Kate Fox, social anthropologist and co-director of the Social Issues Research Centre in Oxford.

Her investigation into the tribe of the British (and specifically the English) was encapsulated in her book *Watching the English*. Though it is not the sort of book that I feel happy to endorse without qualification, her assessment of the English (she is clear to distinguish 'English' from 'British', something that non-British readers are not always well-equipped to do) is fair: and it is worth reading, if only for her insistence that we English suffer from a form of what she terms 'dis-ease' and that "Home is what the English have instead of social skills."

DON'T CALL ME CANTANKEROUS

Outsiders need to be just a teensy bit grumpy. Yes, I want to fly the flag for a particular virtue, and one that is perhaps not usually mentioned in the normal business and self-help books.

Of late, grumpiness has become something of a media conceit. In the UK, the brand started with the TV series *Grumpy Old Men* (not to be confused with the 1993 film with Walter Matthau and Jack Lemmon).

A chatty, conversational format narrated by a suitably grumpy voice-over and usually focusing on one topic, the series ran on the BBC from 2003 and developed spin-offs such as *Grumpy Old Women*. Though the BBC online description gives a disturbingly down-age definition of 'old' ("a series giving a voice to 35- to 54-year-old men, very probably the grumpiest sector of our society"), it permitted a perhaps marginalized group the opportunity to moan and grumble about wide-ranging topics from man-hugging to trips to the supermarket and an increasing list of medical complaints.

As well as the TV diversification, we saw other sub-brands, notably the book *Is it Just Me or is Everything Shit?* by Steve Lowe and Alan McArthur, which was even more bitter and self-righteous in its rantiness. This in turn spawned a sequel, and others such as Richard Wilson's *Can't Be Arsed*, and a counter-tirade called *It Is Just You, Everything's Not Shit.*

The enormous outpouring of material on the subject of happiness has in itself done little to improve overall levels of happiness among those trying to find out how to get more of it themselves.

GRUMP YOUR WAY TO LONGEVITY

There has been substantial evidence to suggest that a more positive outlook on life is associated with longevity, though, as is often the case, it is not always easy to disentangle cause and effect. Much of this it seems to relate to issues of control: if people feel they have some control over their lives (or in other spheres, such as feeding plants or caring for animals) this can engender a greater sense of purposefulness and wellbeing.

According to Dr Howard S. Friedman, Distinguished Professor of Psychology at the University of California, Riverside, cheerfulness is not necessarily correlated with longevity; if anything, a cheery disposition is associated with a shorter-than-average lifespan. Another study looked at pessimists in later life and concluded that older pessimists were less likely to suffer from depression than optimists. A third study even suggested that residents in old-age homes who were more stubborn and cantankerous lived longer than their more placid counterparts.

According to Professor Joe Forgas of the University of New South Wales, writing in the *Australian Science Journal*, a more negative mood is likely to lead to more attentive analysis of the outside world, as well as better communication.

This view is further supported by the writer, philosopher and founder of The School of Life, Alain de Botton, who argues after the likes of French philosopher Blaise Pascal and the Roman philosopher Seneca that optimism is a flawed strategy and can lead to overoptimistic, 'Panglossian' self-delusion.

De Botton also believes that pessimism limits our expectations and enhances our capacity for appreciation (a view shared by psychotherapist Oliver James, who has also argued for limiting our aspirations to improve overall levels of happiness).

This may be why the only people who are found to have a good sense of reality and understand the limits of their importance are those who are clinically depressed. So depression may have an evolutionary and adaptive origin and benefit in that it acts to protect us from wild delusion and disappointment.

GET OUT NOW…

In one of his regular columns for the *Guardian* newspaper, "This Column Will Change Your Life", the journalist Oliver Burkeman discussed a book by John R. Stilgoe, the Professor in the History of Landscape at the Visual and Environmental Studies Department of Harvard University.

A historian and photographer, Stilgoe argues in his book *Outside Lies Magic: Regaining History and Awareness in Everyday Places* that, as we become increasingly sedentary and subjected to screens, we all need to go outside to explore, and see things differently.

This book was written in 1998, so when he talks about escaping the "traps of our programmed electronic age", he had barely an inkling of what that would mean almost 20 years later. I would add him to our happy band of (in his case, literal) outsiders for promoting the view that "Exploration encourages creativity, serendipity, invention."

On the surface an argument to explore our cultural landscapes, Stilgoe's book is an inspiring cry from the heart for the virtues of greater exploration, unstructured incubation and serendipity that we are canvassing for here, for more obliquity and more muddling through. The first three words are "Get Out Now!"

And his plea for unprogrammed awareness chimes with much of the modern (and arguably modish) interest in mindfulness, and what we should and should not pay active attention to.

BEFORE YOU LEAVE…

American psychologist Charles T. Tart specialized in looking at altered states of consciousness. In his book *Waking Up* he introduced the concept of 'consensus trance', a shared consciousness and indoctrinated societal acceptance of a shared narrative, a form of collective confirmation bias or conformity bias that can lead to cases of the Emperor's New Clothes.

So, what have we learned from the Outside Room?

1. Break out of the consensus trance and seek out voids, and people who can stretch across them.
2. Specifically encourage the influx of diverse people and diverse contexts: the French word *L'Étranger* (title of a novel by existential writer, philosopher and goalkeeper Albert Camus) covers a range of meanings which clarify some of the elements we are looking for here: the outsider, the foreigner (the French *à l'étranger* translates as "abroad"), the alien, the outcast, even the unconnected and apparently irrelevant.
3. Be grumpy, cantankerous, Heisenbergian and tumultuous. These are not words normally associated with the standard worldview. But be stroppy with the status quo, pour more of yourself into your work and world and don't worry about mess and chaos. Grumpiness means better decision-making, after all.
4. Remember: you are more likely to be exceptional, original and (strangely) authentic if you have an Outsider point of view.

5. Cultivate naivety: maybe be an expert Monday–Wednesday–Friday but make Tuesday and Thursday naïve days. Or maybe hire a dedicated naïf.
6. Engage with culture that deliberately seeks out the professional alien: watch BBC's *Close Up* documentary series, or find old episodes of *Do They Mean Us?*, a series that looked at the UK through the lens of the foreign press. Better still, make your own version just for you.
7. Notice the negligible: if it's good enough for the world's foremost renaissance-man-polymath, Jonathan Miller, it's good enough for you.
8. Assume the Juxta-Position. Outsiders will be relentlessly putting cats among pigeons to spoil the broth and generally cause a brouhaha.
9. Above all, look – as ever – for influence, meaning and purpose.
10. Be happy with nine rules.

FIRST FLOOR: THE PARLOUR ROOM

5. WORDS AND EXPRESSIONS

On the basis that the parlour was originally the room where people came to talk (as in the French *parler* (speak), though more informally than they would in a parliament), let's snack on some insightful quotations, language and wordplay to incite some preprandial conversation.

LIES, DAMNED LIES AND WORDS

Words may be our friends but they can also betray us, lie to us and conceal their past from us. If we are a bit more inquisitive about the words we surround ourselves with, it can open up new insights and opportunities.

From another perspective, words are a form of literary and mental heuristic – a practical problem-solving device. They are nuggets of history, deep-fried and spiced; all the more tasty if we know who sourced, cooked and prepared them.

Words can operate as heuristics in the sense that they become shortcuts, mental crutches that we rely on in the brain's pursuit of what Daniel Kahneman in *Thinking, Fast and Slow* calls 'cognitive ease'. In the same way that Kahneman (and others such as Gerd Gigerenzer, Director at the Max Planck Institute for Human Development in Berlin) emphasizes the importance of heuristics in saving the brain energy in decision-making, so words and ideas do not need to be freshly brought to the surface, explored and dissected every time we want to use them.

That makes sound evolutionary sense: for us to focus on matters of more pressing evolutionary need (long-term survival, how to defend or enhance our status and impression management), the brain needs to focus its resources where they are most needed. Most of the time that means the brain doesn't have the time to ponder the origins of our feelings towards global warming, saving for retirement or gun control: it simply goes with what is already there.

Language is the same, so let's force ourselves to dig deeper and uncover the hidden riches beneath.

We may expect loyalty from our friends but we must always treat them carefully: words can be ambiguous, deceitful and duplicitous.

Take the word "linguist" itself. Ironically, perhaps, it has two very distinct meanings, depending on whether you are the layperson-on-the-street or a pro.

LINGUISTS (CUNNING OR OTHERWISE)

To most people on the strada, the answer to "What is a linguist?" is likely to be "someone who speaks lots of languages". But within the business, linguists are known as those who study linguistics and are concerned with the science of language rather than speaking multiple languages.

Hence most linguists endure the following conversation at some point in their lives: "I'm a linguist." "Oh. How many languages do you speak, then?"

One way of looking at it is to create a polarity between theory and practice: pros are interested in both but especially the theory of language (singular), speakers primarily with the practice of languages (plural).

If we wanted to build distance between them, we could use alternatives. So, for the popular sense, 'polyglot' serves well enough (from the Greek, meaning 'many tongues'), a word cited as far back as 1645.

Originally, an expert who studied the structure, form and meaning of language was known as a linguistician. However, this seems to have fallen out of favour, one assumes because it falls foul of some of the laws of language: economy of expression and fluency. But linguists themselves (the theoreticians) are famously loath to be linguistically prescriptive (they prefer describing to prescribing). The '-ician' suffix is common enough (my spellcheck directed me away from 'linguistician' and towards 'logician', but it could have offered 'statistician', not to mention 'mathematician', 'physician' or even 'beautician'). The word dates from about 1895, around the time when linguistics became more of a science and the Swiss father of linguistics, Ferdinand de Saussure, wrote his book *Cours de Linguistique Générale*.

On the subject of Saussure, the late English academic and author Malcolm Bradbury wrote a spoof of postmodernism, structuralism and the more fashionable elements of deconstructionism, called *Mensonge* (French for 'lie').

WELCOME TO BRADBURY LODGE

Malcolm Bradbury (1932-2000) was an academic, journalist, reviewer, novelist and TV adapter. He founded the creative writing course at the University of East Anglia, where his first student was one Ian McEwan.

Along with David Lodge, Bradbury wrote a series of novels satirizing academia, such as *The History Man*. But *Mensonge* was a fulminating satire on postmodernism, specifically the likes of Roland Barthes, Jacques Derrida and Michel Foucault. The comic academic novel has a rich heritage, especially in the UK, from Kingsley Amis's 1954 novel *Lucky Jim* through Bradbury and Lodge, to Howard Jacobson.

Jacobson has moved on to weightier matters (2010's Man Booker prize-winning *The Finkler Question*, the dystopian *J* and 2016's *Shylock is My Name*, as well as non-fiction titles such as *Seriously Funny*, an analysis of the origins of humour), but his 1983 debut novel, *Coming From Behind*, was a campus novel set in a West Midlands polytechnic (as the new universities used to be known), Wrottesley Poly.

As a nod to the two great English campus novelists in whose steps he was following, Jacobson refers to a home for literary figures called 'Bradbury Lodge'.

POMO-SEXUAL

Back to Saussure and Bradbury: in *Mensonge*, Bradbury wrote with pen firmly in cheek: "Post Modernism is the move from Saussure to not Saussure after all."

'Linguist' in the amateur sense is attested as far back as the 16th century, in Shakespeare's *Two Gentlemen of Verona* (c.1589-1593), Act IV Scene I"

———

And partly, seeing you are beautified
With goodly shape and by your own report
A linguist and a man of such perfection
As we do in our quality much want –

———

But the professional tribe still resent the label 'linguistician', as evidenced by this comment from professional linguistician Einar Haugen:

———

To … linguistician, I not only cannot subscribe, but feel that any attempt on our part to use such a term and to persuade others to use it will only make us seem ridiculous. It is true that the term linguist is ambiguous, but so is the suffix -ician. It has not only the meaning of "a practitioner of a science", but also that of "a member of an occupation which is seeking for higher status". This meaning, exemplified by such words as mortician and beautician, implies pretentiousness rather than precision.

———

FROM WHORES...

With that warning issued, let's look at some other words that can surprise or inspire us.

'Brothel' is a word that has experienced something of a sea-change over the years. The original Anglo-Saxon meaning referred not to a building but to a vile or worthless person. Significantly, it could refer to either sex and comes from an old English word for a broken or ruined person. In the Middle Ages, the word became entangled with the unrelated 'bordel', originally a small hut or cabin and linked to 'board'.

'Whore' has also glided serenely thorough the waters of semantic change. Several centuries ago it meant 'adulterer'. Before that it seems to have had a root in PIE (meaning the reconstructed Proto-Indo-European language rather than a baked pastry dish) meaning 'dear' or 'sweetheart', putting it surprisingly close to the Latin *carus*, and the Sanskrit *kama* (as in Kama Sutra).

Carus then reminds us of *caritas* (one of the Christian virtues, usually translated as 'charity' or 'virtue').

The French word for 'whore', *pute* or *putain*, has a vernacular meaning of 'damn' (or some stronger expression of your choice). The phrase *putain de merde* is a common one, though the literal translation may seem baffling at first.

The website goutaste.com offers constructive advice on the use of 'putain' in the presence of:
- An older French person
- A French business colleague you've just met
- Children (yours and other people's too, I suggest)
- Someone of distinguished stature.

This is all the more relevant if the older French person is of distinguished stature and his children are listening to the French radio station Radio FG.

Although various explanations have been offered for 'FG' since its launch in 1981 – from "Fréquence Gaie" (Gay Frequency) to "Futur Génération" (Future Generation) to "Filles et Garçons" (Girls and Boys) – these days they are not shy in telling their audience that FG stands for "F***in' Good" music (their Twitter page makes this pretty explicit).

...TO PASTA

On the subject of *putain* and relatives, we need to talk pasta. I hope I can assume that a reader as charming and erudite as yourself is familiar with the delicacy that is *sugo alla puttanesca* – a memorable Italian sauce composed largely of garlic, capers, olives and anchovies.

The sauce may be a later invention than you expect – many trace it back to World War II.

The traditional nudge-nudge explanation for this word is that it derives from *puttana* – 'prostitute' in Italian. To accompany this etymology, proponents of this view have cobbled together a thesis that it was so named because the ladies in question grabbed anything that could be cooked quickly between clients' visits.

But alternative origin stories are available that might cast doubt on this whore-y old story. One is proposed by food historian and blogger Jeremy Parzen. He argues that the sense of *puttana* could be closer to the French use of *putain* we discussed before, as a synonym for 'shit'. In this view, *puttanesca* may be more accurately translated as 'sauce with any old shit in it'. This may be marginally more satisfying than 'whore's sauce', but that might be a manner of taste.

Either way, I think I will remember it as a sauce that can be knocked up easily.

A SERIES OF EXTRAORDINARY BOOKS

Before we dab daintily at our lips and bid *arrivederci* to puttanesca, we have a chance to acknowledge another occurrence of puttanesca sauce and in so doing tip our hats to honour one of the greatest series of books in modern literature, *A Series of Unfortunate Events* by Lemony Snicket (the pen name of Daniel Handler).

This is in fact the only place in recent literature where I can find the preparation of puttanesca sauce occurring as a significant plotline.

That it is labelled "a series of children's novels" by Wikipedia is a heinous understatement of its ingenuity, originality, wit and emotional range (from savage satire to linguistic playfulness to grief and loss).

The gothic universe of the Baudelaire orphans, Violet, Klaus and Sunny, is sharp, smart and more than a match for the worlds of J. K. Rowling or Philip Pullman, or even further back to the creator of *Titus Groan* and *Gormenghast*, Mervyn Peake. The 13-book series debuted in 1999 with *The Bad Beginning* and wove its alliterative journey past *The Ersatz Elevator* (Book 6), *The Carnivorous Carnival* (Book 9) to *The Penultimate Peril*, before finishing with *The End* (the 13th book) in 2006.

What created legions of doting fans of all ages was a winding plot, great characters and villainous machinations addled with adversity, riddles, mystery, incompetent adults and resourceful children, and all suffused with an almost fetishistic love of wordplay, learning and books. If there is a better introduction to the love of language and playfulness, I cannot recommend one.

DARK AND DROLL

The Netflix TV series of *ASOUE* shares with the books a humorously sombre, dark morbidity: glum without being bleak or gruesome, dappled with moments of tenderness, eccentric absurdism and plenty of vigorous fourth-wall breaking.

Directed by Barry Sonnenfeld with every trick he learned working as a cinematographer with the Coen brothers (he then went on to direct the *Addams Family* and *Men in Black* movies and the TV series *Pushing Daisies*), the *ASOUE* world-building is rich, immersive and distinctive.

The character of Lemony Snicket is suitably droll, deadpan and downbeat as he delivers his running commentary.

Take this muted example, at the start of Episode 1:

―――――

If you are interested in stories with happy endings, you would be better off reading some other book. In this book, not only is there no happy ending, there is no happy beginning, and very few happy things in the middle.

―――――

Literary and cultural references, allusions and jokes flow thick and fast in the world of Lemony Snicket. To give a sense of the style, here is an excerpt from the author's note at the back of the first book:

Dear Reader,
I'm sorry to say that the book you are holding in your hands is extremely unpleasant. It tells an unhappy tale about three very unlucky children.

...

It is my sad duty to write down these unpleasant tales, but there is nothing stopping you from putting this book down at once and reading something happy, if you prefer that sort of thing.

A REFERENCE BOOK?

The love of language goes deeper: the love of other references to the literary universe is infectious and inspirational and shows us the pleasure of surprise and juxtaposition. In the universe of Lemony Snicket, for example, the Baudelaires' uncle is Montgomery Montgomery, also known as Monty: as a herpetologist (a student of reptiles and amphibians), he could be a Monty Python.

Older readers and viewers will feel smugly self-satisfied to identify references to *Moby-Dick*, Samuel Beckett, George Orwell, *The Great Gatsby*, Haruki Murakami, Charles Baudelaire, Edgar Allan Poe, Franz Kafka, Shakespeare's *Tempest*, J. D. Salinger, T. S. Eliot (there is a school called Prufrock Preparatory), Dante's Beatrice, Virginia Woolf, Thomas Pynchon, Gustave Flaubert, Vladimir Nabokov, Albert Camus, Mikhail Bulgakov, Philip Larkin and J. R. R. Tolkien.

Digging further, there is a smattering of Greek mythology (the sword of Damocles, Scylla and Charybdis, the Lotus Eaters from *The Odyssey*, Gorgons, the River Lethe) and Plato's allegory of the cave, and even a smattering of Hebrew and Yiddish for good measure.

Oh, and to add to the obliquity and synchronicity on show, Daniel Handler has a cameo in the first TV series and himself plays the accordion, which puts him into a select bunch including John Linnell of the rock band They Might Be Giants and Régine Chassagne of Arcade Fire.

The dish of pasta with puttanesca sauce is featured in *The Bad Beginning*, as part of the meal the Baudelaire children set out to prepare for the evil Count Olaf (Jim Carrey in the 2004 film, Neil Patrick Harris in the Netflix TV series) and his theatre troupe. They set about making puttanesca sauce because it is easy, only for the wicked Olaf to demand roast beef.

SLAGS AND TARTS

While still in the same general linguistic vicinity, let us look briefly at the word 'slag'.

Immediately another world of references and connections opens up, which reminds us of the creative potential of etymology and wordplay.

Generally a term of abuse, more common in UK English than elsewhere, it is seriously disparaging in the sense of sexual promiscuity. Dictionaries still tend to define it in terms such as 'loose woman', a nuance that the all-female UK daytime TV show *Loose Women* has some fun with.

It is tempting to assume that the term comes from the association with 'slag' in the sense of the dross that separates during the process of smelting metal ore (typically iron); but most authorities think that is at best a secondary, reinforcing association.

(It is hard to pin down the nearest US equivalent, but perhaps 'ho' or 'skank' comes closest.)

But the derogatory usage for women seems quite recent, perhaps dating only from the 1950s. If we delve further back, we see again that the term originally had a much more general, and non-gender-specific, use. Lexicographer (and draughtsman) Francis Grose published his *Classical Dictionary of the Vulgar Tongue* in 1785, and defined 'slag' as "A slack-mettled fellow, not ready to resent an affront."

Witness the use of 'slack-mettled' – which means 'weak-willed' – combining slack as in lazy, slow or lax. This in turn comes from the Old English word *slaec*, found as far back as the Old English epic poem *Beowulf*, and ultimately from ancient Indo-European *slegos*, meaning 'loose'. The latter half of 'slack-mettled' also betrays a deeper link between 'metal' and 'mettle', meaning strength or resilience.

On the food front, we can pause briefly to look at another pejorative term for women.

'Tart' started life as closer to a term of endearment for women before assuming the mantle of 'prostitute or immoral woman' in the late 19th century. Opinions diverge – some say it is a shortening of 'jam tart' and rhyming slang for 'sweetheart'. The term 'to tart something up' dates from the 1930s.

But equally interesting is the obsession with food. In Victorian times, there were many expressions likening women to food, especially of the sweet variety: biscuit, cake and confectionery.

BUNS, CRUMPETS AND OTHER BAKERY PRODUCTS

Slightly more extreme [explicitness alert] is the term 'buttered bun', which is again mentioned in Grose's *Classical Dictionary of the Vulgar Tongue*: "One lying with a woman that has just lain with another man is said to have a buttered bun." Over time it has come to refer both to the man who has slept with this woman and to the woman herself.

(The Buttered Bun is also the name of the café where Emilia Clarke's character works in the 2015 film *Me Before You*, based on the best-selling romantic novel by Jojo Moyes. I'm not sure I want to visit it now, even it is fictional.)

As someone who was growing up in the UK in the 1970s, I can confirm that the zeitgeist term for sexually desirable women was 'crumpet'. Dating back as far as the 1930s, and in the long tradition of regarding women as objects of sexual desire through the medium of food (cf. 'she's tasty'), it is quite likely to have emerged at least in part through more rhyming slang, in this case with 'strumpet'.

For example, the British comedian Benny Hill, whose depiction of women would hardly place him in the forefront of feminism, released the single "Ernie: The Fastest Milkman in the West", which became a surprise number 1 hit over Christmas 1971. It was also chosen by the future Prime Minister David Cameron as one of his eight favourite records on a 2006 edition of *Desert Island Discs*.

A selection of the lyrics shows the stream of double entendres for which Hill was renowned:

She nearly swooned at his macaroon and he said,
"If you treat me right,
You'll have hot rolls every morning and
crumpets every night."

Benny Hill's legacy in the UK has been mixed – largely because of what is commonly considered to be his treatment of women – (scantily clad 'Hill's Angels' would regularly be chased around the stage by the leering Hill), but his reputation apparently remains undiminished in the United States.

Many Brits find the US adoration of Benny Hill as baffling as the Americans find the French apotheosis of Jerry Lewis. Potatoes, pot-ah-toes.

QUADRUPLE ENTENDRES

A woman walks into a bar and asks the barman for a double entendre. So he gives her one.

On the topic of double entendres, this meta-joke remains the outstanding exemplar, if only because it operates in so many different ways: the sexual innuendo and the reference to a 'double' as a drink – as in 'double whisky' – make it a candidate for a quadruple entendre.

The other use of 'crumpet', which seems to be more playfully acceptable (at least in middle-class circles), is in the expression 'the thinking man's crumpet'. It can be accurately carbon-dated back to English writer and humorist Frank Muir, who coined it to describe journalist, writer and presenter Joan (now Baroness) Bakewell, presenter of BBC 2's *Late Night Line-Up*.

The additional intellectual veneer took some of the patronizing, sexist patina off the noun, and the phrase became a 'meme' before that term existed, being freely applied to a range of women such as Joanna Lumley, Felicity Kendall, Kate Bush, Jennifer Saunders, Helen Mirren and British TV historian Lucy Worsley.

A 2003 poll in the UK's *Radio Times* magazine saw TV chef Nigella Lawson win first prize ahead of the then *Countdown* star Carol Vorderman.

After the release of *Titanic* in 1997, one UK newspaper went as far as to describe Kate Winslet as "the sinking man's crumpet".

NEW CRUMPET: NOW FOR WOMEN

The media have since attempted to take the sexist tinge out of the phrase by creating the corresponding 'thinking woman's crumpet'.

As far back as 2011, Benedict Cumberbatch, the freshly minted star of *Sherlock*, received this acclamation, even before his performances in Spielberg's *War Horse*, Danny Boyle's stage production of *Frankenstein* and as *Doctor Strange* in the Marvel Cinematic Universe.

Another expression that has changed meaning over time via the soothing effect of mass media is 'Rag, Tag and Bobtail'.

British people of a certain age may just remember being brought up watching a BBC children's television programme of that name that ran from 1953 to 1965 in the Thursday slot of the *Watch With Mother* strand for children.

Yet the makers were presumably unaware that the expression was originally a pejorative term for a disreputable rabble, one of various disparaging terms for the rabble or 'mob' (itself an abbreviation of the Latin expression *mobile vulgus* – the fickle people).

So, file under 'riff-raff' or 'trash'.

MEAT IS MURDER

Another expression hiding a surprising secret is 'Sweet FA', commonly used in the sense of 'absolutely nothing'. (FA here does not refer to the governing body of English football, known as the Football Association.)

But this is a much later exterior, covering over rather more morbid contents.

The original FA was an eight-year-old girl called Fanny Adams, who was brutally murdered in 1867 by a solicitor's clerk named Frederick Baker. His trial was short and he was hanged in front of a mob of 5,000 people. Her grave can still be seen in Alton, Hampshire.

Soon after, the Royal Navy introduced tinned mutton rations for its sailors. They were none too impressed with these rations and the notoriety of the murder was such that with typical grisly humour they began to claim that the mutton ration might contain the remains of 'sweet Fanny Adams'.

So, it was but a small step for it to be equated with mutton or stew, and only some time after did it come to mean 'worthless'. As so often happens, in more modern times the FA came to be understood as 'f*ck all', and much of the original – and far more colourful – story was hidden from view.

TIME FOR AN INTERPOLATION

The Harcourt Interpolation may sound like a discarded episode of *The Big Bang Theory* or a lesser work in the oeuvre of John Grisham, but the word 'interpolation' here has a technical sense denoting the addition of new material into an existing manuscript which came from someone other than the original author.

In fact, the Harcourt Interpolation refers to something altogether more unlikely in the history of swearing and blasphemy. In 1882, a rogue line was scandalously interpolated into an issue of *The Times*.

On Sunday 22 January 1882, the British Home Secretary Sir William Harcourt made a speech in which he referred to an upcoming by-election to be contested by a local tenant farmer. *The Times* decided that it would publish the speech in full the next day, Monday 23 January.

On the day, this was the report filed – complete with an unexpected addition:

———

I saw in a Tory journal the other day a note of alarm, in which they said "Why, if a tenant-farmer is elected for the North Riding of Yorkshire the farmers will be a political power who will have to be reckoned with." The speaker then said he felt inclined for a bit of f*cking. I think that is very likely. (Laughter).

———

NEVER DISGRUNTLE A TYPESETTER

Some context is called for:

The Times, at the time, was in dispute with its compositors, those who are responsible for setting the type. A disgruntled compositor inserted the extraneous line, and it was only after the first edition had been printed that the management sought to recall as many as they could and expunge the offending line from subsequent editions (and presumably, attempted to expunge the offending compositor).

Unsurprisingly, copies of the first edition were later said to be changing hands for hugely more than the original cover price.

The dispute was clearly not fully resolved, as another extraneous insertion (as it were) is said to have been made to an advert for a book, *Everyday Life in Our Public Schools* by Henry Irving, in the same year:

…with a glossary of words used by Henry Irving in his disquisition upon f*cking, which is in Common Use in those schools.

Contemporary sources also suggest other delinquencies in publications other than *The Times*. This is from the *Illustrated London News* of February 1874:

———

A case of the same nature, which occurred in
a daily paper not *The Times* [sense of relief here?]
on the occasion of the birth of one of the royal
children, when the substitution of an 'f' for a 'b' in the
name of the palace where the Queen was confined
gave the heading of the notice a suspiciously
suggestive appearance.

———

Maybe we need a dedicated body to police unruly interpolations.

We could call it Interpol.

According to Stephen Burgen, author of *Your Mother's Tongue*, The British Parliament took a number of actions to limit cursing and blaspheming. As Burgen reports:

"In 1649, the British parliament introduced the death penalty for swearing at one's parents, a statute which, were it revived today, would wipe out an entire generation."

I-WITNESSES AND TESTICULATION

The word 'orchid' comes from the Greek word for 'testicle' because of the resemblance of the tubers to the male testes. *Testis* itself is the Latin word for 'witness' (of manhood), and is still there to remind us in 'testimony'. The medical term for the removal of testicles (apologies if this is too much detail) is 'orchidectomy' (sometimes without the 'd' – 'orchiectomy').

Historically, having an orchidectomy was a more common procedure than it is now. The practice of keeping eunuchs, especially in imperial palaces, was common throughout the ancient world, for example in the court of the Pharaohs and in the Persian empire; it is even mentioned in the Bible.

Though there is no consensus among experts, 'eunuch' is most likely to be a contraction of the Greek for 'bed-holding', a direct reference to their position as trustworthy bedchamber attendants.

In a similar vein, here is a word that is not yet in the *Oxford English Dictionary* but one of which British television's *Countdown* expert Susie Dent is an advocate: the verb 'testiculate'.

As an adjective, this word already exists as a botanical term, referring especially to the twin tubers of some orchids which are shaped like a pair of testicles.

But the verb has gained some currency in the sense of a 'to talk a load of bollocks' (presumably also while gesturing wildly).

PUNKS: SEX CHANGE TO SEX PISTOLS

Returning to *pute* and *putain*, both these words originate from the Latin *putus*, which, as well as meaning 'pure' or 'unadulterated', also meant 'boy' and was in all likelihood linked to the Greek *poustis* (modern Greek for 'gay' and part of a common expression of obscenity: *pousti malaka*).

On the other hand, the word 'punk' has passed *putain* in the opposite direction, starting as synonymous with 'harlot' in Elizabethan times.

According to the *Oxford English Dictionary*, the first recorded usage of 'punk' is in a ballad called "Simon The Old Kinge", composed around 1575.

It warns that drinking is a sin not dissimilar to keeping prostitutes:

"Soe fellowes, if you be drunke, of ffrailtye itt is a sinne, as itt is to keepe a puncke."

Or, prithee witness Shakespeare's *All's Well That Ends Well* (Act II, Scene II).

In this scene we find a reference to a well-dressed prostitute as a 'taffety punk', a term now adopted as the stage name of a Washington, DC theatre troupe.

While in *The Merry Wives of Windsor* (Act II, Scene II) one of Falstaff's followers, Pistol, declares: "This punk is one of Cupid's carriers."

The word also appears in *Measure for Measure* (Act V, Scene I), where Lucio announces: "My lord, she may be a punk; for many of them are neither maid, widow, nor wife."

It was only later that it began to morph into the sense of 'catamite' (boy kept for sexual pleasure) or a young male hustler, via prison slang.

Although 'punk' is found scattered through the works of Hemingway and Burroughs, the hard-boiled author and creator of Sam Spade, Dashiell Hammett, may have been the one to re-popularize the word.

Another sense of 'punk', which seems to have originated in the United States, is of "rotten, dry or decayed wood that can be used for tinder", which may have been behind the nom-de-punk chosen by the leader of the Sex Pistols, John Lydon.

As for the musical use of 'punk', though it was in use in the 1960s, there is a canonical sighting (or citing) in 1971.

American music critic, author and radio talk show host Dave Marsh published the magazine *Creem* in 1971 and in the May issue he used it in talking about the band ? and the Mysterians, most famous for their track "96 Tears", a *Billboard* number 1 in 1966, and covered by various bands such as Primal Scream and The Stranglers.

In the US, punk (or new wave) was associated most with the Ramones, Patti Smith, Television, Blondie and Richard Hell as well as the CBGB venue in New York. (The initialism stood originally for Country, Bluegrass and Blues, a link it soon outgrew as the new and significantly less rural music scene erupted around it.)

Punk UK style was typified by bands such as The Sex Pistols, The Clash, The Damned, and Siouxsie and The Banshees: as we shall see later, The Stranglers do not fit neatly into this category although they arose at the same time.

FROM "TODAY" TO YESTERDAY'S MAN

But punk became a national UK phenomenon on the evening of 1 December 1976, and it was largely Queen's fault.

The band (not Her Majesty) was due to appear on the early evening programme *Today* on ITV, but pulled out at the last minute.

They were replaced at very short notice by their EMI label-mates, punk foursome the Sex Pistols, complete with an entourage that included Siouxsie Sioux (she of the Banshees),with all the interviewees bolstered by some serious backstage drinking.

Soon the interview descended into farce, chaos and copious swearing from guitarist Steve Jones (goaded by presenter Bill Grundy, who admitted to being drunk himself) and an awkward conversation between the middle-aged Grundy and the young Siouxsie Sioux. Though it was only broadcast in London, the newspapers scented a national story: "The Filth and The Fury" was one of the headlines the next morning.

It effectively destroyed Grundy's career, but put punk on the British map.

Outraged ripostes ensued, including this from London councillor Bernard Brook-Partridge:

Most of these groups would be vastly improved by sudden death. The worst of the punk rock groups I suppose currently are the Sex Pistols. They are unbelievably nauseating. They are the antithesis of humankind. I would like to see somebody dig a very, very large, exceedingly deep hole and drop the whole bloody lot down it.

Under the management of Malcolm McLaren, the band built on this reputation for outrageous behaviour, not least in their 1977 album *Never Mind the Bollocks, Here's The Sex Pistols.*

Punk did live on, if only as a caricature: take the character of Vivian in the British sitcom *The Young Ones.*

POST-PUNK TO STEAMPUNK

Before we put our bondage trousers and safety pins back in the loft, let's peek at one particular variant of the punk brand that still seems to be thriving.

'Steampunk' is a mash-up of a quasi-Victorian industrialized, hydraulic retro and fantasy technology with more than a hint of fun and frivolity and some crossover with cosplay, dressing up as favourite characters (as is the custom in comic convention Comic-Con). As a tribe, steampunk has always been on the side of the misfit and the outsider.

US young fiction author Caitlin Kittredge describes it as "sort of Victorian-industrial, but with more whimsy and fewer orphans".

It is a visual style and concept that distinguishes itself from the 'cyberpunk' ethic of sci-fi writers like William Gibson and the style of *Blade Runner*: steampunk looks back to historical roots in steam-powered machinery of the Victorian age, when there was still romance in the hopes vested in science, exploration and the future.

It is one part fashion, one part fabrication and one part storytelling.

The term is said to have been coined by science fiction writer K. W. Jeter, in a letter to *Locus* magazine in 1987:

"Personally, I think Victorian fantasies are going to be the next big thing. Something based on the appropriate technology of that era; like 'steampunks', perhaps..."

Jeter's novels include *Morlock Night* (a follow-on from H. G. Wells's classic *The Time Machine*), *Infernal Devices* (a mad Victorian fantasy) and *Fiendish Schemes*. He has also authored works within the *Star Wars* and *Blade Runner* franchises.

RETRO-PIMP MY SHOW

As with any subculture, the steampunk universe is open and curious, evolving and rebirthing at regular intervals. Retro-pimping involves using more classic material such as copper and brass. It is also healthily non-gender-specific.

And there are lots of bustiers, bodices, top hats, modified armour, gadgets and brass goggles, if you like that kind of thing, or even if you don't. There is even a Steampunk World's Fair, which exuberantly promises "all the joy of the music, clothing, performers, art, literature, culture and general magnificence of steampunk".

Steampunk feels altogether more fun, festive, optimistic and joyous than cyberpunk with its dark, cynical and rather gloomy worldview.

I wish it well. Now where did I put my goggles?

If you want to delve deeper into steampunk, do check the Steampunk World's fair website, where amongst other things you will be able to find the answers to the following intriguing questions and challenges:

- What is the worst thing about being a time traveller who is also magnetic?
- Why scones are vegetables.
- Eat, drink and be merry. For tomorrow you may be teleported back to 1847.

PENNY FOR YOUR THOUGHTS?

But steampunk seems to be creeping inexorably towards the mainstream.

First, the Showtime/Sky series *Penny Dreadful* was both commercially and critically successful. It garnered plaudits among the steampunk community for its gothic Victorian universe including characters from fiction of the era such as Dorian Gray, Frankenstein, Dracula and Dr Henry Jekyll.

Next, the major Netflix series *Westworld* was the subject of much scrutiny, but the jury seemed to feel it was more cyberpunk than steampunk.

Netflix also announced the commissioning of *Altered Carbon*, based on Richard K. Morgan's 2002 novel of the same name.

But most crucial, perhaps, was the arrival of the first steampunk reality show (not a sentence I thought I'd ever see myself write), *Steampunk'd* (*sic*).

Broadcast by The Game Show Network in the United States in 2015, it featured ten so-called 'makers' who are challenged to create a steampunk space and costume. There was the "Punkyard", a set called "The Manor" and teams competing for a $100,000 prize – and there was corset-shaming and elf-ears.

It may not appeal to all the diverse factions with the steampunk community, but it certainly raised the profile of the steampunk genre.

MISQUOTES AND MEMES

The topic of misquotes and memes is a very rich one, so let us take a glimpse at three examples of things that were never actually said despite their memetic longevity.

"Elementary, my Dear Watson" was never actually said by Sherlock Holmes in any of Sir Arthur Conan Doyle's books. It seems to have first occurred in a story by P. G. Wodehouse, *Psmith, Journalist*, published in book form in 1915. It did appear in later Sherlock Holmes movies – it was spoken by Clive Brook in the 1929 film *The Return of Sherlock Holmes.*

Anyone who considers themselves *au fait* with pop culture, let alone a fully-fledged Trekker (I will follow the convention and prefer that to 'Trekkies'), will know that Captain Kirk never actually said "Beam me up, Scotty" to Montgomery 'Scotty' Scott (the second Montgomery we have encountered on this floor of the Inspiratorium). There were close approximations, but never those words in that order.

Michael Caine was long associated with one catch-phrase, which was used by those who managed the not wholly troublesome achievement of doing an impression of his distinctive Cockney tones: "Not a lot of people know that."

But he never actually said it himself. The credit goes to comic Peter Sellers.

On the talk show *Parkinson* in October 1972, Sellers told Michael Parkinson that Caine loved to bore people with useless information:

This is my Michael Caine impression. You see, Mike's always quoting from the *Guinness Book of Records*. At the drop of a hat he'll trot one out. "Did you know that it takes a man in a tweed suit five and a half seconds to fall from the top of Big Ben to the ground? Now there's not many people who know that."

Later, Caine did write a number of trivia compilations – *Not Many People Know That!*, *And Not Many People Know This Either!* and *Not a Lot of People Know This*, and he used the catchphrase as an in-joke in *Educating Rita* in 1983.

Recently, rivalry over who could do the better impersonation of Michael Caine became a thread running through the Michael Winterbottom-directed 2010 TV series *The Trip*, as both Steve Coogan and Rob Brydon vied constantly with each other, often quoting "You were only supposed to blow the bloody doors off," from *The Italian Job* (1969). That line won a 2003 online poll for the best one-liner in cinema.

WHEREFORE ART THOU MISQUOTED?

The only Shakespearean line more commonly mis-quoted (or misinterpreted perhaps) than "Alas, poor Yorick! I knew him..." is "Romeo, Romeo, wherefore art thou Romeo?"

Even the 2016/17 Apple iPhone 7 ad in the UK ("Your movies look like movies on an iPhone 7") perpetuated this misconception.

In the ad, a school production of *Romeo and Juliet* is recorded by an admiring father and what he films is resplendent in cinematic values, rather than the actual ad hoc school-prepared scenery that we observe. But it is that scene, where Juliet says "Romeo, Romeo, wherefore art thou Romeo?" which grates.

For generations, this has been misinterpreted as "Where are you, Romeo?" as Apple's young Juliet intones as she seemingly stretches out as if to look for her absent Romeo.

But this fundamentally mispresents this iconic scene and robs it of much of its meaning.

"Wherefore" is the counterpart of "therefore" and means "for what reason?" or just "why?" Shakespeare used the same term in *Richard III*, Act II Scene III: "Wherefore was I born?"

What Juliet is in truth bemoaning is why Romeo has to be who he is – a Montague, member of the rival clan – which means their love cannot survive the ingrained hostility between Capulets and Montagues. "Why did you have to be who you are?" gives a much better explanation of the sense here, and the following line makes it explicit: "Deny thy father and refuse thy name."

And shortly after, Juliet reinforces the point by looking at the meaning of words and how they should or should not define identity.

———

What's in a name? That which we call a rose
By any other name would smell as sweet.

———

CAPTURE AND RAPTURE

As for the word "catamite", which we encountered a few stories ago, it has been in decline since the early 1800s, but has a strange history itself.

Catamitus was the Latinized form of the Etruscan *Catmite*, which came from the original Greek *Ganumedes*. The Ganymede myth was later the subject of paintings by Rubens (*The Rape of Ganymede*, 1636-8) and Rembrandt (*The Abduction of Ganymede*, 1635). 'Rape' and 'abduction' are synonymous in this instance.

As with the foundational Roman myth, *The Rape of the Sabine Women*, the original Latin term is *raptio*, from the verb *rapere* meaning 'to take forcibly', and similarly visible in 'ravish', 'ravishing' and 'ravage'. It's still there hiding in 'rapt' and 'rapturous'; also in 'raptor', 'rapacious', 'rapine', 'rapid', 'ravine' and the 'Rapture', the taking up of certain Christian believers at the end of times.

Less obviously, it is there in 'ravenous': nothing to do with the bird, but from the same root, accompanied here by the nuance of eating greedily. And with the concealment of a beard and glasses, it is at the heart of 'surreptitious' – one of my favourite almost onomatopoeic words along with 'furtive' (from Latin *furtum*, 'theft') and 'clandestine' ('secretly hidden'), from *clandestinus*, 'secret'. With a bit more make-up, it can also be found beneath 'usurp' (*usurpare*, 'to take or (mis)appropriate').

In the legend of the establishment of the Roman state, *raptio* refers to the large-scale abduction of women after peaceful negotiations had failed, when Romulus gave the signal for the Romans to grab the Sabine women and hold off their menfolk.

In the context of Ganymede, 'abduction' again is the less misleading translation.

The bright yellow flower you see in fields (also known as 'oilseed rape') has a different derivation, from Latin *rapum*, 'turnip'.

A HARVESTER OF 'COMBINES'

More recently, the Ganymede myth was adapted by American artist Robert Rauschenberg.

Rauschenberg was a radical trailblazer. He opposed the move to abstraction and is often claimed to have anticipated Pop Art among other artistic trends. Beyond the art world, he worked in dance with Merce Cunningham, with performances often set to music composed by John Cage, and worked too in the medium of photography.

In the 1950s he created a series of juxtapositions called 'Combines': these were part painting, part sculpture, and often used *objets trouvés* (found objects) that he happened upon on the streets, which helped him to reimagine and reinvent collage.

One such piece was called *Canyon*, in which an American bald eagle perches on a cardboard-box nest, feathered by a pillow hanging below.

As described in the MoMA (Museum of Modern Art, New York) catalogue, it is made of:

"Oil, pencil, paper, metal, photograph, fabric, wood, canvas, buttons, mirror, taxidermied eagle, cardboard, pillow, paint tube and other materials."

The presence of the stuffed eagle (which caused controversy at the time on political grounds) is seen to be a nod to the myth of Ganymede. The work features a picture of Rauschenberg's baby son, Christopher, who is the stand-in for Ganymede to the eagle's Zeus.

In the same year, he created *Pail for Ganymede*, which was made out of sheet metal and enamel on wood with crank, gears, sealing wax and a tin of food.

This was a humorous companion piece to *Canyon*, the pail being imagined as a container for the urine of the distressed victim as he is carried off by the eagle/Zeus.

Canyon also opened up a delicate legal issue: the work cannot be exported from the United States, as it contains a stuffed bald eagle, which would make any such exportation a violation of the country's 1940 Bald and Golden Eagle Protection Act as well as the 1918 Migratory Bird Treaty Act.

INVISIBLE IDIOTS AND STRONG VODKA

There is an elegant Italian expression which concisely sums up the problem of untranslatability and the slipperiness of meaning: *Traduttore, traditore.*

Though the play on words doesn't translate readily into English, the Italian has a concise elegance as "translator/ traitor"; in other words, when you translate from one language into another you betray the meaning or spirit of the original.

While studying French at school, my teacher, Mr Petty, told us the tale of the invisible idiots. As he explained it, it was a demonstration of the perils of literal translation from one language to another. In his version, someone was told to take the well-known English proverb "Out of sight, out of mind" and translate it into Russian, then translate that back into English.

The result: "invisible idiot".

This translation process was tested again using "The spirit is willing but the flesh is weak" (Matthew 26.40). In this case, the resulting translation was "The vodka was strong, but the meat was rotten." This was said to be evidence of the complexity of translating meaning and idiom from one language to another, and perhaps of the limitations of machine translation at a time when artificial intelligence and the power of computing were still in their infancy.

Sadly, however, as is often the case, further excavation indicated that both tales seem to be less than genuine and in all likelihood urban legends, with little evidence of their being based in reality. What they are (apart from benignly amusing) is a flavour of the emerging problems of machine translation, perhaps mixed up with some Cold War neurosis about getting ahead of the Russians, since the CIA is a shadowy presence in this story.

GOSH DARN IT TO HECK: ON EUPHEMISM

A short analysis of religious euphemism and the often bizarre journeys it takes us on.

Taboos having fallen like flies over the last few decades, we seem to be in need of far fewer euphemisms to cover up for them.

'Melon farmer' represents one of the last bastions of euphemism. Swearing is increasingly common (certainly on British television, after an ever-shrinking watershed, and on cable and streaming services in the US, not to mention in the theatre: *Book of Mormon*, anyone?).

But there are channels, especially in the US and on airlines, where swearing is either removed or overdubbed.

The most famous example of this was the film *Repo Man*, Alex Cox's writing and directing debut: one of the best films of 1984 (and beyond) and a long-time favourite on the cult cinema circuit.

On his website, Cox explains:

————

Sometimes for television and aeroplane screening, or for a film to play in prisons or at children's tea-parties, changes need to be made ... by then I'd made Sid and Nancy and I was sick of swearing. It was fine coming up with synonyms for the swear words: "melon farmers' was a particular favourite.

————

There are now various melon farmers websites, dedicated to examining film and TV censorship and beyond.

WTD?

So, in the past, when it was considered socially inappropriate to take the name of the Lord in vain, euphemisms for God and Christ went forth and multiplied, for they were abundant. Before the common meme that is WTF (ask your kids), there was 'What the Dickens!'

'Dickens' had nothing to do with the writer, but was just another alliterative euphemism for the devil which caught on: it preceded the famous novelist by two centuries, occurring for example in Shakespeare's *Merry Wives of Windsor* (Act II, scene II): "I cannot tell what the dickens his name is."

Mark Gatiss is an actor of distinction – defined as having appeared in *Game of Thrones* – and a prolific writer.

He was, and remains, one of the *League of Gentlemen* and was co-creator of the BBC *Sherlock* series, which started airing in 2012 and has already reached the status of national treasure.

He is also a major creative force behind the renaissance (or regeneration) of *Doctor Who*, since its major reboot in 2005.

Gatiss wrote his first episode for *Doctor Who*, now one of the BBC's golden geese, in 2005, entitled "The Unquiet Dead". The ninth doctor (played by Christopher Eccleston, in his first and only series in the role) arrives back in Cardiff, Wales, just before Christmas in 1869 and finds hordes of dead roaming the streets. They team up with Charles Dickens, played by renowned Dickens expert Simon Callow, and together the confront the Gelth (don't ask). In one of many Dickensian in-jokes, Gatiss has Dickens exclaim "What the Shakespeare?" – a play on the common exclamation, "What the Dickens?"

THERE ONCE WAS A LIST OF CONVENTIONS....

It is a challenge for the most creative of minds to take a genre and examine the conventions, before knowing which to break in order create genuine novelty.

We all know and love limericks, even if some of the conventions mean that safety or predictability outweigh the pleasure of surprise.

Someone once defined the conventions of the limerick in the manner of the limerick:

———————

There once was an X from place B,
That satisfied predicate P.
He or she did thing A,
In an adjective way,
Resulting in circumstance C.

———————

English dramatist, librettist and half of the 19ᵗʰ century's Lennon and McCartney, W. S. Gilbert, wrote one of the definitive 'anti-limericks':

———————

There was an old man of St Bees,
Who was stung in the arm by a wasp;
When they asked, "Does it hurt?"
He replied, "No, it doesn't,
But I thought all the while 'twas a Hornet."

———————

In calling on neuroscience to help supply answers for the origin and effectiveness of humour, cognitive scientist Matthew Hurley of Indiana University, Philosopher Daniel Dennett of Tufts University and psychologist Reginald Adams of Pennsylvania State University argue in their book *Inside Jokes* that the root of humour is surprise, or incongruity expressed as the disruption of expectations.

Cognition, in this argument, works because it generates possible futures to ensure our survival and we are rewarded when we realize that an assumption we have committed to turns out to be mistaken.

This unexpected jolt is humour.

THE METALIMERICK

As evidence, they produce this example of what I will call a meta-limerick (original source unknown):

———

There was a young lady called Tuck,
Who had the most terrible luck.
She went out in a punt,
And fell over the front,
And was bit on the leg by a duck.

———

This is a fine demonstration of how the brain finds humour in the upsetting of applecarts, where logic and meaning sometimes go their own ways.

On face value, this particular limerick is entirely without interest: no clever wordplay, no rewarding endlines. The amusement to be gained from it comes from what is missing, the unfulfilled expectation of the rhyme, and what the brain tries to fill in.

Funnily enough, the author of an article on *The Daily Beast* website misses half the gag in declaring that our brain finds it funny because it makes assumptions about the last line: surely this whole limerick works because all lines after the first are pregnant with assumptions of double entendres which don't reach fruition.

Their steadfastness as multiple single entendres is precisely why the brain finds it both amusing and a mark of intelligence.

Before we finish, three favourite instances.

The first is from Dylan Thomas (warning: some might find this offensive):

———

There was an old bugger called God,
who got a young virgin in pod.
This disgraceful behaviour
begot Christ our Saviour,
who was nailed to a cross, poor old sod.

———

Next, another attributed to W. S. Gilbert, but hard to verify:

———

While Titian was mixing Rose Madder,
His model lay posed on a ladder.
Her position to Titian
suggested coition,
So he climbed up the ladder and 'adder.

———

And finally, one for the cricket fans, and with a rhythm of its own:

———

There was a young fellow named Stover
Who bowled 35 wides in one over –
Which had never been done
By a clergyman's son
On a Thursday, in August, at Dover.

———

6. THE HARPOON ROOM

This is the place where we will revel in the appreciation that words are like harpoons, and a good one is hard to extract. Memetic longevity, insight and inspiration are never far away if we have a good word to accompany us.

HOYLE'S HISTORIC HARPOON

Cosmologically speaking, let's start at the very beginning (it's a very good place to start, as a young Austrian woman studying to become a nun once sang).

The British astronomer Fred Hoyle was a believer in the 'steady-state' theory of the universe.

A new countertheory was proposed and he was interviewed by BBC Radio's *Third Programme* in March 1949 for his opinions on the rival idea. As much, one assumes, because of the scientific version of confirmation bias as anything, he soundly rejected the new theory. In so doing, he mockingly referred to it as ... "the big bang theory".

However, much to his alleged annoyance, the term caught on as a way of referring to the new idea and has become the default nomenclature for it (not to mention the best sitcom since *Friends* or *Frasier*).

In a later BBC interview, Hoyle explained that part of the reason for his rejection was the grandiose association of the term:

"The reason why scientists like the 'big bang' is because they are overshadowed by the Book of Genesis. It is deep within the psyche of most scientists to believe in the first page of Genesis."

But more relevantly to us, he later mused – perhaps with some ruefulness – on the impact of his interview and the effect of his inadvertent coinage: "Words are like harpoons. Once they go in, they're very hard to pull out."

Despite the explosion in media and content, we still sometimes forget to dig beneath our words and expressions to see the other layers that lurk underneath.

Why do some words seem to have that harpoon-like intractability?

WORMS OF THE YEAR 2015

One only has to look at words and terms in the news to appreciate their memetic power to propagate virally and keep us hooked.

A good neologism becomes a linguistic earworm that burrows its way into our individual and collective consciousness, despite our best intentions to shake ourselves free from it. And for as long as it lasts it irritates and provokes, roaming widely across the media landscape before suddenly disappearing until the next one comes along.

Moreover, words are deeply powerful and often capture our mental and political worlds better than we realize.

Let's consult an authority.

In 2015, the *Oxford English Dictionary* made a bold choice with its Word of the Year: not a word at all but an emoji, known technically as 'face with tears of joy'.

This unpronounceable symbol beat the likes of 'lumbersexual', 'Brexit', 'dark web' and my personal favourite, 'on fleek'.

The *OED*'s rather clinical entry for this latter expression is:

"Early 21st century: apparently an arbitrary formation; popularized in a 2014 video post on the social media service Vine by Kayla Newman ('Peaches Monroee')."

Ms Monroee was using it to describe her eyebrows as being 'on point' but appears to have revived the expression in a big way. It is attested as far back as the prehistoric era of 2003, where its meaning seems to be in the area of 'smooth, nice or sweet'; but, as with so many terms, a process of linguistic attrition rendered it yet another hollowed-out synonym for 'awesome'.

Soon everything and everyone was 'on fleek', from Ariana Grande, Kim Kardashian and Nicki Minaj to the inevitable marketing brandwagon: hello Taco Bell. Subsequently, a search for #onfleek revealed over 86,800 posts on Instagram alone.

As so often happens, it is now one of a growing collection of cultural curiosities abandoned in the dark corridors of 'The Museum of Whatever Happened to...'

WORMS OF THE YEAR 2016

The following year was different. The broader political and cultural turmoil of 2016 was reflected in many of the *OED*'s choices.

One of its candidates, 'Brexiteer', reflects the UK's tumultuous year of political self-examination, and the result of the referendum on remaining in/exiting from the European Union. We needed a word for those in favour of leaving, and for the likes of Boris Johnson and Michael Gove 'Brexiteer' was an adequate description.

The US equivalent (at least in terms of influence) was 'alt-right', an expression for the ideological grouping of various strands on the far right of US politics who came to prominence before and during the election of President Trump and who exploited social media to operate in a 'post-truth' universe.

'Glass cliff' was an agenda-setting coinage reflecting a widespread and significant phenomenon. It was created by two psychologists on the model of 'glass ceiling', to denote the situation where a large number of women have been promoted to prominent but precarious positions of leadership. Oddly, the term was not in itself new (the *New York Times* identified it as one of their key words as far back as 2008), but in 2016 it seemed to enjoy a rebirth.

At the other end of the spectrum (and perhaps as a response to the existential darkness behind many of the events of 2016) we find a concept from Denmark which also seemed to be having a moment.

Hygge (loosely or broadly pronounced 'hew-ga') is a specifically Danish idea, which has followed other

Scandinavian exports from Volvo and Lego to TV series such as *Wallander*, *The Killing*, *Borgen* and *The Bridge*. Call it the Scand-wagon if you must.

Hygge lies somewhere in the space inhabited by cosiness, warmth and intimacy; it is etymologically linked to 'hug' and relates to *Gemütlichkeit* and *gezelligheid* in German and Dutch, but has a special cultural foothold in Denmark. The fact that Denmark regularly tops the list of happiness in the world rankings may have increased interest in it.

The publishing industry's obsession with the concept was manifested in a browse of my local bookshop, which revealed about a dozen books covering the topic, making it the natural successor to boy-wizards, teenage vampires and mindfulness.

LAGOM: ACHIEVING PEAK MODERATION

The ever-voracious media and publishing world constantly crave the latest trend-fix, especially in the blush of New Year, and Scandinavia has proved to be surprisingly obliging. The latest from this luxuriantly bountiful source is already sowing its seeds far and wide.

So, as hygge recedes cosily into the distance, incoming... *lagom*.

This is the new Swedish lifestyle trend to pursue: simple, understated, unpretentious and based on moderation, contentment, balance and a typically Scandisocial orientation.

Etymologically, the consensus is that it is a contraction of *laget om* meaning 'laws of common sense', or the result of a folk etymology based on the concept of 'around the team', when a horn full of mead would be passed around and everyone would take what was right and appropriate. The archetypical Swedish proverb *Lagom är bäst* literally means 'The right amount is best' – close to the English expressions 'Enough is as good as a feast' or 'There is virtue in moderation."

Elliot Stocks, the co-editor and creative director of Bristol-based magazine *Lagom*, contrasted the two terms, proposing that whereas hygge is a momentary state of bliss, lagom is more a way of living.

According to Charlotte Ågren, and founder of LondonSwedes.com, writing in *Time Out London*:

"That's the Swedish word for 'just the right amount'. Sweden is sometimes called 'lilla landet lagom' ('little lagom land') by us Swedes, and this is the way a lot of us live our lives: in gentle moderation."

But let's not get carried with too much moderation. As Oscar Wilde said:

"Everything in moderation. Especially moderation."

But then he also added:

"Moderation is a fatal thing. Nothing succeeds like excess."

NOT GIVING A FIKA

One aspect of lagom that has come to the fore is the custom of *fika*, a break for coffee and a pastry, especially a cinnamon bun (*kanelbulle*). But it's flexible: call it elevenses, a tea break with a distinct social component, or a pause for quality time.

Fika is probably back slang from *kaffe*, perhaps an illicit code used during one of the many times when coffee was banned in Sweden from the late 18th century onwards, when King Gustav III believed that it might cause health problems, or even prompt an overthrow of the monarchy. We will meet Gustav soon.

The concept has already been branded and monetized in the United States by Gevalia, a Swedish gourmet coffee brand, in whose adverts a handsome Swedish man talks of how "We fika every day... once in the morning and once in the afternoon."

Perhaps the idea of slowing down and pausing is more radical in some parts of the world than in Europe, in which case the Americans' embrace of fika may owe something to their association of beverages with energy and excitement rather than relaxation and social time.

SLACK BANG

Back slang involving the reversal of syllables, as in *fika*, is particularly common in French, especially in hip-hop, rap and across 'yoof' culture, but tends to go in cyclical waves of popularity and obscurity. The French word for it, *le verlan*, is itself a back-slang creation from *l'envers*, meaning 'the reverse'.

As with many forms of slang, argot or other minority dialects, much of the reason for its existence lies in a sense of tribal community in which playful creativity becomes a shared and vibrant code amongst the in-group, and both puzzling and alienating to the out-group (generally, anyone over 27).

It is intended to be cryptic (from the Greek for 'hidden') precisely to denote the need to hide. Some examples of verlan:

- *Céfran* – from *français* ('French')
- *Meuf* – from *femme* ('woman'; ma meuf = 'my girl')
- *Ripou* – from pourri ('poor-quality', 'rotten')
- *Tromé* – from *Métro*
- *Cimer* – from *Merci* ('thank you')
- *Ouf* – from *fou* ('crazy')
- *Portnawoiq* – from *n'importe quoi* ('nonsense')
- *Chébran* – from *branché* (literally 'connected', 'switched on' or 'plugged in' but from there a small step to 'cool', 'hip' or 'trendy')

Another example of tribal slang, or 'cryptolect', was polari (from Italian parlare, 'to speak'), a favourite slang among the gay subculture in the UK after World War II.

THE GREAT TEA AND COFFEE EXPERIMENT

As we saw above, fika dates from the time when the king of Sweden, Gustav, attempted to hold back the tide of hot beverages among his subjects. His story will repay the telling.

Gustav III was King of Sweden from 1771 until his death in 1792. By most accounts, he was quite progressive: he was an advocate of the Enlightenment, he scrapped the practice of torture in Sweden, encouraged freedom of the press, and promoted religious tolerance. He was a celebrated patron of the arts, founding the Swedish Academy and the Royal Swedish Opera.

But history will, perhaps sadly, remember him primarily as the implacable enemy of hot beverages.

He believed that tea and coffee were the enemies of good health. In 1746, a royal edict had already been issued against them due to the misuse and excesses of tea and coffee drinking, but it had failed to halt the tide of intellectuals discussing big issues of the day over a flat white.

Gustav came to the conclusion that a simple edict banning the drink would fail, so he engaged in a surprisingly modern-sounding experiment to test his hypothesis. He got hold of two prisoners who were identical twins and were scheduled to be executed (they had both been convicted of murder). Gustav commuted their sentences to life imprisonment, but on one condition.

For the rest of their lives, one of the prisoner-twins had to drink three pots of coffee every single day, while the other had to drink the same amount of tea.

Gustav's hypothesis was that both would fall ill (and likely die) quickly, proving once and for all that the health effects of coffee and tea were both dramatic and calamitous.

His experiment, however, was a massive failure, for him if not for posterity.

Firstly, both brothers defiantly outlived the doctor who administered the doses. Secondly, they both outlived Gustav III as well, who would be assassinated at a masked ball in 1792, at the age of 46.

In the final coup (cup?) de grâce, the first of the twins to die was the tea drinker – but not till he had reached the ripe old age of 83. The coffee drinker outlived his tea-twin, but we have no evidence of how much longer he survived.

In any case, it is fair to conclude that Gustav III's experiment had little effect on social policy (other than perhaps 'Avoid masked balls if you are a monarch') and Sweden's current per capita (per cupita? per cup'o'tea?) consumption would have Gustav turning in his grave.

And if you so fancy, you can see the stomach contents of one of the conspirators in Gustav's death at the Royal Armoury Museum in Stockholm.

A GREAT FINNISH

On the subject of Scandinavia, we can look back at Finland with an even deeper sense of wide-eyed admiration. For Finland recently became the first country in the world to publish its own set of country-themed emojis.

In my youth, these would have been published as stamps. A note for readers under the age of retirement: a stamp is a "small piece of paper that is purchased and displayed on an item of mail as evidence of payment of postage" (Wikipedia); they come from the snail mail era where people would write things down on paper, often accompanied with other physical items, and 'post' them, often involving a process known as walking. This could take a period measured in days not nanoseconds, stretching out into the horizon of infinity.

The Finland emoji collection contains 56 proudly tongue-in-cheek expressions and customs, which were created to explain and export some hard-to-describe Finnish emotions, words and habits and other meaning-frustrations that the Finns seem to have sorted out quite satisfactorily.

It may be that these are not peculiar to Finland, but that the Finns have merely created an exotic name for something that the rest of us either take for granted or didn't even realize we didn't have a word for.

Let's examine a few of them to see what we can learn.

TORILLA TAVATAAN

The literal meaning here is "Let's meet at the Market Square." For Finns, the square is the location of big celebrations, such as ice hockey world championship victories (one Finn breathlessly exclaimed that the "genuine bliss after the 2011 hockey final ... was pretty unmatched"), and whenever Finland appears in the global media spotlight.

The term is often employed sarcastically in a small-town way to suggest that the Finns are obsessed by international recognition and what others think about them.

One example was when Finland triumphed against all the odds at the Eurovision Song Contest in 2006.

The band Lordi made history (or at least Eurovision history, which may not strictly speaking count) on 20 May 2006 by becoming the first, and to date the only, hard rock act and the first Finnish artists to win the Eurovision Song Contest, with the song "Hard Rock Hallelujah".

Not only was Lordi's victory a total surprise, but the total of 292 points was greater than the accumulated points of all Finland's entries since 1985.

UNDERWEAR-DRUNK IN THE POLAR NIGHT

Kalsarikännit: this Finnish term translates as 'underwear-drunk', and is used to describe the time or mood when you are going to stay in and get drunk in your underwear without any intention of going out.

Surely a brilliant example of something that we all know we do – yes? – but it took the Finns to imagine a dedicated expression for it.

Time to reclaim, everyone.

More distinctively Scandinavian is the sunless period which typifies Finnish winters. In Lapland, the sun doesn't rise at all between December and January, though there is twilight between 10am and 3pm, and the sky is often suffused with a blue glow or 'blue moment'. The word for this is *kaamos*, or polar night.

(This was also the name of a Finnish progressive rock band in the 1970s and a Swedish death metal band from 1998 to 2006.)

UNBREAKABLE NOKIAS

Another Finnish emoji is for the concept of 'unbreakable'.

Not the 2000 superhero movie directed by our friend M. Night Shyamalan. No, this is an impressive boast largely based on the Nokia 3310 mobile phone.

Nokia itself is a Finnish tradition, though one that has sadly struggled to adapt to the times. Nokia was originally a paper mill set up in 1865, and named after its second factory based in the town of Nokia on the banks of the River Nokianvirta.

In September 2013, Nokia announced the sale of its mobile and devices division to Microsoft, who subsequently chose to rebrand the handsets as Microsoft Lumia before discontinuing that brand at the end of 2016, and focusing instead on their profitable network equipment division.

But an abiding fondness for the Nokia 3310 lives on. The star of a million memes, and named by Techradar as the greatest phone of all time, its resilience and durability have become legendary since its launch in 2000. Not only sturdy but sleek and light with that 'candy bar' feel, the iconic handset had a reliable SMS (text) system, was pleasingly responsive with hard buttons rather than relying on swiping, and introduced many to the joys of the game 'Snake'.

For many it is part of the revolving door of nostalgia, a memory of a simpler time when 'dumbphones' were exciting, sexy and cool yet still had a battery life measured in weeks, not hours. And of course, they were modestly priced.

Some 126 million units later, HMD, the Finnish company that now owns the Nokia brand license, relaunched the 3310 at the Mobile World Congress in early 2017, targeted at those looking for a second or so-called 'burner' phone to make calls and send texts, but without internet connectivity. The new phone has a slightly bigger screen than the original, and it is in colour this time. It also has a camera on the back, which the original did not. Though recognizably the child of its parent, the new 3310 is about half the thickness of the original. But it has ten times the talk time (some 22 hours), and twice the standby time: no less than one month. And of course, it has Snake.

But will we ever want to abandon our glossy smart-phones for some nostalgia-doused, retro-simplicity? Especially those who took to social media to claim that their original was still in perfect working order.

MINE'S SEVERAL COFFEES

Before we leave Finnish consumption-based emojis and the topic of hot beverages, one of their emojis is a coffee mug.

This is to honour the fact that despite other, more obvious candidates (hello again, Sweden), Finns turn out to be the largest consumers of coffee in the world at an average of 12kg per person per year, or 2.6 cups per day. For comparison's sake, coffee aficionado Italy comes in at only 5.7 kilos per year while Spain consumes only 4.5 kilos annually.

A report from Nordic Coffee Culture found that 6% of Finnish women and 14% of Finnish men drink more than ten cups of coffee per day.

But this is still not at the level attributed to French novelist and playwright Honoré de Balzac, whose work habits were legendary and whose bursts of creativity were fuelled by up to 50 cups of coffee a day.

Take this example of a love letter to coffee:

––––––––––

Coffee glides into one's stomach and sets all of one's mental processes in motion. One's ideas advance in column of route like battalions of the Grande Armée. Memories come up at the double, bearing the standards which will lead the troops into battle. The light cavalry deploys at the gallop. The artillery of logic thunders along with its supply wagons and shells. Brilliant notions join in the combat as sharpshooters. The characters don their costumes, the paper is covered with ink, the battle has started, and ends with an outpouring of black fluid like a real battlefield enveloped in swaths of black smoke from the expended gunpowder. Were it not for coffee, one could not write, which is to say one could not live.

———————

Paul Erdõs, the famously collaborative Hungarian mathematician whom we will meet later, also had a serious caffeine habit, powered by 10 to 20 milligrams of Benzedrine or Ritalin, strong espresso and caffeine tablets. Hence the famous quote said of (but not by) him:

"A mathematician is a machine for turning coffee into theorems."

MOOMINS AND MÄMMI

As the French have Asterix – whom we shall rejoin later – and the world now has Harry Potter, the Finns grow up with the stories of the Moomins.

Created by the Swedish-speaking Finnish illustrator, painter and author Tove Jansson, the hippopotamus-like creatures were enormously popular from the 1950s onwards in their native Scandinavia as well as extending into other media (a TV series and a theme park in Turku, in southwest Finland). From the end of 2017 into early 2018, London's Dulwich Picture Gallery put on the first major retrospective of Jansson's art.

Mämmi, on the other hand, is a sludgy-looking dark brown pudding made of malt and rye flour, traditionally served at Easter as a desert after roast lamb. Finns are sharply polarized themselves as to whether it is manna from heaven or engine sludge, but all agree that like many foodstuffs it is vastly improved when eaten with cream and sugar.

First mentioned in a 17th-century Finnish dissertation in Latin, mämmi was traditionally served in birch-bark trays, but is now available from food shops around the country every spring in prepacked cardboard cartons.

Finally, before we leave the Finns it is time for a traditional Finnish saying. The Finns don't say something "vanished into thin air"… they say it "disappeared like a fart in the Sahara" (Kadota kuin pieru Saharaan).

WOOD, FORESTS AND SCARY CLOWNS

From a publishing point of view, the hygge section took over the shelf space that had only recently been occupied by one of those break-out books that seemed not so much to defy convention as to lock it up in a basement, surround it with snakes and throw away the key.

Norwegian Wood: Chopping, Stacking and Drying Wood the Scandinavian Way is a paean to the wonders of felling, chopping and burning trees by journalist and novelist Lars Mytting. It sold 300,000 copies in its native Norway, achieved significant sales in the UK (some 20,000 within a few months) and has been published in at least 16 languages to date.

It was, on top of all this, the winner of the British Book Industry award for Non-Fiction Book of the Year in 2016 and BBC Radio 4's Book of the Week over Christmas 2016. To call it a surprise best-seller qualifies as a monumental understatement. I haven't been able to establish whether any editing was necessary when it was published in English, but at least one assumes Mytting had no problem with cutting.

Such was its success that it spawned a franchise, with a *Norwegian Wood Activity Book* for armchair enthusiasts and active woodcutters alike including a game for all the family of 'Top Trunks' (kudos for that). The perfect fireside companion, indeed.

In another part of the cultural forest (a deeper, darker part of the forest), coulrophobia had its moment.

In case you missed it, the 'killer clown craze' that started in the United States migrated to the UK in October 2016 and again in October 2017, in time for Halloween. Creepy or killer, there were sightings of clowns (or at least, people, in clown masks) all over the UK, leading to some genuine Stephen King-like moments for those who suffer from coulrophobia: the fear of clowns.

Though the British media was over-eager to use terms such as "UK high streets being blighted", the sinister clowns clearly did have some effect – though perhaps not so much a wave of intimidation as a fit of opportunistic anarchy.

The craze even reached presidential heights when the 30 October 2017 cover of the *New Yorker* depicted the incumbent of the White House as a scary clown.

The *Oxford English Dictionary* defines coulrophobia as 'extreme or irrational fear of clowns', but many might argue that there is nothing irrational about fearing a character with such a twisted history.

As a character in D. J. MacHale's young adult novel *The Quillan Games* says:

"There are two types of people: people who fear and hate clowns. And clowns."

POST-POST-TRUTH

But none of the worthy entrants we have so far examined were deemed deserving of Oxford Dictionary's coveted Word of the Year for 2016.

That went to a compound word that had been circling around the zeitgeist for some time: 'post-truth'.

Again, this was not a freshly minted novelty from 2016 (it can be traced all the way back to an essay by the Serbian-American playwright Steve Tesich in *The Nation* magazine in 1992). It became the umbrella term for a range of fears and concerns about the ideology of truth in a media climate where it was being pulled one way and another, especially in the context of both the Brexit vote in the UK and the 2016 US Presidential Elections.

The American *Late Show* host and critic Stephen Colbert coined (or at the very least repopularized) 'truthiness' on "The Wørd" segment of *The Colbert Report* in 2005, and it was named Word of The Year in 2005, by The American Dialect Society, and in 2006 by Merriam-Webster dictionaries.

'Post-truth' is heavily indebted to Colbert's concept of truthiness (a fact that he was not slow to mention on his show). But what both terms share is a sense that increasingly perception is strangling reality; image and emotion are trumping (*sic*) fact and allowing our brains to skew the facts according to how we see things rather than how they might actually be.

A rival publisher, Collins, chose as its word of the year for 2017 the closely related term 'fake news'.

UNWITTING REPOPULARIZATION

On the subject of repopularizing, a number of years ago I started to use the term 'arithmocracy', and I still do to this day.

It was intended to describe a system and class that I believed was becoming increasingly important in the worlds of business and marketing. It was rooted in an obsession with numbers and measurement, prediction and control, and had seeped into my world of advertising as it had from the broader world of business, government and public policy.

I'm not sure where it came from: to me as a classicist the term seemed quite an obvious one, but occasionally people would say I had invented the word. Immediately, my social media channels would clog up with those pointing to the origin of the word in the 19th century.

I will settle for 'repopularizing', especially as my meaning was actually rather distinct from its original use.

MY FAVOURITE HARPOONS:
THE DISTANCE BETWEEN REINDEER PEES

Let's revisit the region of Scandinavia and look at reindeer. But rather than Santa and Rudolph, let's explore some of the more down-to-earth facts about Lapland's favourite mammal, and in particular how long they can travel between what some people might prefer to call 'toilet stops'.

Buried away at the end of an article from December 2013 "So You Think You Know Reindeer?" is a comment about how reindeer need to stop to pee.

Apparently, reindeer are unable to walk and pee at the same time, so they have to pause to do so. These pauses are of great concern to locals and there is even a traditional word in Finnish to describe this interval: *poronkusema* is that word and it translates as 'reindeer piss'.

The approximate distance for a reindeer dragging a light sledge is in the region of 6 miles (7.5 kilometres) so this has now become the term for a distance of about that length.

As far as I am aware there are no marathons in Lapland (the weather may be a factor), but I would like to imagine a series of races based on 1, 2 and 4 poronkusema.

ALMONDS AND SEAHORSES

Some of the most memorable word-coinage has come with the onset of neuroscience.

If we just focus on the brain for a moment, we can see some clues as to the origins and meaning of many terms used to describe the various parts of the brain, and how we may be already familiar with many of them.

- 'Caudate', from the Latin for 'tail'. The same word that can be discerned underneath the various romance language words for 'queue' (*coda* in Italian, *cola* in Spanish, *coada* in Portuguese). Pronounced 'caw-date' and not to rhyme with 'Gaudete'.

- Part of the limbic cortex is the cingulate cortex: 'cingulate' means 'belt' or 'girdle' and can be seen underneath the word *ceinture* in French.

- 'Cortex' itself is the Latin for the bark of a tree.

- Still on the topic of arboriculture, the extensions of neurons are 'dendrites'. This comes from the Greek root (as it were) meaning 'tree', as in the relatively well-known flower rhododendron ('rose tree') and the rather less commonly used 'acrodendrophilous' (describing creatures that like to live in treetop areas) or 'dendromania' (the obsessive desire to be among trees or forests).

- The term 'limbic' comes from the Latin *limbus*, meaning 'border' or 'edge', or, particularly in medical terminology, a border of an anatomical component. The French 19th-century physicist and anatomist Paul Broca coined the term based on its physical location in the brain, sandwiched between two functionally different elements.

However, my two favourite terms are the almond and the seahorse.

The *amygdala* (plural *amygdalae*) is a ganglion of the limbic system within the temporal lobe of the brain, which is involved in the emotions of fear and aggression. It is named after the Greek word for an almond (because of the visual resemblance).

For the same reason, *amygdala* is also used to describe the tonsils. Then there is the *hippocampus* (Greek for 'seahorse'), a technical term for the two regions located in the medial temporal lobe of the brain. It is known to be key in the formation of long-term memories, and specifically in translating short-term into long-term memory.

"I 'AD THAT HIPPOCAMPUS IN THE BACK OF MY TEMPORAL LOBE"

One famous experiment was carried out with a sample of London cab drivers, famous for their need to pass a test nicknamed 'The Knowledge', where they have to master 320 routes within a 6-mile (10-km) radius of Charing Cross in Central London, a challenge which takes an average of two to four years to master.

Using FMRI scans, the researchers concluded that the posterior hippocampi of London cabbies were indeed larger than a corresponding sample of non-cabbies, and this was probably a result of their brains responding to the vast amount of navigational learning and experience they had undertaken. Amongst other things, this oft-cited study is evidence for neural plasticity and against the straw man of 'hard-wiring'. It establishes how, rather than being fixed and immutable, the brain is extraordinarily plastic (that is, malleable and adaptable) and can make quite dramatic changes over a lifetime.

Before we leave the world of science and medicine, let us look at two more etymologies.

Bacterium (plural *bacteria*) is a Latin word for 'stick' (from the Greek *bakterion*), and again it was a visual analogy that led to its naming: when these organisms were first observed by German naturalist Christian Gottfried Ehrenberg in 1838, the obvious image was that of a stick, rod or small staff.

'Cell' we may forget also is a metaphorical description.

The credit for the discovery of the cell is usually given to the polymath Robert Hooke.

In 1665 Hooke coined the term to describe the building blocks of biological organisms, suggested by the resemblance of plant cells to the cells of a honeycomb. 'Cell' comes from the Latin word *cella*, meaning a small room in which monks lived.

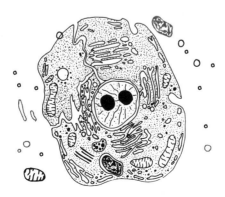

WISH I'D THOUGHT OF THAT

Another beautiful harpoon takes us back to 18th-century France.

The term is *l'esprit de l'escalier*, literally translated as 'the wit of the staircase'.

The French philosopher, encyclopaedist and prominent enlightenment thinker, Denis Diderot, composed an essay on acting called "The Paradox of the Actor", around the mid-1770s.

The founder of the Actors Studio and pioneer of the Method, Lee Strasberg, remarked that, "It has remained to this day the most significant attempt to deal with the problem of acting."

In the course of the essay Diderot cites an anecdote concerning a dinner he attended at the home of the Swiss banker, and later French finance minister, Jacques Necker.

Diderot recalled that during the meal, someone made a remark that left him stunned and speechless at the time, and he could only really re-gather himself at the bottom of the stairs on his way out.

Some familiarity with architectural conventions of the time is necessary here. Eighteenth century grand houses in France had their principal public rooms on an upper floor, so to leave would require coming down the stairs.

So *l'esprit de l'escalier* came to mean the sense of missing the moment, a despair at conjuring up some dazzlingly witty repartee which comes frustratingly too late to have the desired impact. The nearest equivalent English expressions – 'afterwit' or 'escalator wit'

– both lack the charm and elegance of the original, not to mention the effect of assonance that helps to make the French phrase more memorable. The Yiddish term *trepverter* ('staircase words') comes closes but still feels a poor carbon copy.

For younger readers: behind the email convention 'cc' – used when copying a message to someone other than the main named recipient – lies the palimpsest of a far older technology. Anyone under the age of (say) 40 is unlikely to be familiar with carbon copies.

A sheet of carbon paper would be inserted between the 'top copy' and another blank page beneath. The pressure of pen, pencil or typewriter key would cause the pigment in the paper to produce an identical impression on the page below.)

PALIN-OBSESSED

'Palimpsest' itself is a great term and one that reveals several layers beneath its surface.

Another Greek etymology ('scratched or scraped again'), it refers to the ancient practice of reusing a writing surface after scratching or washing away the original text. The term can then refer to the idea of something that remains hidden beneath layers, waiting to be rediscovered.

The same prefix can also be seen in 'palindrome', a word that reads the same backwards as forwards. More adventurous souls have also developed palindromic sentences, of which "A man, a plan, a canal: Panama" is one of the least meaningless and irritating.

There are, of course, at least two well-known examples of Palin as a surname, and they couldn't be more different.

On the one hand there is Sarah Palin, Governor of Alaska and Tea Party champion, perhaps best known as the subject/victim of Tina Fey parodies on *Saturday Night Live* in 2008.

On the other side of – well, pretty much everything – Michael Palin: former *Monty Python* actor, seasoned TV traveloguer, CBE and BAFTA (British Academy of Film and Television Arts) winner, and activist.

As far as I know he is not especially athletic, but I have often thought that maybe his hometown of Sheffield (also home to the now-retired British heptathlete world and Olympic champion Jessica Ennis-Hill) should dedicate their local sports stadium to him. They could name it the Palin-drome.

INTERLUDE

From a quiz I once compiled, I offer you these ten palindromic questions: answers on page 358.

1. The most famous Scandinavian band.
2. One of their biggest hits, from 1975.
3. The name of an album recorded by Black Sabbath and Miles Davis (separately).
4. Another famous Scandinavian Band, Norwegian specifically.
5. Walter O'Reilly's nickname in MASH.
6. Dictionary definition: "made into, or treated as, a god".
7. A one-man canoe.
8. Kevin Kline's character in "A Fish Called Wanda".
9. The main character in "Holes".
10. "My brother's keeper's" mother.

A QUESTION OF STEREOTYPES

We know of the word 'stereotype' as a way in which we establish preconceived views, conventions or overly formulaic classification, especially of groups of people.

But the word has come a long way on its journey to the heart of the political, social and cultural agenda.

Coming into English from French, the term is originally from the Greek *stereos* meaning 'firm' or 'solid' and *typos* meaning 'impression'.

So, before you ask, stereophonic speakers have nothing to do with two separate directions, but rather with the feeling of sound being more solid. The term was coined in 1927 by Western Electric, by analogy with the word 'stereoscopic', which related to creating the illusion of depth in vision.

Now, 'stereophonic' is perhaps best known in the plural, as the name of a band formed in Cwmaman, one of the former mining villages in Cynon Valley, Wales, whose version of "Handbags and Gladrags" , (written originally by Mike D'Abo of Manfred Mann and performed by Chris Farlowe in 1967), had been used by Big George as the theme tune of the UK version of *The Office*.

Farlowe's biggest hit, incidentally, was a version of The Rolling Stones' "Out of Time", which hit the top spot in the UK in 1966.

BITTERSWEET SYMPATHY

While on the subject of the Rolling Stones, let's examine a bittersweet experience from someone who sampled their music.

When writing "Bitter Sweet Symphony", Richard Ashcroft of the band The Verve obtained a licence to use a short five-note sample of "The Last Time" by the Rolling Stones (1965), specifically an orchestral version of the track performed by the Andrew Oldham Orchestra from their *Rolling Stones Songbook* album.

Andrew Loog Oldham was a talent impresario and manager of the Stones, who positioned them as the anti-Beatles and encouraged Mick and 'Keef' to write their own material.

The Verve track reached number two in the UK charts and was voted best single of the year in the 1998 Brit Awards. In the US, it reached number 12 and was nominated for best rock song at the 1998 Grammy awards.

But Richard Ashcroft has now had to forfeit all of the royalties for the track, because the former manager of the Stones, Alan Klein, heard the track and concluded that it relied on more than just a short snippet of "The Last Time". As his company ABKCO owned the royalties to the Stones' pre-1970 releases, he went to court to argue that The Verve had broken the arrangement and used more than the agreed snippet.

There was an out-of-court settlement, the result being that The Verve lost all royalties and songwriting credits are now "composed by Jagger/Richards/Ashcroft".

UNCOMMON MUSICAL WORDS: 1

The lyrics of many modern bands tend to concentrate on the usual themes of love, attraction and other more bodily concerns. But some writers have managed to escape these mundane limitations and play with language.

Bob Dylan's recent award of the Nobel Prize for Literature "for having created new poetic expressions within the great American song tradition" can at least remind us that wordsmiths are still operating even today in the field of popular (and rock) music.

Let's consider examples of lyrics that employ words not traditionally found in the oeuvres of Taylor Swift or Kanye West.

"Verisimilitude" is a track by Scottish band Teenage Fanclub, on their 1995 album *Grand Prix*, their fifth and most commercially successful release. As used in the track, 'verisimilitude' means something near to, but not quite the truth (perhaps an early lyrical reference to 'truthiness'?), from the Latin, meaning 'similar to the truth'.

The chorus complains:

"I hate verisimilitude."

UNCOMMON MUSICAL WORDS: 2

Next we come to Frank Black, another musical hero.

Born Charles Michael Kittridge Thompson IV, he is still best known as the front man of the extraordinarily influential garage/surf/space/rock/indie band, Pixies.

Performing with them under the name of Black Francis, he created a body of work on their early albums which influenced a generation of songwriters and performers, starting with Nirvana and Radiohead. After the first dissolution of Pixies, he embarked on a solo career as Frank Black. As a lyricist, many of his lyrics for the Pixies are influenced by Biblical themes, and some are in Spanish.

The track "Thalassocracy", from his second post-Pixies solo album, *Teenager of The Year* (1994) is one of his more eyeball-slicing, up-tempo power-rock numbers, and at only 1 minute 33 seconds long, it is one of his typically obscure and surreal pieces, lyrically speaking.

From the Greek meaning 'rule or empire by sea', or 'naval or commercial mastery of the sea', thalassocracy is a word used to refer to the Athenian empire under Pericles in 5th century BCE Greece, which led in part to the Peloponnesian war (430 to 404 BCE) and pitted Athens' mastery of the sea against Sparta's land-based dominance. It could also refer to other naval empires, such as Carthage and more latterly those of the Netherlands, Britain, Spain and Portugal.

UNCOMMON MUSICAL WORDS: 3

Third comes the US band They Might Be Giants.

A pair of Johns from New York (Linnell and Flansburgh), they are a disconcertingly strange blend of Seuss-like nursery rhymes, comical wordplay and sublime melodies, post-punk rock riffs and moments of genuine beauty. They are wonderfully and purposefully uncategorizable, and for those who only recall their 1990 hit "Birdhouse In Your Soul" (from the album *Flood*), or their return to more mainstream appeal with the theme tune to *Malcolm in The Middle* ("Boss of Me"), their genre-crossing is not to everyone's taste: some people find their endless parading of parody and pastiche tiresome.

(These people are entitled to their opinions, but they are wrong.)

Their 2002 release *No* was a children's record, an unusual move for a rock band. But it is perhaps the culmination of their work: wildly varied, full of ludic joyfulness and some sweeping music with songs about robots, rebellious brooms, balloons, sleeping and fibbing.

But they are called up here because they are, as far as I know, the only band to include the words "filibuster vigilantly" (as a lyric on "Birdhouse in Your Soul", their 1989/1990 track from the album *Flood* and their biggest hit to date).

FILIBLUSTERING?

The word 'filibuster' has an exotic story in line with its origins.

It is mostly used now for politicians who deliberately 'talk a bill to death' – a practice going back at least as far as Roman senator Cato the Younger. A fierce opponent of Julius Caesar, he once spoke until nightfall to prevent a Senate vote on the issue of whether or not Caesar should be allowed to stand for consul in absentia.

The word 'filibuster' has ended up in English, via the late 18th century French words *fribustier* and *filibustier* and the Spanish *filibustero*. It is a small step away from the Dutch *vrijbuiter* ('freebooter'), referring to pirates who pillaged the Spanish colonies in the West Indies. And there may be a later link to the idea of inciting revolution.

This sense of a tactic deliberately designed to 'pirate' or sabotage is probably what led to its later, less glamorous use in political proceedings.

Therefore, behind the political obstructiveness for which it is now known, is a history of adventure and (let's be honest) piracy.

UNCOMMON MUSICAL WORDS: 4

Which brings us finally to the English rock band The Stranglers.

Emerging in 1974, just before the UK punk explosion, they stood aside from and then outgrew punk to create a body of work which has endured for over 40 years; minus Hugh Cornwell, who left acrimoniously in 1990, they have continued to record and tour.

Choose from their growlingly aggressive mood ("London Lady", "Bitching", "Peaches", "5 Minutes", not to mention "Bring On the Nubiles" or "Ugly") or the elegiac, lyrical and even beautiful ("Strange Little Girl", "Don't Bring Harry", "La Folie" and of course, their biggest and most MOR track "Golden Brown").

But from the start they were not your average punk or punk-y band, in that the topics they covered ranged from broad-brush critiques of Sweden ("Sweden: All Quiet On the Eastern Front" – guitarist Hugh Cornwell did postgraduate research at Lund University), songs about the Japanese poet, playwright and film director Yukio Mishima ("Death and Night and Blood"), genetic manipulation ("Genetix" – Cornwell was a biochemist), the 1979 revolution in Iran that brought in Ayatollah Khomeini ("Shah Shah a Go Go"), Odin's two ravens ("Raven"), alien visitations (most of their *Meninblack* album), as well as songs wholly or partly in French – bassist Jean-Jacques Burnel has French parents).

Also in the long line of coded songs, there was a track about drugs, "Don't Bring Harry", on the subject of the band's experimentation with heroin, an association that was lost on the producers of Britain's premier teatime music programme, *Top of The Pops*, where the band played it in December 1979.

NUCLEAR GERRYMANDERING

One of Hugh Cornwell's most political lyrics was for "Nuclear Device (The Wizard of Aus)", a track on the *Raven* album. After a traumatic experience touring in Queensland, Australia, the band wrote "Nuclear Device" about the then premier of Queensland, Joh Bjelke-Petersen. It makes references to excavating uranium, genetic mutation in animals and the premier's alleged strong-arm policing tactics.

But I include it here for one special reason: that it is, as I have been able to detect, the only mainstream pop/rock track to mention 'gerrymandering', the process of obtaining political advantage by manipulation of electoral districts.

And 'gerrymander' itself has an interesting etymology.

It was named after the 18th-century American politician and later vice president, Elbridge Gerry, who redrew various districts in Massachusetts.

(Some US dictionaries use the term 'redistricting'.) The *Boston Globe* responded to this in 1812 with a cartoon which satirized one particularly oddly shaped district, South Essex, in the shape of a strange dragon.

Others developed the thought, suggesting the image of a salamander: and the 'gerrymander' was born. Since then the suffix '-mander' has gained a life of its own (mainly in the US) in the same way as the more recent '-gate'.

Tufts University in Massachusetts is exploring how to minimize gerrymandering and to reduce electoral dysfunction. Under the tutelage of Associate Professor of Mathematics and director of the Science, Technology and Society programme at Tufts, Moon Duchin, Tufts announced a five-day summer school in August 2017, with the principal purpose of training mathematicians to be expert witnesses for court cases concerning redistricting and gerrymandering.

As this involved something called the Metric Geometry and Gerrymandering Group, I declared myself unavailable.

The issue of gerrymandering is a hot topic in the US and also in the UK, where boundary commissioners are on the verge of agreeing a massive redrawing of the electoral map.

Additional note: Vice-President Gerry's name was pronounced with a hard 'g' (as in 'gun') but evolved into the soft 'g' of 'genius'.

LATIN MUSIC FOR BEGINNERS

Next up, some classical examples of Latin music.

Not the smooth, samba, merengue, salsa-inspired sounds of Ricky Martin, Gloria Estefan or Shakira, romantic ballads sung in Spanish or *Tejano* (Spanish for 'Texan' or 'Tex-Mex') or infectious mariachi bands.

No, here we can have a glimpse of a much more niche musical genre: popular songs entirely or partly sung in either classical or medieval Latin.

We can start with some modern reworkings of hymns or religious anthems, such as "Gaudete", a 16th century Christmas carol that was a surprise hit for electric folk band Steeleye Span, reaching number 14 in the UK charts in 1973. It was sung *a capella* (from the Latin meaning 'in the manner of the chapel', i.e. unaccompanied).

We will also include "Pie Jesu" from Andrew Lloyd Webber's Requiem, recorded originally by Sarah Brightman and Paul Miles-Kingston in 1986, and secondly as a minor hit for a 12-year-old Charlotte Church in 1998.

Then there is Mike 'Tubular Bells' Oldfield, who had a top ten hit in 1975 with "In Dulci Jubilo" ('In sweet joy'), an instrumental version of a 14th century Christmas carol attributed to the mystic Heinrich Seuse or Henry Suso (no relation to Theodor Seuss Geisel, alias Dr Seuss). Oldfield's version (now a staple of Christmas radio) has no Latin lyrics other than the title. Another distinctive feature of "In Dulci" is that it is an example of a 'macaronic' text, using a mixture of languages – in this case, Latin and German. This term comes from the rather pejorative late Latin *macaronicus* ('dumpling', or 'vulgar fare').

HARRY POTTER AND THE LATIN PIG

These days the best-known examples of pig Latin (Latin-ish but not quite correct Latin) are to be found in the Harry Potter series: for instance, *expelliarmus*, *expecto patronum*, *lumos* or *deletrius*.

J. K. Rowling studied French and Classics at the University of Exeter, so she should know Latin well enough to teasingly subvert it.

Following her dramatic rise to global prominence, there seems to be some debate about exactly how much Latin, Greek and classical civilization she actually studied and passed, but we can ignore that for the moment.

THE DUMMY TEXT

Arguably the most commonly used manifestation of pig Latin is *Lorem ipsum*, at least if you work in the advertising or publishing worlds.

Sometimes known as 'lipsum' or 'greeking' (strangely), it is used as dummy or filler text in the printing and typesetting industries and increasingly on desktop publishing software and websites that are visibly 'under construction'.

It has two main advantages that have seen its place remain unchallenged for some five centuries. It is similar in format and letter distribution (consonant/vowel balance, word size, punctuation) to real text; but to all but the most devoted Latinist it has no meaning, so readers won't be distracted by reading actual words and can focus fully on the visual representation. Usually, the text is modified and mixed up from the original passage to render it completely nonsensical.

So where does it originate?

A contraction of *dolorem ipsum* ('pain itself'), it comes from sections 1.10.32 and 1.10.33 of Marcus Tullius Cicero's treatise on ethics, *De finibus bonorum et malorum* ('On the ends of good and evil'), written in 45 BCE. His most developed philosophical work, over five books it explores the three ethical systems which were most prominent at the time: the Epicurean, the Stoic and that of the Academy under Antiochus.

The full sentence in the original Latin goes as follows:

Neque porro quisquam est, qui dolorem ipsum,
quia dolor sit amet consectetur adipisci velit.

The English translation (based on the 1914 Loeb edition) runs:

Nor again is there anyone who loves or pursues
or desires to obtain pain of itself.

We need to thank Richard McClintock, a Latin professor at Hampden–Sydney College in Virginia for locating the source of the line (as opposed to the source of the Nile).

He was in the process of looking up the obscure Latin word *consectetur* and in so doing found the 1914 Loeb Classical Library edition of *De finibus* and spotted that, because of a line break in the text, page 36 started with *-lorem ipsum*.

A LATIN CAT

And finally to our Grand Prix, or more Latinistically, *Victor Ludorum*: Cat Stevens's, "O Caritas" (before he assumed the name Yusuf Islam).

From 1972's *Catch Bull at Four*, I think it is the only (or at least the best) original song by a major artist composed and sung almost entirely in classical Latin.

Written by Stevens with Jeremy Taylor and Andreus Toumazis, it is a Flamenco and bouzouki inflected melancholic reflection on the end of the world and the need for love.

There is also a direct reference to the line that Roman gladiators are said to have uttered before fighting: *Nos morituri te salutamus* ('We who are about to die salute you').

ELEPHANTS AND CASTLES…

Another well-known harpoon is the story of the Elephant and Castle district of London: the origin of the name leads to some intriguing byways.

Elephant and Castle was historically, and still remains, a key transport hub for London. It has two underground stations, a mainline rail station, 28 bus routes, excellent road connections as well as one of London's first Cycle Superhighways, linking 'the Elephant' to King's Cross.

To many Londoners it is a familiar, if tatty, landmark and home to thousands of people. But it is also an area in transition, with a major regeneration programme underway, where over £3 billion of public and private money is being invested in the area.

And it is home to the London College of Communications, part of UAL (University of the Arts, London), which is in the midst of a major redevelopment into a new cutting-edge university campus complete with exhibition and cultural space.

At its heart is the first covered shopping mall in Europe, built in 1965, but now felt by many to be a remnant of that era's architectural predilection for ugly brutalism and overwhelming misery.

When the Polish kitchen and bar, *Mamuśka*, announced its move across the road from the shopping centre, it labelled the centre "The Pit of Despair".

…AND SPANISH PRINCESSES

But we are to here to investigate the origin of the name 'Elephant and Castle', and in so doing expose another folk etymology.

There are still people who earnestly declaim over a hot beverage that Elephant and Castle is a corruption of *Infanta de Castile*.

This is then usually said to be a reference to Eleanor of Castile (1241–1290), the wife of King Edward I (in Spain and Portugal, *infanta* was the title given to the eldest daughter of the monarch without a claim to the throne).

But it looks like another exotic but false etymological dawn.

Lexicographers have shown that Eleanor of Castile wasn't an infanta (or at least wasn't known as that – the term only appeared in English about 1600).

The one infanta that any British schoolchildren have heard about is Maria, the daughter of Philip lll of Spain. But she had no connection with Castile. So, another dead end.

Rather more prosaically, it seems to have taken its name from the 'castle' carried on the back of an elephant – an alternative name for the *howdah*, a seat traditionally used by hunters in India.

What is commonly agreed is that there was a local pub called the Elephant and Castle. Most sources (including our Wiki friends) draw a link between that pub and the Worshipful Company of Cutlers, a London craft guild founded in the 13th century which represented workers who made knives, scissors, surgical instruments and the like. The guild used emblem of an elephant with a castle on its back. The link here is the Indian elephant ivory used for knife handles, in which the Cutlers' Company dealt.

MEET THE WORSIFIER

Someone who recognized the power of a good harpoon in the cause of wit and inspiration was Ogden Nash.

Nash (1902-1971) was a comic poet or writer of humorous verse ('light verse' really doesn't do it justice).

He came from a prominent American family and was a descendant of Francis Nash, the Revolutionary War general after whom Nashville, Tennessee is named. He published his first verse in *The New Yorker* in 1931.

A former ad man (a copywriter), he was also a lyricist, screenwriter and author. He collaborated with S. J. Perelman (who worked with the Marx brothers among other achievements) and the composer Kurt Weill (who enjoyed a prolific partnership with Bertolt Brecht) on the Broadway musical *One Touch of Venus*.

But Nash's reputation stands on his creation of wit and whimsy that was nimble, terse and pointed. From couplets to limericks to longer stanzas, crammed with unconventional rhymes and irregular lines. No friend to spellcheck he.

Nash called himself not a poet but a 'worsifier', a sparkling example of his art, not to mention his humility.

He was a playful iconoclast, a breaker of rules: making up, misspelling and distorting words for the sake of a pun. He saw his field as the minor idiocies of humanity, and deserves respect as an observer of human foibles and philosopher of words. His love of language, wit and imagination put him in the same droll elite as Tom Lehrer.

I WISH I COULD BE LIKE OGDEN NASH – IT'S HIGHLY UNLIKELY BUT I'LL GIVE IT A BASH

It would be a minor felony not to showcase some of Nash's work here.

Some short-form work:

———

The Bronx? No Thonx!
Candy is dandy, but liquor is quicker.
Parsley is gharsley.
Too much Chablis can make you whablis.
A bit of talcum Is always walcum.
If called by a panther, don't anther.

———

INTERLUDE: NEOLOGISM CORNER

The rule is to take an existing word, change one letter and devise a new definition. Rules may be interpreted with a degree of latitude in pursuit of glorious comedic effect.

By all means create your own and send them to the author.

1. Zenophobia: Hatred of hippies
2. Unspire: To demoralize
3. Maverink: Renegade ice-skater, like Tonya Harding
4. Ostendatious: Proud of being Belgian
5. Cravado: Daring to wear bold ties
6. Reteriorate: To get worse again
7. Felodrama: *Cats*
8. Beardroom: Where aged directors meet
9. Breadcast: Hovis commercial
10. Batricide: Dropping the remote control
11. Premiscuous: Having many sexual partners before marriage
12. Fuelgood factor: Relief at having enough petrol
13. *Carmon*: Opera about small Japanese animated characters
14. Figarette: minor character in opera
15. Pomosexual: Having many sexual partners, ironically
16. Antepathy: Hating something before you see it
17. Barberic: Particularly vicious hair styling
18. Internit: Source of information about head lice
19. Cropaganda: The anti-GM lobby

20. Wasdom: Outdated knowledge
21. Nonversation: Talking to a teenage child
22. Ambidextrose: Able to eat sugar with both hands
23. Cinegogue: Place to view Jewish films
24. Coup de grâce: French for 'lawnmower'.

So we have come to the end of our whirlwind word tour of words, their meanings and the layers and links they reveal.

- We have covered Latin, Finnish, French and Dutch and found the value of a good harpoon in becoming an earworm.
- So learn never to take them for granted: they may look like friends while deceiving us with their cunning.
- The most inspiring words are ones that have a great back-story, such as gerrymander, filibuster and palimpsest. So always dig beneath them to see what riches you might uncover.

SECOND FLOOR: THE SCIENCE LAB

7. COMPLEXITY, CONTROL AND LETTING GO

The laboratory of science can make even those of us who are dedicated to the arts more inspired and surprised.

But first we must learn to be less certain and start letting go...

Science has not remained still, stuck in the rut of reductionism, mechanism and physics envy. The boundaries between biology and physics, for example, are blurring.

New fields – from evolutionary psychology, cognitive sciences and AI/A-Life to small-world thinking and what started as econophysics and has evolved into behavioural economics – can give us new frameworks more in tune with the new, broader ways of seeing the world.

Let us start with the notion of networks.

CAPRA'S IT'S A WONDERFUL LIFE

Fritjof Capra's book *The Web of Life* (1996) announced itself as "A new understanding of life at all levels of living systems". It sought to cement the paradigm shift taking place in the scientific world. Following on from his controversial book *The Tao of Physics* (1975), which sought to re-enchant physics by exploring the similarities between new insights in physics and Eastern religions, he gathered together a breadth of writing and thinking, both scientific and philosophical.

Another, less obvious, development was the series of insights derived in the 1920s from the new science of quantum physics. Although on the surface this seemed to be more about even tinier subatomic particles, the most subversive implications of quantum theory were just emerging. For a start, the notion of superposition and probability theory meant that the process of observation and measurement muddied the clear waters of interpretation. In the light of Heisenberg's celebrated Uncertainty Principle, it was no longer possible to know where a particle was and what its velocity was at the same time. Or at least that's what I think he meant.

Secondly, the actual act of observation appeared to affect the outcome of experiments, as demonstrated in the thought experiment of Schrödinger's Cat. This was a manifestation of the claim that said feline could be both dead and alive, until the observer opens the box and both states collapse into a specific reality.

One of my favourite *New Yorker* cartoons features an anxious vet announcing: "About your cat, Mr Schrödinger – I have good news and bad news."

The third connection was the ecology movement, beginning with the study of groups of organisms and the relationship of organism to environment. From there the concepts of the ecosystem and biosphere were conceived. This also changed, or at least supplemented, the orthodox perspective based on an architectural view of physics and saw the burgeoning of research into communities and networks. In *The Tao of Physics*, Capra had already got up the collective noses of much of the scientific establishment by arguing that Western science had much to learn by adopting many of the ideas of the East (or 'Eastern mysticism' to his critics), namely, those of Hinduism, Buddhism and Taoism.

So, Capra concludes, instead of being like a machine, Nature turns out to be more like human nature in that it is unpredictable and sensitive to its environment and small fluctuations around it.

FROM CAPRA TO KAFKA

Which leads us by a thread through the author of *The Metamorphosis* to the perennial Christmas favourite, Frank Capra's film *It's a Wonderful Life*, and ending at the Academy Awards and the 12th Doctor Who.

Franz Kafka's It's a Wonderful Life was the name of a short satirical comedy made for BBC Scotland in 1993. It is set at Christmas Eve, when Kafka (played by Richard E. Grant) is suffering writer's block, not unlike Barton Fink in the eponymous Coen Brothers 1991 movie.

Kafka is frustrated in his attempts to determine the beginning of *Metamorphosis*, specifically what Gregor Samsa should turn into, in the face of increasingly absurd interruptions from dancing girls, a threatening knifeman and dreamlike visions.

Some of the options he considers are a giant banana and a kangaroo. It is, admittedly, a one-gag film over 23 minutes but it is a good gag, especially when shot in such a Gothic and Burtonesque style. The film later received an Academy award (Oscar) as Best Live Action Short Subject of 1995, as well as a BAFTA award.

The film was written and directed by Peter Capaldi and is an example of the sort of creative serendipity and mashing that we have been eulogizing here. The idea for the film came about when his wife accidentally said in conversation "Franz Kafka's *It's a Wonderful Life*" when she meant to say "Frank Capra".

Before Capaldi assumed the mantle of the 12th Doctor Who, which he relinquished at the end of 2017, and all of the global promotion that went with it, his first big break was in the Bill Forsyth 1983 film *Local Hero* alongside Burt Lancaster, Peter Riegert and Jenny Seagrove, famous also for its Mark Knopfler soundtrack.

His most famous TV role before Gallifrey's Time Lord was that of a different type of doctor, the foul-mouthed spin doctor Malcolm Tucker in Armando Iannnucci's *The Thick of It*, which became a spin-off movie, *In The Loop*, in 2009 (paving the way for Iannucci to create *Veep* and the movie *The Death of Stalin*). Capaldi's third medical outing came when he directed several episodes of the 2009 BBC Four sitcom *Getting On*, set in a National Health Service hospital (in one episode of which he appeared as a doctor).

SYSTEMS ARE DOING IT FOR THEMSELVES

There are a number of exciting developments in the science of complexity. One of the many popular expositions of this area, called, helpfully, *Complexity*, was a book written by Roger Lewin (1992).

During his study, Lewin meets many of the scientists at the heart of the then new theory, including many who were creating the new ecosystem of Artificial Life (A-Life) from their computers. Among these was Thomas Ray, who was responsible for the Tierra program, the goal being to create artificial, digital life to replicate the biological model as closely as possible.

All this followed, in terms of complexity theory, from the emergence of global patterns from simple rules.

One of the central tenets of complexity and systems thinking is that small-world networks may lack an organizational centre, yet global interactions still take place. What this means is that old, cherished notions of hierarchical control do not apply: the assumption inbred into generations of scientific managers that their role is based on controlling their organizations, their brands and their cultures needs to be revised.

So, from the few simple rules imposed on the A-life by the likes of Tom Ray and Chris Langton – the American theoretical biologist who coined the term 'artificial life' in the 1980s – massively varied 'life' arose from the mere workings of a complex adaptive system. In other words, complexity could create these conditions without the need to import any extraneous explanations.

The number of popular books published on the related areas of complexity, chaos, ubiquity, universality and small worlds testifies to the strength of its popular appeal. It is no accident – since theorists admire deep-seated, architectural coincidence (or, rather, organizing principles or power laws) – that Malcolm Gladwell's *The Tipping Point* may well prove to have been the point at which interest in these domains tipped.

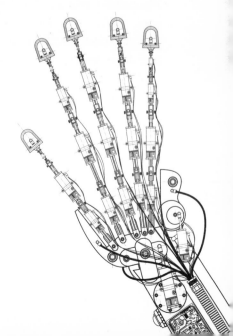

Its talk of 'leverage' strikes a chord with many who see that like does not always generate like: sometimes small movements can have massive effects (and vice versa).

THE END OF ESSENCE, THE PRIMACY OF PATTERN

One of the many pillars supporting the new paradigm emerging within science is the move away from substance and towards pattern and relation.

It is now common knowledge that the way we perceive our world and our place in it has changed drastically since the impact of the cumulative insights of Darwin, Gödel, Einstein and Heisenberg. Old certainties about our place in the cosmos, our relationship to the rest of creation or our grasp of the smallest and largest boundaries of our conception were shaken forcibly by their work.

First of all, many scientists have come to define our species as 'pattern-makers'. Take the Nobel-laureate physicist and Santa Fe complexity guru, Murray Gell-Mann – the man who coined the word 'quark'. He talks of people as being 'complex adaptive systems' (CAS).

In this way, he believes, there are universal similarities among some of the most crucial processes on earth – biological evolution, ecological systems, the mammalian immune system, the evolution of human societies and sophisticated computer software systems, to name but a few. What links all these processes is that each relies on gathering information about itself and its interactions with its environment, building as it goes a model or schema of the world around it based on the regularities it perceives. So, in the case of human beings, we think, learn, use symbolic language and generate new generations of CASs in our wake (chief amongst which are powerful computers and their descendants).

Later, Gell-Mann adapted the term to include a CAS that acts as an interpreter and observer of the information: this he called an IGUS, an information gathering and utilizing system.

According to this thinking, through both our biological inheritance and our culture, we are primed to seek patterns. The desire to link all things together and create patterns goes back as far as Pythagoras with his belief that numbers were gods, and the concept of the harmony of the spheres.

Patterns work as editing devices, maps of a world too complex, chaotic and swollen with information for us to cope. Our minds seek out patterns in order to let us expand our mental powers and move on to higher planes. It is the relationships that are primary, and a new lexicon is being created to foreground the role of the relationship or network.

Charles Darwin

PLUS ÇA CHANGE,
PLUS C'EST LA 'MEME' CHOSE

The word 'meme' fits well into the notion of pattern and connectivity. It has already been absorbed by (or, perhaps more appropriately, it has colonized the minds of) some within the broader media and communications world.

'Meme' was coined by Richard Dawkins in a chapter of his book *The Selfish Gene* to postulate cultural transmission as analogous to genetic transmission. Acknowledging the notion of memes means locating power in ideas as entities in themselves, and seeing them as active agents spreading virally from brain to brain, without the (conscious) involvement of the carrier.

This provides a vital link in an intriguing chain: between psychology and neurology; epidemiology and the power of viral communication promoted among others by Gladwell in *The Tipping Point*; and the sort of universal patterns described in fashion, history, seismology and forest fires by Mark Buchanan in *Ubiquity*.

The fact that the media world and the internet find the concept of meme so seductive and flattering is due to its power in prioritizing the value of the idea over factual, rational content, and its insistence on the social side of communication. Moreover, recent research, carried out by Giacomo Rizzolatti and interpreted by V. S. Ramachandran, into the mirror neurons in the ventral premotor area of monkeys hints at imitation being a driving force behind learning, empathy and the development of language. The communications industry has picked up on the role of imitation and cultural infection and how it supports research models based on saliency and involvement, but adds the new dimensions of imitability, catchiness or virality (like virility but for ideas).

IT'S HARD MAKING PREDICTIONS, ESPECIALLY ABOUT THE FUTURE (YOGI BERRA)

The Lebanese-American former financial analyst-turned-professional author, controversialist and Cassandra-like seer, Nassim Nicholas Taleb, is perhaps best known for his global bestseller, *The Black Swan*.

It became something of a business bible for the way in which it seemingly foretold the recent financial meltdown. But before that, in *Fooled By Randomness* he had investigated similar territory: the extent to which we are so deluded in our belief that we did in fact predict what happened in the past that we believe we can do the same with the future.

This is because we are hardwired to ignore all evidence that we do not see and are programmed to be blind to the possibility of randomness.

One of our many design faults is a failure to forecast or deal with the notion of unpredictability, and a general aversion to the non-linear, or the unknown unknown (what Taleb calls the 'Black Swan', based on English philosopher David Hume's theory of induction: that if we only ever see swans that are white, we conclude that all swans are white, until we spot one that is black).

Taleb's *Antifragile* outlines a philosophy where systems should not just resist knocks to achieve robustness, but be 'antifragile' enough to be strengthened by the knocks.

WALK THIS WAY…

Speaking on much the same subject is Leonard Mlodinow. As both a physicist who helped develop a new type of perturbation theory for eigenvalue problems in quantum mechanics (me neither) and a screenwriter who has written for *Star Trek: The Next Generation*, he immediately commands a significant amount of awe as another notable hyphenate.

In his book *The Drunkard's Walk*, he explores the concept of the 'hot hand' – the idea that success breeds success, especially in the sense that a sports player on a great run is more likely to succeed again.

He concentrates on the case of Sherry Lansing, who was the boss of Paramount Studios during a golden period of both critical and commercial success for the studio: *Braveheart*, *Forrest Gump* and *Titanic* were all produced under her aegis in the 1990s.

In looking at whether these lucky streaks are anything more than that, as an expert in probability his conclusion is clear: that the law of large numbers will throw up these patterns and sequences, but that over time there will always be what is known in the trade as 'regression to the mean'.

We love to think about 'hot hands' or the curse of *Sports Illustrated* (there is a myth that appearing on the cover of this magazine brings bad luck), but this is often just our pattern-oriented brain seeking to make order out of what is simple, unstructured chaos.

So, things fluctuate but generally will flatten out again in the longer term and revert to something approaching previous normality. When Lansing lost her job after a string of 'poor numbers', she was – in Mlodinow's words – just at the "wrong end of a Bernoulli series", the fact that in any large series of numbers there will be exceptional peaks and troughs.

Though I'm guessing that wasn't spelled out in the email that fired her.

THE EVIL GENIUS

For further evidence of the power of large numbers, just hunt out some of the experimental psychology created by British master-illusionist, mind-controller and all-round evil genius, Derren Brown.

In *The System*, he built a television programme around the concept of a foolproof way of winning on the horses. As the programme reached its conclusion, it was revealed that rather than being a scam or (heaven forfend) a miracle, it was merely a demonstration of a number of psychological and statistical truths.

The power of large numbers suggests that if enough people are recruited and given money and a camera, then eventually – by the sheer law of large numbers – there will have to be someone who has bet on all of the winners. This person then became the centrepiece of the programme.

The psychological truth at work here is our old friend confirmation bias. We assume that there must be some special pattern or luck at work, but in fact it is our blindness to the larger picture – our failure to realize how broader causality can work itself out without relying on anything other than large numbers.

A simpler example was a scene where Brown is shown tossing a coin and getting 'heads' 10 times in a row.

Not impossible, not even magic, but the result of patience: all that was required was hours of filming until statistical probability eventually came up with the goods.

KNOWING NOTHING

The Swiss mathematician Jakob Bernoulli, who explored probability theory and devised the law of large numbers, said, "One should not appraise human action on the basis of its results."

Now, anyone who has spent time working within a business culture and has a central atrium with a shrine devoted to the Five-Year Plan has figured out in their heart of hearts that much of it is a concocted blend of wish-fulfilment, rationalization of job functions and existing systems of finance and corporate culture.

Yet once there is a plan – which in my experience has in all likelihood been based on "what we did last year +3%" – everything is deemed to be accomplished in pursuit of that plan. Meanwhile, the world on which that plan was based – perhaps including an unpredictable Black Swan or two – has almost certainly moved on, leaving the plan stuck on its own island of self-serving certainty.

It seems that we are just unable to accept the reality that human behaviour's natural unruliness is something that simply cannot be explained and encompassed perfectly by theoretical models.

MODEL CITIZEN

Talking of models, Emanuel Derman is a trained physicist who later became Head 'Quant' (quantitative analyst) at Goldman Sachs before returning to academia as head of Financial Engineering at Columbia University.

In *Models. Behaving. Badly.*, he distinguishes between theories and models. Theories, in his eyes, are defined by the way they describe the natural world. They can be discovered, but they behave as though they were a kind of fact, and exist on their own terms. Models, on the other hand, are little more than simplistic metaphors or analogies, and we must accept their limitations. For Derman, economics suffers from "its dark love of inappropriate scientism".

The map, as scientist Alfred Korzybski said, is not the territory. The model is not reality, and we must remain alert to that potential confusion.

In this context it is enough to say that we need to be aware of our instinctive desire to create models of the future, and recognize exactly how constrained by our own prejudices and expectations they are.

TAKING BACK CONTROL

The campaign to take Britain out of the European Union in 2016 notoriously relied on a number of tactics. But the slogan used in the campaign was fascinating: "Take back control."

This is not a political analysis, but it is hard to argue against the visceral power of that rallying cry – after all, who doesn't want to have more control in their lives?

And not only was this echoed in President Trump's call to "Make America great again," but it can also be seen in the rush of other states such as India and China to recover past glories.

'Control' is central to our self-belief and self-worth. So many self-help books, especially those offering the secret to happiness, emphasize the need, if not to take control, at least to understand the limits of control.

Unsurprisingly, it is one of the central topics of psychology, especially with the new emphasis on the essential irrationality at the heart of human behaviour – often labelled under the rubric of 'behavioural science' or 'behavioural economics'.

This body of works emphasizes the many self-serving biases we are loaded with or construct in order to maintain the veneer of control and authority – such as confirmation bias, cognitive dissonance, the status quo bias and the heuristics we saw earlier – everything from the self-justifying historian that is memory, to other engines of self-justification.

CERTAIN?

> It's not what you don't know that kills you,
> it's what you know for sure that ain't true.
> **– MARK TWAIN**

Part of the construction of control is the drive for certainty. Most scientists would agree that certainty is dangerous. The 2016 publication by Marcus du Sautoy, the UK's newly installed Professor for the Public Understanding of Science (a role he assumed from Richard Dawkins) is *What We Cannot Know*, his refreshingly honest attempt to explore what he calls the "seven edges of knowledge".

Data has only got bigger, algorithms have got more algorithmic and there is a militant tendency among forecasters and thinkers that Dataism, or the singularity (where humans and AI merge), is only a matter of when rather than if.

We talked earlier about the need for failure and error, and here again, certainty must be resisted if it closes doors rather than opens them.

In *Man for Himself*, the psychoanalyst and social philosopher Erich Fromm put it like this:

"The quest for certainty blocks the search for meaning. Uncertainty is the very condition to impel man to unfold his powers."

MISTAKES WERE MADE…

Carol Tavris and Elliot Aronson's book *Mistakes Were Made (But Not by Me)* is another impeccably alluring title.

The most prominent citation of the expression appears to be Henry Kissinger's in the 1970s, "Mistakes were quite possibly made by the administrations in which I served." But other sources indicate it has an older and nobler heritage, dating back to Ulysses S. Grant in an 1876 report to congress when he admitted his shortcoming in his administration: "Mistakes have been made, as all can see and I admit it."

The list of similar usages covers Nixon's press secretary, when apologizing to journalists Woodward and Bernstein in 1973, Ronald Reagan in 1987 on the Iran-Contra affair, Jamie Dimon (CEO of JPMorgan Chase) in 2009 and Jeb Bush in March 2016.

In March 2017, the expression reared its slippery head when the British cycling team, Team Sky, were in the midst of a PR maelstrom in relation to a mystery package delivered to Bradley Wiggins (now Sir Bradley) at the 2011 Critérium du Dauphiné in France. They had claimed repeatedly that it contained a legal decongestant. Amidst the row over therapeutic use exemptions (TUE), Wiggins' use of the decongestant came under intense scrutiny from the media and the government's Culture, Media and Sport Select Committee. Team Sky claimed there was no official record of what was delivered, and it was a matter of "process failures rather than wrongdoing".

"Self-evidently, the events of recent months have highlighted areas where mistakes were made by

Team Sky", began the letter from Team Sky Principal Sir Dave Brailsford sent to members of Parliament on 7 March 2017.

This expression is what grammarians call an example of the 'exculpatory passive': the use of the passive voice ('were made') rather than the active voice, which requires a subject ('basically, I did it').

…BUT BLAME COGNITIVE DISSONANCE

Elliot Aronson is considered one of the most important psychologists of the 20th century.

His work on cognitive dissonance built on that developed by his mentor Abraham Maslow, and Leon Festinger (who coined the term).

One of Aronson's definitions of cognitive dissonance is "anything that contradicts 'I am nice and in control'". Elsewhere in his article "Theories of Cognitive Consistency", he argued that:

"Dissonance theory does not rest upon the assumption that man is a rational animal; rather, it suggests that man is a rationalizing animal – that he attempts to appear rational, both to others and to himself."

So, we go out of our way to seek information and evidence that makes us feel good and right.

I will look at any additional evidence to confirm the opinion to which I have already come.
– LORD MOLSON (1903-1991)

FUTURE, HAPPINESS AND THE DEVIL

Future: that period of time in which
our affairs prosper, our friends are true
and our happiness is assured.
– AMBROSE BIERCE (1842–C.1914)

This is a view of the future which is anything but rosy-cheeked, and would in all likelihood receive a Stoic stamp of approval. The Greek and Roman Stoics believed that every day we should prepare ourselves for the worst and thus moderate that unbridled optimism which so often leads to disappointment.

Bierce was an American Civil War veteran and journalist who also wrote short stories (war stories and ghost stories) as well as poetry. He was the tenth of thirteen children born to Laura Sherwood and Marcus Aurelius Bierce (named, one assumes, after the Roman Emperor of the 1st century, a devout practitioner of Stoicism).

In 1868 he met Mark Twain, became editor of the *San Francisco News Letter*, and began writing the column "The Town Crier", where he honed his blend of critical observation and savage wit. Later he worked for William Randolph Hearst's *San Francisco Examiner* and *Cosmopolitan*. In 1913, he set off on a tour of some of his old Civil War battlefields, and travelled to Mexico before making a complete and mysterious disappearance.

He is best known as a mordant satirist (to such an extent that he was characterized during his lifetime as 'Bitter Bierce'). His biting but unceasingly droll observations and lexical definitions were originally published in weekly instalments and later collected in a volume entitled *The Devil's Dictionary*.

A selection of entries demonstrates the bleak tone and accuracy of his worldview:

- Apologize: to lay the foundation for a future offense.
- Birth: the first and direst of all disasters.
- Consult: to seek another's approval of a course already decided on.
- Fashion: a despot whom the wise ridicule and obey.
- Religion: a daughter of Hope and Fear, explaining to Ignorance the nature of the Unknowable.

GIVING UP CONTROL?

The human need for control is deep-rooted and seemingly ineradicable. Whatever we believe about the existence of a single self or the presence of consciousness, we all have a need to feel "This is who I am" and "I am in control of this self and all that goes with it." And sometimes beyond.

Stoic philosophy is very much in vogue at the moment, with books by philosophers Alain de Botton (*The Consolations of Philosophy*) and Martha Nussbaum (*Anger and Forgiveness*), journalist Oliver Burkeman (*The Antidote* and *Help!*) and from the evil genius Derren Brown (*Happiness*). All explore the modern relevance of Stoicism, while a series of books on the Roman Stoic philosopher Seneca is also due for publication.

You can find Stoic principles underlying many modem psychological and psychotherapeutic treatments, especially cognitive behavioural therapy (CBT).

Stoicism was founded by Zeno of Citium (in Cyprus; c.334-c.262 BCE). Among its most important disciples was Epictetus (c. 50-135 CE). Epictetus' thinking also influenced the Roman Emperor Marcus Aurelius (121-180 CE).

The key insight from the Stoics can be summed up as: "You can't control the world but you can control your evaluation of and response to it. Accepting the fundamental uncontrollability of the world and freeing ourselves from the obsession of trying to control it is the Stoic insight par excellence.

Seneca said that we consistently act as if we have more control over the world than is the case. All we can control are our judgements.

As Derren Brown puts it in his book *Happy*, the secret is not to visualize what we want to achieve, but to take control of our life stories.

IRONICALLY OUT OF CONTROL?

Modern neuroscience even suggests that our sense of mental control is not what we think. As David Eagleman put it so eloquently in his book *Incognito*, "We don't think the way we think we think."

One example of the potency of the cognitive unconscious is 'ironic process theory', a term coined by the late Daniel Wegner, Professor of Psychology at Harvard and author of *The Illusion of Conscious Will*. In his book, he describes the tendency to say or do precisely the thing we are trying to avoid when under what psychologists label 'mental load', such as stress, time pressure, distraction or a bulging inbox.

One of the papers Wegner wrote outlining his theory is worth reading if only for the title: "How to think, say or do precisely the worst thing for any occasion" (*Science*, July 2009).

The most famous demonstration he gives goes as follows:

Close your eyes.

No, really (yes, you at the back with the hipster beard, cardigan and glasses).

Now for 30 seconds ... don't think of a polar bear.

In his *Science* article, Wegner shows a range of other contexts in which the imp of ironic process can be found.

For example, sports psychologists and coaches are familiar with 'ironic movement errors', that is, movements which accomplish precisely the opposite of what they are intended to achieve. Wegner cites former major league baseball player Rick Ankiel and his wild throws, which Ankiel called 'the Creature'. In golf putting for example, the ironic tendency is so prevalent that is has a nickname ('the yips').

Wegner presents evidence from studies that show that golfers who are instructed to avoid a particular error (e.g., 'Don't overshoot') are in fact more likely to make that very error when under pressure.

Of all the many psychological tricks and truths that are labelled and reach the general public, this is one that resonates for us all.

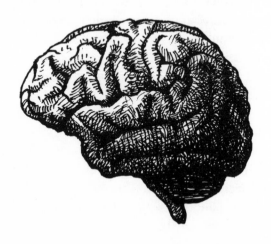

DON'T MENTION THE SWISS

Comedians are, as we have seen, some of our greatest thinkers and mappers of the human condition.

Basil Fawlty (played by John Cleese) famously put this into practice in "The Germans" episode of *Fawlty Towers* in 1975. After sustaining an injury from a moose head, Fawlty urges his staff to be careful around a group of German guests: "Don't mention the war," he implores. He then goes on to make a series of increasingly cringe-making references and puns on the war. "Don't mention the war" has enjoyed a long afterlife in popular culture beyond *Fawlty Towers*.

More recently Bill Bailey, the British stand-up, musician, actor, presenter and ornithologist, explored this to notably comedic effect in his *Tinselworm* show.

Ironic process theory provides the punchline for a story he tells about preparing to do a corporate gig for the Swiss bank, UBS, and the concerns he had about its association with hiding Nazi gold:

She told me not to mention Nazi gold,
and of course if you tell a comedian not to do
something, they'll immediately go and do it.
So, I went out on stage on a giant, neon swastika,
and sang "Gold, gold/always believe in your soul/
you're indestructible – like the Third Reich."

IMPS AND IMPLICATIONS

As is so often the case, artists articulate and explore a human truth before the scientists can identify and label it.

So, decades before Wegner's ironic process theory (or even Freud's identification of subconscious repression), the master of the macabre, Edgar Allan Poe, published a story called "The Imp of the Perverse" in 1845.

In this work, which is part essay, part short story, the narrator explains how his conviction for murder was a result of his theory that there exists a demonic force, an 'imp of the perverse', which often compels us to follow a clearly self-destructive path and act against our best interests. For the narrator, this ultimately means making a full confession and going to the gallows.

He is narrating the story from his prison cell.

As Poe puts it, "The more reason deters us from the brink, the more impetuously we approach it."

We all know and fear the imp, don't we?

There are also profound implications here for behaviour change. Many campaigns, be they government, social or commercial, rely on telling people what not to do, or aim to discourage a particular form of behaviour: don't smoke, cut down your fat intake, reduce your drinking, don't bully, don't buy the rival brand.

Ironic process theory – and its literary and metaphorical incarnation, the Imp of the Perverse – should warn campaigners and communicators that we might be promoting the very behaviour we are trying to repress.

Studies from the US suggest that "Cut down on binge drinking, which is prevalent on campus" may in fact be ironically processed as "Binge drinking is prevalent on campus, so it's OK."

Why is thought suppression so hard? And what does this say about our ability to control our mental processes, about the rational and conscious System 2's arrogant assumption that it is in control of the unconscious and stealthy System 1?

OBLIQUE HOUSE REVISITED

The British economist John Kay wrote a sharp book called *Obliquity*. His big idea is that the direct path to many of our objectives may not necessarily be the most effective and that indirect means may often be more productive. He covers a number of domains, from the need for commercial success to the search for happiness, via evolutionary theory and David Beckham.

Kay readily acknowledges his debt to Yale Economics Associate Professor Charles Lindblom's classic article (1959) "The Science of Muddling Through", written at a time when rationalism was at its peak and the feeling was about that everything could be solved with a positivist scientific bent.

Kay suggests that 'obliquity' might be a more acceptable euphemism than the perhaps shambolic-sounding 'muddling through'. His argument is that obliquity is more effective in an uncertain and complex evolving environment.

With conclusions that accord with those of many experts studying happiness, he proposes that the more we search for happiness, the more it eludes us.

The American poet Emily Dickinson put it elegantly:

―――――――

Tell all the truth but tell it slant –
Success in circuit lies.

―――――――

AGENT SHERMER…

Like Derren Brown, Michael Shermer was a zealous Christian in his youth, but later abandoned religion to become a prominent sceptic. He is now best known as a science writer, historian of science and Editor in Chief of *Skeptic* magazine.

His insight into talking to the dead, from his 2006 TED talk *Why People Believe Weird Things*, is worth quoting here:

"The whole business of talking to the dead is not that big a deal. Anybody can do it. Turns out that it's getting the dead to talk back that's the really hard part."

But in his book *The Believing Brain*, Shermer uses the word 'agenticity' to describe the universal human tendency to infuse patterns with meaning, intention and agency. In other words, we are naturally driven to seek out patterns which indicate that the world is governed by invisible intentional agents.

Along with our ingrained 'patternicity' – a tendency to seek meaningful patterns to explain often meaningless noise – Shermer argues that this is why so many of us believe in God, Intelligent Design, magic, the supernatural, aliens and all manner of conspiracies.

"SOMETHING BETTER CHANGE": FROM PUNK TO PINK

On to change.

In so many ways, change is the immovable object, faced with someone else's irresistible force. The sweep and influence of our mental short-cuts mean that so much of our behaviour, so many of our attitudes are inbuilt, hardwired, automatic and almost beyond the power of new rational input, however relevant it may appear superficially.

"And so this general approach remained intact, because it was after all easy to understand, simple to monitor and straightforward to enforce," says Daniel Pink in *Drive*.

Pink is referring to the conventional model (which he calls "Motivation 1.0") rooted in F. W. Taylor's remarkably enduring theory of scientific management, which saw workers as inert cogs in a giant machine.

What makes Pink's observation such a powerful and universal insight is that it is applicable to so many other spheres.

For example, there remains a stubborn insistence that human behaviour is still Taylorian in essence. This Neo-Classical model (sometimes caricatured as Homo economicus) suggests that humans are essentially rational and consistent – that their behaviour can be changed by appealing to their rationality and

243

by using conscious persuasion in order to achieve this. It is the goal of those who operate in the field of behavioural economics (sometimes called behavioural science) to point out the work of Daniel Kahneman, Dan Ariely, Richard Thaler, Cass Sunstein and Barry Schwartz, and show the fallacy of this view, but its longevity and potency have endured precisely for the reasons Pink outlines.

The guardians of this theory have enforced it ruthlessly across the marketing and communications world. It does have a beguiling simplicity in that it can be exemplified in acronymous mottoes like AIDA (awareness, interest, desire, action).

Setting this up as the default model for decades meant that research, theory and methodologies were established, cementing the belief that recalled information and propensity to change behaviour should be measured.

Now that there is a coherent body of evidence to show that the 'easy, simple and enforceable' model is not actually valid, we can start dismantling it and replacing it with something that is closer to the empirical truth.

We can add to an observation of J. B. S. Haldane.

Haldane was a British (later naturalized Indian) scientist and Marxist, whose work in genetics, evolutionary biology and mathematics led to the development of 'kin selection theory', a type of natural selection where individuals will sacrifice their own lives in an effort to save closely related organisms, thereby ensuring the survival of genes that they both share. He famously joked, when asked if he would give his life to save a drowning brother, "No, but I would to save two brothers or eight cousins."

As well as these fields of expertise, in 1929 he originated the 'primordial soup theory', which led sci-fi guru Arthur C. Clarke to call him "perhaps the most brilliant science popularizer of his generation", and prompted the renowned biologist Peter Medawar, who won the Nobel prize in Physiology or Medicine in 1960, to announce that "His genius was to enrich the soil, not to bring new land into cultivation."

Haldane stated, "I have no doubt that in reality the future will be vastly more surprising than anything I can imagine. Now my own suspicion is that the Universe is not only queerer than we suppose, but queerer than we can suppose."

FOUR STAGES OF ACCEPTANCE

Haldane wrote in a 1963 review in the Journal of Genetics:

———————

I suppose the process of acceptance will pass
through the usual four stages:
(i) this is worthless nonsense;
(ii) this is an interesting, but perverse, point of view;
(iii) this is true, but quite unimportant;
(iv) I always said so.

———————

Again, a very important insight into the nature of human change and the passing on of new wisdom. Any great change will be met with resistance. Haldane intuited that there is a default formula, which moves from irrational reception to mild acceptance to the triumph of confirmation bias: "I was never wrong in the first place."

This is also not dissimilar to Planck's Principle, as elucidated by Max Planck, the German theoretical physicist and polymath who was also a musician and philosopher of science and did much to lay the foundations of quantum theory:

"A new scientific truth does not triumph by convincing its opponents and making them see the light, but rather because its opponents eventually die, and a new generation grows up that is familiar with it."

Perhaps in this era of social media, where the pressures of the echo chamber tend to drive us to seek out what reinforces our worldview, Planck's Principle should be sacrosanct. Whatever our beliefs or theories, we should always be aware of our immunity to looking for anything that is at odds with them.

W IS FOR WORDSMITH

Another giant of scientific thinking and popularization is E. O. Wilson, biologist, thinker and generally considered to be the world's leading myrmecologist (specialist in ants), so here we have a rare example of a Venn diagram of etymology and entomology. In his book *Consilience*, Wilson argues for a rapprochement between what C. P. Snow defined as 'the Two Cultures': the sciences and the humanities.

The word 'consilience' in this sense had been revived and re-energized as the unification of different branches of knowledge by William Whewell, another English polymath and a man rated by contemporaries as one of the most influential thinkers of the 19th century.

Another intellectual colossus, Whewell ranged across terrains as diverse as mechanics and mineralogy, astronomy and political economy, to theology and educational reform, international law and architecture, as well as writing a number of works that remain relevant today in the philosophy of science, history of science, and moral philosophy. One of his massive works was *The Philosophy of the Inductive Sciences*, which he completed after *A History of the Inductive Sciences*.

And he still had time to be an Anglican priest and translate the works of Goethe. One of his contemporaries remarked of him, "Science is his forte, omniscience is his foible."

'Consilience' is not the only word this great word-smith was responsible for. He coined and bequeathed the terms 'anode', 'cathode', 'electrode' and 'ion' to his great friend Michael Faraday.

THE ORIGIN OF SCIENTISTS

One of our assumptions about language is that words are either of indeterminate age, or that they are trendy coinages. We take so many for granted that it comes as a shock when we can point to a word and say: "That word was created by that person, at that time."

One such word is 'scientist'.

In response to a challenge by the poet Samuel Taylor Coleridge in 1833, William Whewell invented the English word 'scientist'.

Before then, the most commonly used term was 'natural philosopher', which dated back to Aristotle and was synonymous with the idea of the systematic study of nature.

Isaac Newton happily called his 1687 work *Mathematical Principles of Natural Philosophy* (*Philosophiae Naturalis Principia Mathematica*), in which he developed his theories on motion and gravitation.

The term 'natural philosopher', Whewell argued, was too wide and too lofty. He argued the need for a new, more specific term. As part of his belief in consilience, he also believed a single term was needed in order to prevent the fragmentation of science that seemed to flow from its specialization. And eventually he came up with the word 'scientist', by analogy with 'artist'.

BENTHAM: LOOKING GOOD FOR HIS AGE

Let's turn to another neologist of note, Jeremy Bentham, jurist and fabricator of philosophies and words.

He devised utilitarianism, whereby he stated, "It is the greatest happiness of the greatest number that is the measure of right and wrong."

Brilliantly inventive and wide-ranging, he devised the 'panopticon' (a model prison-cum-school-cum-poorhouse), outlined the need for something like the UK's modern National Health Service, designed a *frigidarium* for storing food at low temperatures and a plan for a Nicaraguan Canal to be dug to connect the Atlantic and Pacific oceans, called the *Junctiana*.

He died in 1832 but made elaborate plans (as was his wont) for his body to be preserved in the form of what he called an 'Auto-Icon' (Greek for 'self-image'). Unlike most people, his wish was mostly granted. If you visit University College London (UCL), and find the end of the South Cloisters of the main building, you will be confronted by a wooden cabinet. Within the cabinet sits Bentham's preserved skeleton, dressed in his own clothes and surmounted by a wax head. (His real head was also preserved but deemed unsuitable for display.) Bentham requested that his body be preserved in this way and it was moved to UCL in 1850. UCL helpfully remarks that he is woken up at 8am and put to sleep at 6pm. If you want to see what it looks like from Bentham's point of view, the box (obviously) has its own live Twitter account (@PanoptiStream).

Some of the other stories surrounding the Auto-Icon turn out rather disappointingly to be myths:

for example, the claim that Bentham is brought out to College Council meetings and is declared in the minutes to be "present but not voting".

Jeremy Bentham was also a prolific nomenclaturist and classifier, in works like *An Essay on Nomenclature and Classification*. He left us with a host of words that seem part of our linguistic furniture, including 'maximize', 'minimize', 'international' and 'codify' to start with, but also 'exhaustive', 'monetary', 'percentage' and 'secretarial'.

BREAKING GOOD

From fossilized neologists to fossilized thinking.

In *Life's Grandeur*, Stephen Jay Gould cited the Latin motto of the US Palaeontological Society:

'*Frango Ut Patefaciam.*'

Though I have not been able to validate the expression beyond Gould's citation, it is something that deserves wider coverage because of its breadth of applicability.

It translates literally as "I break in order to reveal," and works at a number of different strata.

In that hammers are the tools of the palaeontologist's trade for excavating fossils and learning what lies beneath, it works elegantly at the literal level.

But what gives it a deeper reverberation is the metaphorical sense, one that resonates with anyone seeking understanding and wisdom in their private or professional lives.

We should always be seeking to break things open to reveal what lies beneath (though parents of toddlers may wish to defer transmitting this message to their children).

SACKS, LIES AND VIDEOTAPE

Until he passed away in 2015, Oliver Sacks was Professor of Neurology at the New York University (NYU) School of Medicine.

He was also another arresting communicator and graceful popularizer, through books such as *The Man Who Mistook his Wife for a Hat*, *Awakenings*, *A Leg To Stand On* and *An Anthropologist on Mars*, as well as writing some tender memoirs.

He was a very special example of a scientist (and polymath) whose belief in personal history and the integrity of the personal over and above the diagnostic courses through his books. His whole professional ethos had been rooted in avoiding the victimization of patients with neurological disorders and in looking holistically at the person rather than merely at the deficiency.

His holistic and compassionate tone is evident from the following quotation:

———

To restore the human subject at the centre
– the suffering, afflicted, fighting, human subject
– we must deepen a case history to a narrative or tale;
only then do we have a "who" as well as a "what",
a real person, a patient, in relation to a disease
– in relation to the physical.

———

More than that, Sacks was an impassioned humanist who understood the human need for meaning and pattern:

"To live on a day to day basis is insufficient for human beings; we need to transcend, transport, escape; we need meaning, understanding and explanation; we need to see overall patterns in our lives."

WRITING, THINKING AND DOING

In *Aspects of the Novel*, E. M. Forster bequeathed to posterity another timeless quote (though, as so often, there is a dispute as to the exact origin and progenitor of the expression):

———————

How can I tell what I think until I see what I say?

———————

If you're not satisfied with Forster, try any of these alternatives, which cover similar territory:

Writing has got to be an act of discovery…
I write to find out what I'm thinking about.
– EDWARD ALBEE

Writing a play is thinking, not thinking
about thinking.
– ROBERT BOLT

I write entirely to find out what I'm thinking,
what I'm looking at, what I see and what it means.
– JOAN DIDION

This quotation has always been a great source of illumination, and is advice that should be taken liberally. As a cure against too much reinforced echo-chamber confirmation bias (as discussed before) and as a means of exploring ideas and how we feel about them, it is exceedingly useful to start writing.

If you are interested in the process of writing and want to be a writer (or produce any form of writing), there is no substitute for actually getting on with it, structuring your thoughts, finding a thread, uncovering your point of view.

This chimes very well with certain aspects of behaviour change theory, which could be briefly summarized in the slogan of a well-known sportswear producer.

ONE WISE MAN AND MANY JOKES

Richard Wiseman is one of most visible faces of popular academic psychology, equally at home appearing on CNN and the BBC and fronting his own shows and social media channels.

But he started out and remains a performer of the dark psychological arts of magic, and is one of a select group of magicians who have found fulfilment and tenured employment as psychologists.

As well as being a full paid-up member of the Magic Circle in the UK, he is Professor of the Public Understanding of Psychology at the University of Hertfordshire. He is also good chums with evil genius Derren Brown, on whose TV shows he has often acted as an adviser.

Wiseman is a great exponent of social media (especially YouTube, where many of his clips have received millions of viewings: find his "Amazing Colour-Changing Card Trick"), has written several best-selling books on popular psychology such as *The Luck Factor*, *Quirkology*, *59 Seconds* and *Paranormality*, and has carried out many mass-participation experiments.

Given our interest in comedy, we must mention his 2001 experiment to find the world's funniest joke. Over 40,000 jokes were submitted and over 1.5 million ratings were contributed.

(Maybe it would have been simpler if they had just set up their own dedicated search engine, called Giggle).

The winner was:

Two hunters are out in the woods when one of
them collapses. He doesn't seem to be breathing
and his eyes are glazed. The other guy takes out
his phone and calls the emergency services.
"My friend is dead! What can I do?"
he screams. The operator says: "Calm down. I can
help. First, let's make sure he's dead." There is a
silence, then a shot is heard. Back on the phone, the
guy says: "Ok, now what?"

The winning joke was almost certainly based on
one written by Spike Milligan for the BBC radio series
The Goon Show in 1951.

One of the other insights Wiseman uncovered was
that the funniest animal is considered to be the duck
– I assume because of the rhyming potential lurking
beneath, although the duck is also the subject of one
of my favourite jokes:

Two ducks are sitting on a pond.
One of the ducks says "quack".
The other duck says, "I was going to say that."

Incidentally, scientists of humour also tend to agree
on the 'K' effect, there being something inherently
amusing about the letter.

WISEMAN THE DEBUNKER

Not a fan of the self-help industry, Richard Wiseman's book *Rip It Up* is both practical and gently polemical, with his usual blend of light-touch education and entertainment. It takes aim at self-help gurus who encourage different thinking by going in for radical attitude change. We know this is difficult and often fruitless, and Wiseman goes back to psychologist William James for inspiration.

Rip It Up isn't necessarily the clearest of titles, and later editions were re-named *The As If Principle*, to reflect the core tenet of the book: the belief that if you act 'as if' you are a certain person with certain behaviours, you are more likely to achieve the changes that enable you to become that person. This runs contrary to the trend in the self-help world of thinking yourself into being happier, thinner, smarter, or President of the Free World.

Wiseman breathes new life into insights from William James and modern psychological research from Paul Ekman and Ellen Langer, as well as looking further back to work by psychotherapist and founder of individual psychology, Alfred Adler.

His book is an exhilarating read and its emphasis on action over thinking means that it really should be more widely prescribed for those interested in behavioural science.

THE FATHER (AND UNCLE) OF PSYCHOLOGY

William James, whom we have already encountered, is often hailed as the 'father of psychology'.

His brother was the novelist Henry James (*The Portrait of Lady*, *The Wings of a Dove*, *The Turn of the Screw*); this presumably makes Henry the uncle of psychology.

As one contemporary wit put it, Henry wrote novels like a psychologist while William wrote psychology texts like a novelist.

William James's book *The Principles of Psychology* is a classic and still widely read and taught today.

His foundational insight was that we tend to have the arrow of causality the wrong way round. We are taught that our emotions cause us to behave in certain ways. So, we are told, when we feel happy we smile, when we feel sad we cry. This is all common sense, surely.

But James was the first to elucidate a coherent theory to support the notion that this might be completely topsy-turvy. He theorized that the relationship between emotion and behaviour might be more complicated, and that behaviour might cause emotion. According to James, smiling can make you feel happy and frowning can make you feel sad. As he put it, "If you want a quality, act as if you have it." Aristotle had said something similar 2,400 years previously: "Whatever we learn to do, we learn by actually doing it. By doing brave acts we become brave".

Or, to use James's favourite way of putting it: "You do not run from a bear because you are afraid of it, but rather become afraid of the bear because you run from it."

BEARING UP TO EVOLUTION

In evolutionary terms, the relationship between emotion and behaviour described by psychologist William James makes perfect sense. If evolution designed our emotions to trigger survival responses above every other imperative, it looks like good design if the first thing we do is carry out the behaviour that will maximize our chances of passing on our genes to future generations.

In the case of danger, that means running first.

The sequence is likely to be:

1. Run ... then...
2. Experience bodily sensations ... then...
3. Feel the emotion of fear.

The action is triggered first, followed by a bodily signal and finally, as its reaches our conscious awareness (what Daniel Kahneman describes as System 2 in his book *Thinking, Fast and Slow*), we experience the behaviour and become consciously aware of it.

Converging on this view is the philosophical system devised by Russian theatre theorist Konstantin Stanislavski. His concept of the 'magic if' is still used widely as a creative tool for inspiration by actors.

The power of the 'magic if' is that it allows actors to transcend the confinements of realism by asking them what they would do if they were in an imagined set of circumstances.

Examples from one theatre website include:

- What if the world were ending?
- What if I'm not alive?
- What if this is a game?
- What if I'm secretly on medication?

So write, do, and explore what happens when you do.

In the same way, Richard Wiseman suggests a number of practical tips which emphasize the prioritization of behaviour over thinking.

One of the figurehead demonstrations of this principle is to smile in order to make yourself feel happier. Plenty of research has been conducted which suggests that the act of smiling and the muscle movements involved in the action can fool the brain into creating the sense of wellbeing associated with happiness: so actions do indeed speak louder than words.

STRIKE A POSE

Though often caricatured, there does seem abundant evidence to suggest that certain displays, such as acting out a power pose, can help build or reinforce self-confidence.

An infamous paper was published in *Psychological Science* in 2010 by Dana Carney (then at Columbia University and now an Associate Professor at the Haas School of Business at the University of California, Berkeley), and her colleagues Amy Cuddy and Andy Yap. The team suggested that when people are asked to stand in typically power-related poses they can symbolically assert power and authority.

The original paper claimed that:

In short, posing in displays of power caused advantaged and adaptive psychological, physiological, and behavioural changes, and these findings suggest that embodiment extends beyond mere thinking and feeling, to physiology and subsequent behavioural choices. That a person can, by assuming two simple 1-minute poses, embody power and instantly become more powerful has real-world, actionable implications.

Since then Carney has distanced herself from the stronger implications of this study, but there seems other evidence that such displays can have some effect.

MOSTLY MINDLESS

The research paper "The Pull of the Past: When Do Habits Persist Despite Conflict with Motives?" by D. T. Neal, W. Wood, M. Wu and D. Kurlander, published in the *Personality and Social Psychology Bulletin*, suggested that much of our behaviour is heuristic, automatic and mindless, often cued by patterns and contexts rather than purposely chosen.

By way of example, it is clear that much of our food-related behaviour is hardwired into our environment by a combination of habit and context. I remember my late mother would always offer me biscuits with a cup of tea, as she said she could never just have a "bare cup of tea". As such, any notion of tea without an accompanying confection remains the source of much personal psychic distress.

In "The Pull of the Past", snackers were offered popcorn and were divided into two groups. Half were asked to eat with their non-dominant hand, and the results showed that this group consumed less popcorn than those who ate with their dominant hand. It also revealed that habitual popcorn eaters when in the right environment are more likely to eat popcorn that is noticeably stale.

This disruptive manipulation, which obstructs the automatic execution of a habit, had a similar effect to changing the environmental context of the snacking. It also forces us to focus attention on something that is normally automatic; hence we are more likely to ask ourselves "How long have I been eating this popcorn for the sake of eating?"

There is evidence to suggest that freeing ourselves of our embedded habits and the illusion of control is the way to achieve lasting behavioural change. If we try to alter the environment that triggers mindless behaviours (such as eating), we are more likely to succeed.

So, use smaller plates and utensils, hide the addictive food or use the other hand.

THEORY IN PRACTICE

Let us dig a little deeper into the relationship between theory and practice.

> In theory there is no difference between theory and practice, but in practice there is.
> **– ATTRIBUTED TO BASEBALL LEGEND YOGI BERRA,**
> **BUT PROBABLY COINED EARLIER**

A witticism I was introduced to when I was deeply absorbed in the details of postmodernism was concerned with two French philosophers:

———

"It works in practice," said one.
"But does it work in theory?" said the other.

———

I then came across a story about the outgoing US Federal Reserve Chairman, Ben Bernanke, from 2014:

The problem with QE [quantitative easing] is that it works in practice, but it doesn't work in theory.

Since I am about as capable of explaining the niceties of economics as my cat is of distinguishing the gerund and gerundive in Latin, I will leave the explanation of quantitative easing to the Bank of England:

"[QE] is an unconventional form of monetary policy where a Central Bank creates new money electronically to buy financial assets, like government bonds. This process aims to directly increase private sector spending in the economy and return inflation to target."

The quote seems to be an old saw used for demonstrating how out of touch a particular group can be: hence the frequency of its use in the context of economists, traditionally perceived as being theory-reliant philosophers who think empiricism means conquering foreign territories. In their defence, economists can now point to the use of Big Data as the basis for deriving their models.

8. CHANGE AND CHOICE BLINDNESS

LUND'S END

Let us look at the work of two Swedish researchers, Petter Johansson and Lars Hall, now at the Choice Blindness Laboratory at Lund University.

Lund University should not be confused with Sarah Lund, the main character in the international breakout hit Danish TV crime drama *The Killing*, played by Sofie Gråbøl, mainly in a Faroese sweater.

Lund, the university, has over 40,000 students and celebrated its 350th anniversary in 2016. It is one of the top 100 ranked universities in the world and is where – as we saw above – Hugh Cornwell of The Stranglers did his postgraduate research in the early 1970s.

It has as its motto *Ad utrumque*, meaning "prepared for either option", which comes from Book II line 61 of Virgil's *Aeneid*, telling the story of The Trojan Horse: "He was ready for either course: to engage in deception, or find certain death." Lund's use of the motto refers to the turbulent history of Sweden and Denmark, and one specific era in the 16th and

17th centuries after the province of Skåne was ceded to Sweden by Denmark in the treaty of Roskilde in 1658.

The motto was originally a clandestine reminder to the Danes that they were prepared for either book or sword, an allusion which is broadly ignored in the modern era. Though please feel free to watch *The Bridge* to observe that Swedish–Danish tensions have not disappeared entirely.

MAGIC, SUBTERFUGE AND PSYCHOLOGY

Swedish researchers Petter Johansson and Lars Hall carried out a series of experiments, using unorthodox techniques from the world of stage magic to help answer the question of how we make decisions, which they later published in *Science* mazagine in 2005. Apart from the scientific value, it's a cracking story involving industrial amounts of subterfuge, surreptitiousness and stratagems in the pursuit of science.

For example, in an early study they showed volunteers pairs of pictures of faces and asked them to choose the more attractive of the two. (They had been preselected to be approximately matched for attractiveness.) The cards with the faces on were then held up, and the subject was asked to point to the one they considered to be more attractive. Then, both photos were placed face down on the table and the chosen photo was pushed across the table, the subject then being invited to take a closer look and ponder the reasons for their selection.

Here the trickiness, manipulation and magical sleight of hand begins. Unbeknownst to the subjects, the double-card magic trick means that in a number of cases the magician/experimenter had covertly swapped one face for the other, so in fact the subject ended up with the face they had not actually chosen.

Now, we'd like to think that we would all notice such a big change in the outcome of a choice. Wouldn't we? But the result showed that in 75% of the trials our participants were blind to the mismatch, even offering reasons for their (new) choice. Most notable excuses included "I prefer blondes" (said by someone who had initially chosen a brunette) and "I really like earrings" (the statement of a subject who had in fact chosen a woman without earrings).

So, the killer twist was that most people would give perfectly reasonable, thought-out arguments in defence of their choice. But most of them had actually chosen the other face in the first place, so they were in fact defending the indefensible. (Before you ask, only a quarter of subjects detected the swap.)

Johansson and Hall labelled this effect 'choice blindness', consciously (if that's the right word) echoing 'change blindness', the phenomenon identified by psychologists where a significant number of people fail to spot a major change in their environment.

STRANGERS TO OURSELVES?

This is sometimes termed the 'introspection illusion' because it illuminates a problem that science has with the concept of subjectivity. As Timothy Wilson argues in the book of that name, we are *Strangers to Ourselves*. It is just really hard to know about decision-making from the inside.

What was especially insightful about the work of the Swedish neuromagicians was that they created a mechanism that not only showed their subjects that what we believe to be solid, contemplated choices are often hastily achieved, but that, even when our choice is shown to have been falsely created, we can still convince others (and, more worryingly, ourselves) that there were legitimate grounds for our bogus choice.

Their research has opened up the mechanism known as 'confabulation' so we can see it for what it is: a natural byproduct of the brain's irresistible urge to explain and justify. Further analysis by their team revealed that this can lead in some cases to a long-term change in preferences, once a feedback loop has been generated: "I have made this choice, I proclaimed it publicly, therefore I must stand by it, like it and convince myself and others of that fact." As we fool ourselves, cognitive dissonance rears its head again. One consistent finding from the Lund studies is that whenever people are asked if they would guess whether their selection had been switched, around 80% claim they definitely, certainly and indubitably would have spotted the change. The researchers use a suitable meta-term for this, calling it 'choice blindness blindness'.

Another experiment involved two pots of jam, seemingly different. But they were both double-ended, so both pots contained different flavours of jam. When respondents were asked to confirm their choice, they were given the other jam to taste and would happily confabulate till the cows came home.

The Swedish duo have extended their work to look beyond consumer choices and the results appear both robust and replicable, while also being relevant in the political and social domains (with similar, and equally alarming, results).

THE DISPOSITION OF THE LINEN

In the mid-1970s, Timothy Wilson, Professor of Psychology at the University of Virginia, and Richard Nisbett, who held the equivilant role at the University of Michigan, conducted one of the most famous and widely cited social psychology experiments of all time, using little more than some ladies' hosiery.

Taking a stall outside a thrift store just outside Ann Arbor, Michigan, they stood under a banner that said "Consumer Evaluation Survey: Which is The Best Quality?" Displayed on the table were four pairs of tights (pantyhose), labelled from A to D from left to right. As women passed by they were asked to examine the four pairs and say which they preferred. Over the course of the day a clear statistical pattern emerged: pair D was the most preferred and pair A, the least.

Moving from left to right, the percentage of those rating each pair of pantyhose the best quality was 12%, 17%, 31%, 40%. This did not surprise the researchers, because – as is known to the inner circle of magicians – this is a manifestation of the 'recency effect', a tendency noted by psychologists where we are more likely to be affected by what we have seen or heard last.

But at the beating heart of this experiment was the fact that all four pantyhose were identical. Respondents tended to attribute their decision to so-called 'dispositional factors': the inherent qualities of the available choices, rather than the situational factors which in fact were what dominated choice. Thus, Wilson and Nisbett concluded that "What matters … is not why the [position] effect occurs but that it occurs and that subjects do not report it or recognize it when it is pointed out to them."

Wilson and Nisbett then asked the women to explain their decision (effectively, "Why did you choose something that was identical?"). Some 80 different reasons were given, including the knit, weave, sheerness or elasticity. No-one mentioned the position of the hosiery, except one subject who confessed that she was taking three psychology courses and had recently been introduced to the order effect.

As Wilson describes it in his book *Strangers to Ourselves*, this set him on the road to exploring why it is that we seem to have "little or no introspective access to our higher cognitive processes". This effect is often known in the psychology world as the Fundamental Attribution Error – our bias towards privileging personality-based answers over those based on situation or context.

So, we all need to acknowledge that while we think there are rational reasons for our choices, in reality, we are often just post-rationalizing a decision making process of which we are unaware.

A BRIDGE TOO FAR

In 1974, two Canadian psychologists, Donald Dutton and Arthur Aron, conducted an experiment on the spectacular Capilano River Bridge in British Columbia, which rises some 230 feet (70 metres) above the river.

A female research assistant approached lone male tourists at the entrance to the bridge. They asked the men to walk to the middle of the bridge and write an imaginative story in response to a drawing. Afterwards, the researcher gave each participant a telephone number to call if he wanted to find out the results of the research project.

Dutton and Aron then repeated their experiment on another nearby bridge. This one was also wooden, but it was quite sturdy and was only 10 feet (3 metres) above the river. This time the tourists would write their stories in the middle of a bridge that posed no threat and therefore aroused no fear.

Subsequently, 65% of the men on the first bridge rang the telephone number provided and asked for a date, while only 30% of those on land did. The researchers concluded that this was due to a "misattribution of arousal". The men on the scary bridge felt an adrenalin surge and a rush of blood to the head, both physical responses associated with fear – but they had mistaken vertigo for lust.

A study by Gregory White of the University of Maryland also examined misallocation of emotion. In his experiment, he got a group of men to run on the spot to elevate their heart rate, before asking them to rate the attractiveness of a woman. The control group ran for only a few seconds. The result was the same: the rush of adrenalin (this time prompted by physical exercise) was mistaken for sexual ardour.

What this phenomenon also demonstrates is that our arrow of causality is often sadly misdirected. We know that when we find someone attractive our hearts beat faster. But what these arousal experiments also prove is that the converse can be true: when our hearts beat faster, we are more likely to find someone seductive.

INATTENTIONAL BLINDNESS

Another striking incidence of change blindness was shown in a BBC documentary, *How You Really Make Decisions*. Psychology Professor Christopher Chabris set up another experiment to test the level at which 'inattentional blindness' occurs. He wanted to probe a hypothesis he had developed based on a 1995 court case where a Boston police officer, Kenneth Conley, was accused of perjury and obstruction of justice. Some back story is needed.

On a January night, the Boston police had been summoned to a suspected shooting. A whole group of police officers ran and cornered the suspects' car in a cul-de-sac. A black undercover officer named Michael Cox went after one of the suspects, but in the darkness and chaos, another officer mistook him for the perpetrator and "did a Rodney King on him" (in the words of the journalist who wrote a book about the events).

Conley, in his car, witnessed another suspect escaping, and as he pursued that suspect he ran right past the scene of the policemen attacking Cox. In court, he swore that he had seen nothing, but he was accused of deliberately lying to protect his fellow officers (all of whom were vigorously perjuring themselves by claiming they hadn't witnessed – let alone been involved in – the beating).

Chabris later set up a re-enactment on campus where a subject was asked to run for three minutes behind a jogger and follow them at a distance (to ensure they had a fixed focus of attention). They were required to concentrate on a specific cognitive task:

to count how many times the runner tapped their head with their hand. Then, shortly after the run started, a team of Chabris' accomplices began a mock fight as the runners passed by, at a distance of only about 25 feet (7 metres) from the path of the runners.

You should be able to guess the conclusion. About half of the guinea pigs did not notice the fight at all, even when prompted – and the figure was barely better when the experiment was conducted in the daylight hours compared to nighttime. Chabris believes this research has wide-ranging implications, and as long as driving while under the influence of a mobile phone is in the news, it is hard to dispute his claim.

9. SELF-ASSEMBLY

> The self is a shaky edifice we build out of scraps,
> dogmas, childhood injuries, newspaper articles,
> chance remarks, old films, small victories,
> people hated, people loved.
>
> **– SALMAN RUSHDIE, *IMAGINARY HOMELANDS* (1991)**

The modern and ancient arts of neuroscience and philosophy are much vexed by the nature of the self. Is it singular, is it continuous and is it powered by free will?

Much of our self is composed, modified by and codified in story.

Storytelling can lead us to think in the following way:

- The self is a fractured and fractious thing, and it is hard to find an essence to or for it.
- Stories are key to the construction and maintenance of our sense of self and identity. It is no surprise that we feel so at home with stories.
- New thinking from the world of neuroscience indicates that memory is malleable, that we are open to influence with our memories and that we need to elaborate to save face.

- All this gives our brains permission to create and embellish fictional narratives around ourselves (or 'confabulate').

THE MANY MES

> How could anyone know me,
> when I don't even know myself?
> **– THE THE, "GIANT"**

The UK band The The made several influential albums with lyrics that always scratched beneath the surface of the quest for human identity and self-knowledge. "Giant" was the final track their 1981 album *Soul Mining*.

> So much of who he was was involuntary
> **– JOSHUA FERRIS, THE UNNAMED**

Joshua Ferris received significant acclaim for his debut novel *And Then We Came to the End*.

This quotation from his 2010 novel *The Unnamed* is pertinent because it encapsulates something that neuroscientists are increasingly coming to assert: that much of who we are, what we do and how we construct ourselves is actually happening beneath the surface without our knowledge or complicity.

> There used to be a me
> but I had it surgically removed.
> **– PETER SELLERS**

English actor Peter Sellers was famous for his comic work with the Goons and later as a straight actor in the likes of 1979's *Being There*, in which he portrayed Chance, the simple gardener who is mistaken for a guru.

In his more thoughtful moments, Sellers was accustomed to talking about having no identity of his own, but merely inhabiting his roles.

AN 'I' FOR ILLUSION?

That we each have a single, unified and consistent self may be a proposition that sounds beyond dispute. But here again the twin and often diametrically opposed spheres of neuroscience and postmodernism seem at one in questioning this most basic of assumptions, helped by some modem philosophers such as Alain de Botton and historians such as Yuval Noah Harari.

The idea that everything, including our 'selves', may be subject to change is, of course, not new.

The notion of eternal change is found as far back as the Greeks, particularly Heraclitus. This accorded with his belief that dynamism and change were the ways of the world.

He famously said: *Panta rei*. This may best be translated as "Everything flows", or "All is in flux", or even more simply as "Things change."

Heraclitus also asserted "You can never bathe in the same river twice."

This is usually taken to have two complementary meanings.

In the first place, that the nature of rivers and matter is such that they are in a constant state of transformation and renewal, so that the river you dip in today cannot be the same as the river you swam in yesterday.

But by the same token, Heraclitus may also be alluding to the principle whereby you are not the same person as you were yesterday. With the benefit of modern discoveries, we can see this as demonstrating the perpetual flux of our bodies as cells grow, decay and die.

Looking with a neuroscientific eye, there seems to be remarkable consensus on the view that the single self is not scientifically proven.

V. S. Ramachandran, Professor of Neuroscience at University of California, San Diego, has his doubts about the sanctity of the self:

"Here and elsewhere when I say that the self is an 'illusion', I simply mean there is no single entity corresponding to it in the brain. But in truth we know so little about the brain that it is best to keep an open mind."

Though it is often hard to detect irony in the written word, it seems to me that the last few words in this sentence are written without any ironic sheen.

The question of what constitutes the self, how it is arranged and what is its relationship with consciousness are ones which still vex the neuroscientists, cognitive scientists and philosophers.

THE TWO SELVES

We have already seen the work of psychologist Timothy Wilson and his book *Strangers to Ourselves*.

So, we are not self-transparent because of the processes that experts call the 'adaptive unconscious', the 'undermind' or even TASS ('The Autonomous Set of Systems') and, chiefly, what Daniel Kahneman popularized as System 1.

Many of our inherent dispositions, traits and temperaments belong to the adaptive unconscious, to which we have no clear access. So, we find ourselves constructing theories about our own personalities from other sources, such as our own creation myths (what we learn from our parents, our faiths, our culture) and our aspirations.

One of the foremost experts on the neurophysiology of emotion is Antonio Damasio. He discusses two types of consciousness, mirrored by two forms of self. He labels these the 'core self' and the 'autobiographical self'.

The core self is "a transient entity, ceaselessly recreated for each and every object with which the brain interacts". The autobiographical self comes from the "idea of identity and corresponds to a non-transient collection of unique facts and ways of being which characterize a being".

In discussing his concept of core consciousness, he outlines why he believes that wordless storytelling is natural:

"Telling stories precedes language, since it is, in fact, a condition for language, and it is based not just in the cerebral cortex, but elsewhere in the brain and in the right hemisphere as well as the left."

"I AM UNDER CONSTRUCTION"

There are plenty of reasons why the idea of the single self seems attractive to the point of being self-evident. We have mentioned before the drive for 'agencity', the instinct that things happen for a reason.

We all have a single body with physical boundaries. It explains the 'I' when 'I' do or see things and why I feel things you cannot.

It allows a sense of moral responsibility; it endows us with an overdeveloped sense of causation. The 'I' becomes the centre of attention and focus for what we call the stream of consciousness; and it provides a model for us all to share a social connection. But is it any more than a convenient fiction, a self-assembly-self built by our brain's IKEA?

As the neuropsychologist and writer Paul Broks put it:

"They [our mental processes] come together in a work of fiction. A human being is a story-telling machine. The self is a story ... but who tells the story of the self?"

The 'I' is a principle of biological organization, a product of biological and social forces arising from the interaction of individual, isolated brains.

There is no 'abiding I' or permanent self. The self, it seems, is a work in progress; its webpage a placeholder with two words: "under construction".

We also know now that much of what we think is simple and coherent in our brains has been composed and reconstructed.

We are 'unreliable witnesses' and various experiments have been carried out which demonstrate how easily we can create memories that were not there, and alter existing ones to fit the moment.

The insight usually attributed to French-Cuban writer Anaïs Nin seems ever more apposite:

"We don't see things as they are. We see things as we are."

REWRITING HISTORY

It seems that much like historians, or composers of our own autobiography, we are constantly rewriting our own history and moulding the world to ourselves.

There are a number of reasons this makes sound biological and cultural sense. As we saw earlier, we lack self-transparency, so that much of what lies beneath is not accessible to the conscious mind. We inject what we can see and describe – such as our feelings, our (claimed) memories, our behaviour and how other people see us – into the fabric of a narrative that may reflect and capture what lies beneath.

But it also makes sense to compose stories about our lives as a way of minimizing the awkwardness known as 'cognitive dissonance'. This is rooted in the need to maintain a position on any topic (say global warming, abortion, our favourite football team or a political party) based on a central core of beliefs, and to do this by seeking only validatory evidence and discarding anything that conflicts with that position.

There is no denying the fact that not only are we (more obviously) storytellers, but we are equally 'storyvores': we devour, consume and construct stories with even more readiness than we tell them.

We are storytelling animals and we use narrative as an organizational principle for constructing our life-stories. To say selves are wholly fictional, as American philosopher Daniel Dennett and others suggest, may do us a disservice. The idea that we have no 'I' certainly feels strange as is it runs counter to our central concept of consciousness, of what it feels like 'to be me'.

But is undoubtedly true, in that our selves are not rigid and timeless. As we gather more stories (or meaning and purpose) we constantly refine and elaborate our story.

So, in many ways the 'self' will always be open-ended as it is forever undergoing revisions and edits.

10. BIKE SHEDS AND HUMAN COMPUTERS

BEWARE THE BIKE SHED: A WORD OF WARNING

Returning to decision-making, the analysis of group decision-making owes much to civil servant, historian and theorist, C. Northcote Parkinson.

He may have gained his fame largely for his observation that "Work expands so as to fill the time available for its completion," but he was also responsible for another blinding truth about commercial (and more broadly, human) behaviour.

Known as the Law of Triviality, and more informally as 'bikeshedding', it states that in any group decision-making, a disproportionate amount of time will be spent on what is trivial.

The example Parkinson gave was the committee which has to make an informed decision on building a nuclear reactor, and then whether to build a hypothetical bike shed.

Because no-one knows anything about nuclear reactors and the issues surrounding it are complex and likely to highlight people's ignorance, the decision is made almost immediately. On the other hand, a bike shed is within everyone's compass and so everyone feels they are an expert and is entitled to their view. So, it takes hours for the group to debate, decide (and often defer) the policy on bike sheds.

There is thus an inverse relationship between the cost and importance of a project and the time spent on it. The trivial trumps the non-trivial.

HIDDEN FIGURES

One of the big movies of late 2016/early 2017 was *Hidden Figures*, the "Why didn't I know that?" story of the unsung African American women who came to work at NASA's Langley Research Center, Virginia, starting during World War II. While most people have some idea of the 'space' element of the space race, the 'race' aspect has remained largely underreported.

Margot Lee Shetterly's book, on which the movie was based, tells the story of the female mathematicians and engineers who worked behind the scenes at NASA Langley to support the men traditionally credited with making the major advances in America's aeronautics and space programmes.

Langley began recruiting African American women in the 1930s, initially for the forerunner of NASA, but due to strict segregation laws in Virginia they were kept away from their white counterparts and had to use separate dining and toilet facilities – something the film does much to emphasize.

The film focusses on three of these pioneers: Katherine Johnson, Dorothy Vaughan and Mary Jackson.

One of the pivotal moments in the film (and confirmed as authentic, though the timeframe is compressed for dramatic purposes) is when John Glenn is moments away from becoming the first American to orbit the Earth in 1962.

While waiting at Cape Canaveral, moments away from lift-off, he anxiously awaits details of his launch trajectory and rings Langley for final confirmation. In so doing, he demonstrates how he trusts Katherine Johnson "to do the math" more effectively than the newly arrived IBM computer:

"Get the girl to check the numbers. If she says the numbers are good … I'm ready to go."

COLOURED COMPUTERS

Hidden Figures is a great film, but here we will consider the linguistic aspect of this story: the use of the word 'computer' to describe a human being.

For many, the word is automatically associated with machines, especially if, like the author, you grew up in the 1960s and 70s watching Bond movies and spy series where the computer occupied most of a large building.

But since the 1630s 'computer' had been used to denote a person who calculates, from the Latin (via French) *computare* meaning to calculate (together) or count or determine through mathematical means.

The root word *putare* is one of the first words Latin students learn as it means 'to think' (originally to clean or prune) and is visible in everything from 'putative' to 'repute', 'reputation', 'impute', 'dispute', 'depute' or 'deputy' and 'amputate'.

There is a strange System 1 and System 2 link here: the Old French word *counter*, from which the English 'count' derives, means both 'to count' and 'to tell a story' (nowadays the resemblance in English is preserved in 'count' and 'recount' and shared in the word 'account', though modern French spelling distinguishes *compter* (count) from *conter* (tell)). Perhaps the shared link is from enumerating being the same as reciting a list.

One final mathematical footnote: *calculus* was originally a small pebble used for counting, the diminutive of *calx* (limestone), the genitive of which is *calcis*, giving us 'calcium'.

English chemist Sir Humphrey Davy coined 'calcium', as he was the first to name it after isolating the substance using electrolysis in 1808, alongside strontium, magnesium, barium and boron in that same year (he had knocked off potassium and sodium the previous year).

11. THREE WISE MEN

CHARLES DARWIN:
ELOQUENCE AND ELEGANCE

Charles Darwin was one of the greatest thinkers and visionaries of his age, whose visit to the Galápagos Islands to observe finches (amongst other species) changed the way we see our world and our place within it.

The Darwinian revolution was arguably one of the foundational reframing revolutions of humanity. Along with Copernicus and Freud, Gödel and Einstein, Darwin's theory demonstrated that humans are not the centre of the universe nor specially positioned in creation, and that there are forces that we struggle to understand: descent with modification, variation and chance are far more significant than we would like to concede.

It is hard for us to imagine quite what the world was like when scientists assumed that the natural world was suffused with design and purpose, now that evolution by natural selection has developed beyond just a theory (at least for most people).

Darwin chose to wait for more than 23 years before publishing, for fear that his theory of evolution by natural selection would offend those (including his wife) who believed in the literal story of Genesis.

But, apart from the elegance of his thinking, the elegance of his writing remains undiminished by time. Take this, the last paragraph of *The Origin of Species*:

There is grandeur in this view of life,
with its several powers, having been originally
breathed into few forms or into one; and that,
whilst this planet has gone cycling on according to
the fixed law of gravity, from so simple a beginning
endless forms most beautiful and most wonderful
have been, and are being, evolved.

In those days of the gentleman scholars, erudition and education went hand in hand. Take this thought:

"Men are called creatures of reason: more appropriately, they would be creatures of habit," as Darwin also noted.

DAN, DAN, THE THINKING MAN

Daniel Dennett, whom we met a few sections ago, is a leader among the AI (Artificial Intelligence) community. He has made major contributions to the study of Darwin, evolution and the mind–brain debate.

Like many others, he draws on a wide variety of disciplines to make his points: anthropology, AI, biology, evolutionary theory, game theory, physics and philosophy occupy the bulk of his intellectual output.

A great spinner of metaphors, he ranks alongside his esteemed colleague in the Darwin wars, Richard Dawkins, as the militant atheists' branch of what Gould termed the 'Ultra-Darwinists'.

(For more on the feuding over Darwin's legacy, see Andrew Brown's thorough and witty analysis, *The Darwin Wars*).

In *Darwin's Dangerous Idea*, Dennett attempts to prove that Darwinism (specifically the modern synthesis of Neo-Darwinism) is indeed the "single best idea anyone has ever had". In fact, Dennett tries so hard he almost makes Darwinism a theory of everything, a solution to the Meaning of Life. He would claim that what he is attempting to carry off is a grand demystification of such traditions as the origins of life and the evolution of consciousness, and a lucid analysis of the implications of taking Darwinism to its logical conclusions: the possibility of design without a designer, meaning deriving from meaninglessness and the human self as a product of the same blind algorithms.

As well as exploring Darwinism, free will, memetics and other mind–body issues, he is also a great neologist, a coiner of words and deployer of metaphors. He defines Darwinism as a 'universal acid' that eats through any domain it comes into contact with.

When discussing Darwinian complexity as opposed to faith and miracles, he distinguishes between those who believe in 'skyhooks' (miraculous top-down philosophy with no foundation) and 'cranes' which are founded in bottom-up Darwinian thinking (which he espouses). For many, this thinly veiled attack on religion and philosophical espousal of atheism puts him in the same demonized category as Richard Dawkins.

DAWKINS: THE GENE GENIE

One of the most eminent heirs of Darwin is the ethologist, biologist and outspoken atheist, Richard Dawkins. Similarly to Charles Simonyi, Professor for the Public Understanding of Science at Oxford University, he came to stand for the view that science is the unique standard-bearer of enlightenment and rationality.

He made his name with *The Selfish Gene*, which promoted a gene-centred view of evolution, with humans as mere 'survival machines', empty vehicles or 'lumbering robots' for the transmission of genes. This was not universally popular and there are those who think that the gene-centred view of Darwinism remains incomplete, for example in terms of epigenetics or group selection.

At the end of *The Selfish Gene* he posited the idea of a cultural unit that could self-replicate in the same way as the gene: thus was born the 'meme'.

But you can look through his work and find other great metaphors and language, such as *The Blind Watchmaker* or *Climbing Mount Improbable*. In the latter, he used a geographical metaphor to illustrate how evolution proceeds incrementally and to dismiss claims that miracles are needed to create complexity.

In his TED talk and in his book *The God Delusion*, he described how humans are living in the 'Middle World'.

Dawkins argued that we are equipped to explain, understand or imagine neither the world of the submicroscopically small (quarks, atoms and the like) nor the astronomically vast or geologically timeless.

But the Middle World is the 'middle-scaled realm' or relatively narrow range of reality between the atomic and the cosmic, through which we are designed to navigate. But even here we are blinded by fictions that make it easier for us to swim economically and effectively through a world of social beings than a world of scientists, for whom quantum mechanics or the cosmological constant are facts of everyday life. Much may be forever beyond our grasp.

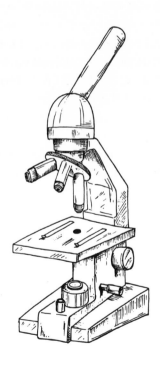

12. ERDŐS, BACON AND SABBATH

THE EBS: 3 MEASURES AND 6 DEGREES

Is there an index for versatility, polymathy and inspirational influence with some serendipitous playfulness?

We could do worse than look at those who perform well on the Erdős Bacon Sabbath (EBS) scale, a measure of creative diversity, connectedness and polymathy, albeit channelled through a mathematical lens.

To perform well on this measure you must demonstrate creative links to the mathematician Paul Erdős, the actor Kevin Bacon and heavy metal legends Black Sabbath. It is a source of pride for many to see what their EBS number is.

The index was the brainchild of Sean O'Connor (one of the self-declared "handful of over-educated dorks" behind *Timeblimp*, a science-related blog) and Ross Churchley, a graduate student from Vancouver, British Columbia, whose research field is graph theory. The two geeks joined up a couple of well-known indices of connectivity and added a new dimension.

Their website proudly proclaims:

"Anyone with a well-defined EBS number must have many talents and a fascinating backstory, but they turn out to be more numerous than you might think. The goal of this website is to discover these Renaissance men and women and to tell their stories."

Pure mathematicians had already lovingly designed a fun game ('fun' as defined by mathematicians at least) in honour of the Hungarian mathematician Paul Erdõs (1913-1996), who is said to have written around 1,500 articles alongside some 500 collaborators. Described in his *New York Times* obituary as "a mathematical pilgrim with no home and no job", Erdõs was famous for appearing on colleagues' doorsteps, staying for a few days, working on a paper, and then leaving suddenly.

At some point around the late 1960s, it became an exercise to see how close mathematicians could be to Erdõs. If you were one of the original collaborators, you had an Erdõs number of one; if you had co-written a paper with one of the originals you had a two, and so on.

This was based on the so-called 'six degrees of separation', also known as the mathematical principle of 'small world theory', an exploration of human interconnectedness characterized as a series of short paths and social networks. One of the seminal experiments was carried out by Stanley Milgram, though much of the thinking dated back to the 1920s. The expression 'six degrees of separation' was itself only popularized by the play of that name by John Guare, which premiered in 1990. The 1993 movie starred Donald Sutherland and Will Smith.

A BACON AND BAT SANDWICH

After Erdõs, the second and more mainstream component of the EBS index centred around the prolific actor Kevin Bacon and the calculation of one's 'Bacon number' (proximity to the legend).

Building on the notion of connectedness and a similar application to the world of Hollywood movies, it started with a claim in 1994 from the *Footloose* star that he had worked with pretty much everyone in Hollywood. Three students from Pennsylvania took him at his word and turned it into a parlour game for movie buffs: it led to an appearance on the Jon Stewart and Howard Stern shows, and A Meme Was Born. (That could be a remake of the classic Hollywood for the viral age.)

In 1999, Brett Tjaden established the 'Oracle of Bacon' using data from the *Internet Movie Database* to quantify the computation. As it turns out, Bacon is not the centre of the Hollywood universe: the most recent holder of that title was Eric Roberts, brother of Julia and star of *Star 80* and *The Coca Cola Kid*, yet labelled a "risky, no holds-barred actor" by the Internet Movie Database (IMDb).

The third leg of the cultural triumvirate is British band Black Sabbath. Famous for having more rotating members (35 including touring) than albums (19), their place at the centre of rock's pantheon was cemented when they played their final concert in their home city of Birmingham on 4 February 2017.

Despite all their successes, the larger-than-life antics of Ozzy Osbourne have always loomed over the group to such an extent that a Google search still offers "Ozzy Osbourne bat" as one of its top-ranked associations.

Yes, he did actually bite the head off a bat that was thrown on stage, in Des Moines, Iowa, on 20 January 1982. It was reported locally thus:

"Out of more than 18,000 nights in the 50-year history of the Veterans Memorial Auditorium [now the Iowa Events Center], the landmark night turned out to be a bloody decapitation."

And it was not his first decapitation either, this honour having been bestowed upon a dove in 1981.

Incidentally, in an ornithologically mixed metaphor, the *Des Moines Register* claims that subsequently the bat incident "became something of an albatross" for Ozzy.

And the EBS is a rare occasion where Bacon and Sabbath are such close neighbours.

EBS NEWS

What the Erdõs Bacon Sabbath index demonstrates is that there are elite polymath's, heroes of the Inspiratorium, the polymaths' polymaths.

In the light of the 'mathiness' of the measurement system, we could expect a plethora of scientists and mathematicians to have low EBS numbers (that is, close proximity to the heart of each of the three domains).

Indeed, we find Einstein, Thomas Edison, Stephen Hawking (who has performed alongside Pink Floyd, as well as appearing on *The Simpsons* and *The Big Bang Theory*), and Carl Sagan with arresting EBS numbers, as has the renowned theoretical physicist Professor Lawrence Krauss of Arizona State University. Another not altogether surprising contender is rock god and astrophysicist, Queen guitarist Brian May.

"I don't know a scientist who looks as much like Isaac Newton as Brian May," said Martin Rees, Britain's Astronomer Royal since 1995, and now Baron Rees of Ludlow.

Another star of EBS is Brian Cox, the English physicist and musician. Known for his work on the ATLAS experiment at the Large Hadron Collider at CERN, and for presenting a number of science programmes for the BBC, fans of 1990s Britpop/dance will recall that before that he was the keyboardist for the pop band D: Ream, whose track "Things Can Only Get Better" topped the UK charts when re-released in 1994 and was then borrowed by the Labour Party as their theme music for the 1997 General Election.

His Bacon score comes from the *Valiant* animated film about a pigeon with Jonathan Ross, who appeared in Cox's first series of *Stargazing* (2011). In *Valiant*, alongside a parade of British talent such as Ewan McGregor, Ricky Gervais, Hugh Laurie, Jim Broadbent and Rik Mayall, was John Hurt; Hurt provides the link to Kevin Bacon from *Jayne Mansfield's Car* (2012), a family drama set in 1969 Alabama, directed and co-written by Billy Bob Thornton.

SOME SURPRISING CONNECTORS

But as part of our exploration of inspiration, connectivity and serendipity, the EBS throws up some rather more unlikely cross-cultural connectors, especially among the acting fraternity.

The British actor and star of *The King's Speech*, Colin Firth, gets a Bacon score of 1 for starring alongside Kevin in *Where The Truth Lies*, directed by Atom Egoyan (2005), and his appearance in the Abba movie *Mamma Mia* allows him access to a 4 on the Sabbath scale. Rather more surprisingly, he can claim an Erdõs 6 score on the basis of being named one of four co-authors of a paper on the neuroscience of political leanings ("Political Orientations Are Correlated with Brain Structure in Young Adults"), published in the journal *Current Biology* in April 2011, after he edited a BBC Radio 4 programme and commissioned the research.

Lisa Kudrow may have shot to stellar fame as Phoebe Buffay on *Friends* and may be remembered for "Smelly Cat"; but before her break into acting, she graduated in biology from Vassar College, New York, and spent eight years researching headaches. A 1994 paper she co-authored with her father on the effect of handedness on headaches boosts her EBS index.

Another scientist who has since achieved spectacular sitcom stardom is Mayim Bialik. Before appearing as the neurobiologist and long-suffering consort of Sheldon Cooper, Amy Farrah Fowler, she played the young Bette Midler in *Beaches*, having made her big break in the sitcom *Blossom*, several episodes of which were directed by Bill Bixby (Bruce Banner in *The Incredible Hulk*, 1978). She appeared in Michael Jackson's video "Liberian Girl"; Michael Jackson's "Give in to Me" featured Guns 'n' Roses guitarist Slash. From Slash it is but one small step away to Black Sabbath.

Before all this, Bialik gained a PhD in neuroscience and contributed to an article titled "Sensorimotor Integration in Agenesis of the Corpus Callosum".

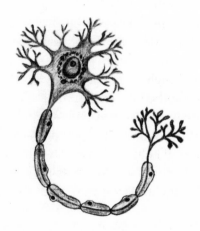

THE OTHER BLACK SWAN

Another surprising scientist with an impressive EBS score is Natalie Portman.

In 1994, Portman came to prominence in the role of an orphaned 12-year-old child who befriends a middle-aged hitman (played by Jean Reno) in Luc Besson's film *Léon: The Professional*. Soon after getting the part, she abandoned her original surname of Hershlag and adopted her paternal grandmother's maiden name, Portman. This role was followed by that of Padmé Amidala in the *Star Wars* prequels.

In 2010, she won the Oscar in Darren Aronofsky's *Black Swan*, a psychological horror about a young ballerina and not (as some readers might imagine) a big-screen version of Nassim Nicholas Taleb's book on the unpredictability of outlying events referred to earlier (though I would pay good money to see that movie, maybe with Robert Duvall as Taleb).

But her appearance on the EBS scale dates back to her student days when Portman co-authored two research papers that were published in scientific journals: a 1998 high school paper, "A Simple Method to Demonstrate the Enzymatic Production of Hydrogen from Sugar", co-authored with scientists Ian Hurley and Jonathan Woodward, and a study on memory called "Frontal Lobe Activation During Object Permanence: Data from Near-Infrared Spectroscopy" during her psychology studies at Harvard.

THE ELEMENTS OF CONNECTIVITY

In *The Big Bang Theory*, Amy's companion and uber-geek Sheldon Cooper is prolific with his science and pop-science references. The show itself is littered with suitably geeky guest-stars: from Stephen Hawking, to Neil deGrasse Tyson to Apple cofounder Steve Wozniak and astronaut Buzz Aldrin.

But true science aficionados will appreciate the moment when Sheldon goes on stage and starts to perform "The Elements" by Tom Lehrer (Series 3 Episode 18). Written in 1959 by the Harvard lecturer turned musical satirist and performer, it lists all elements known at the time to the tune of the "Major General's Song" from Gilbert and Sullivan's *Pirates of Penzance*.

As evidence of Lehrer's satirical bent, witness the title of one of his albums, *An Evening Wasted with Tom Lehrer*, or have a listen to songs like "Poisoning Pigeons in the Park" or "The Masochism Tango".

"The Elements" was also performed by Daniel Radcliffe on the BBC's *Graham Norton Show* in 2010, one of many virtuoso performances Radcliffe is wont to deliver: on the *Jimmy Fallon Show* in 2014, Radcliffe delivered a rendition of "Alphabet Aerobics" by rap duo Blackalicious.

Perhaps the finest acknowledgement of Lehrer's influence was his own comment:

"If, after hearing my songs, just one human being is inspired to say something nasty to a friend, or perhaps to strike a loved one, it will all have been worth the while."

After our scientific odyssey, we have found:

- The limits of our control, how far our desire for certainty can mislead us.
- The Hidden Figures behind NASA and how 'computers' have changed.
- We've looked at the role of memes and models and covered everyone from Darwin, Dennett and Dawkins to Derren Brown and the Black Swan.
- The Erdős Bacon Sabbath index has been a metaphor for the Inspiratorium: a measure but also a demonstration of the virtues of genre and domain-hopping.

THIRD FLOOR: THE ARTS ROOM

13. THE CLASSICS LIBRARY

Now let's spend some time in the company of the arts, the humanities and one side of what C. P. Snow, the English novelist–scientist, famously defined as "The Two Cultures", in a 1959 speech in Cambridge.

Historically, a solid grounding in the Classics was a crucial component of an education in the arts. Without necessarily having to cling on to that idea, let us look at the abiding influence of the Classics, and uncover a few surprising classicists and classical influences.

ADVENTURE OF A LIFETIME?

Shall we start with Chris Martin?

Formerly 'Pectoralz', then 'Starfish', Chris Martin, Jonny Buckland, Guy Berryman and Will Champion settled on the name 'Coldplay' in 1998. "Yellow" was released to massive acclaim and sales in 2000, and since then they have won pretty much every music award on the planet.

Martin is their frontman, multi-instrumentalist and chief songwriter. He also seems to be up there with the likes of Michael Palin as a candidate for Britain's Nicest Man.

While at University College London (where he met Buckland), he read Ancient World Studies and graduated with First-class Honours in Greek and Latin.

There may be some vestige of his classical education in his religious views. Having claimed in a 2005 *Rolling Stone* interview that he definitely believed in God, he later elaborated by claiming to be an

'all-theist' (his term for 'Omnism', a word coined in 1839 for those who recognise and respect all religions, and counting among its few followers the actress Ellen Burstyn).

But he suggested that, rather than Mohammed, Jesus or Buddha, he'd "go for Zeus".

THE BRAINS

Susan Greenfield, now Baroness Greenfield, is a British neuroscientist and writer, specializing in consciousness and Parkinson's disease.

One of the 'people's peers' introduced into the House of Lords by Prime Minister Tony Blair in 2001, she is equally at home in the commercial sector and is president of a biotech company called Neuro-Bio. She also has 30 honorary degrees and is not afraid of courting controversy, either with her dress sense or her views on technology-induced mind change.

Another multidisciplinary wanderer, her academic beginnings were with the Classics: she took Latin, Greek and Ancient History (as well as Maths) at A-level and took entrance exams to Oxford in Classics before switching to philosophy and psychology.

From her interview with *Prospect* magazine, her response to "If I ruled the world" was a heartfelt plea for the Classics:

If I ruled the world, I would reintroduce the Classics into all schools. I get very angry when people label Greek and Latin as elitist, or dismiss them as simply dead languages. It's my firm belief that everyone would benefit from studying them, irrespective of the path they choose in life afterwards.

She is a former President of the Classical Association and currently Senior Research Fellow at Lincoln College, Oxford.

Lincoln was founded in 1427 by Bishop Fleming (and is my old alma mater, since you ask), and famous alumni include the American writer Theodor Seuss Geisel, who met his wife Helen at Oxford. She suggested he abandon his plan to become an English professor in favour of following his art as Dr Seuss.

Another alumnus is David Cornwell, who would later assume the name of John Le Carré; he ended his time at Lincoln with a First-class degree in Modern Languages as well as gathering information for British Intelligence, which inspired his later career as an author of espionage novels.

DIDO (NOT AENEAS)

Or to give her full name, Dido Florian Cloud de Bounevialle O'Malley Armstrong. Her debut album *No Angel* in 1999 was an immediate hit and she achieved popularity first in the US where one of her tracks, "Here With Me", was used as the theme for the TV series *Roswell*. Her brother Rowland (a.k.a. Rollo) is part of electronic band *Faithless*.

Interest in Dido accelerated after the opening verse of her track "Thank You" was also sampled by Eminem for his 2000 track "Stan". She also featured in the video as the girlfriend of the Eminem-obsessed fan, Stan.

But in this context, we know her as someone who studied Latin, Greek and philosophy for A-level.

Named after the founder and queen of Carthage, in modern-day Tunisia, she carries her classical antecedents lightly.

YOU CAN BANK ON TELLER

Penn and Teller are rather special American magicians and entertainers.

They have worked as a team since 1981, and to categorize them just as magicians or even illusionists is to do them a major disservice.

I saw their Las Vegas show with my family back in 2007, and we were privileged to talk to them backstage (and talk, as even the famously silent Teller spoke to us).

Penn Jillette, known for his association with Teller, is also an actor and musician as well as a prominent atheist, Libertarian and sceptic to boot; he is enormously indebted to arch-debunker, sceptic and Darwin lookalike, James Randi. Penn and Teller hosted several seasons of the debunking documentary *Penn and Teller: Bullshit!* between 2003 and 2010 on the US Showtime channel.

But it is Penn's long-term partner and famous mononym who interests us here. Sharing the same sceptical, atheist Libertarian leanings as his partner, he has also co-directed Shakespeare and a documentary film, *Tim's Vermeer* (2014), about inventor Tim Jenison's obsession with 17th-century Dutch painter Johannes Vermeer.

As Raymond Joseph Teller, he studied Latin in high school and college and taught the subject at Lawrence High School, New Jersey.

A CLASSICAL MARVEL

Tom Hiddleston is one of the new group of young British actors whose rise to the global acting pantheon has been astronomical.

Stephen Colbert (he of 'truthiness' fame) invited the British actor onto his *Late Show* in March 2016 to promote Hiddleston's movie about Hank Williams, *I Saw the Light*.

During the interview, he invited Hiddleston to duet with him in a rendition of Williams' song "I Saw The Light", which is a genuinely moving moment.

If we can find it in ourselves to forgive him the 'Hiddleswift' debacle – the coupling and uncoupling of the relationship between Hiddleston and singer, songwriter and celebrity Taylor Swift – and assume charitably that it was a show-mance or faux-mance, this is more evidence of the rashness of becoming a celebrity blend.

Before he entered the Marvel Cinematic Universe, he played F. Scott Fitzgerald in Woody Allen's 2011 *Midnight in Paris*, appeared alongside King Kong in *Skull Island* and was the hero of the AMC/BBC series *The Night Manager* (based on the novel by Lincoln College, Oxford, alumnus John Le Carré). He even appeared in the Superbowl 2014 ad break as one of the three British villains in the Jaguar campaign (alongside Mark Strong and Sir Ben Kingsley).

But before all that, he was another fully licensed classicist, having achieved a double first in Classics at Pembroke College, Cambridge.

HOW TO BE HANDY

Charles Handy is one of the most renowned management thinkers.

A significant segment of the public may have even heard the term he coined in the 1980s, 'portfolio career.'

"If Peter Drucker is responsible for legitimizing the field of management and Tom Peters for popularizing it, then Charles Handy should be known as the person who gave it a philosophical elegance and eloquence that was missing from the field," says organizational consultant Warren Bennis.

Son of an Irish Protestant vicar, Handy sought a different path. He left Ireland for Oxford University, where he graduated in 1956 with First-class honours in Greats, the study of Classics, history, and philosophy, before starting his career at Shell.

His first book, *Understanding Organizations*, was written in 1976. This was followed by *Gods of Management*, in which Handy vividly deployed the metaphor of the Greek gods, learned from his classical education, to explain four different organizational cultures and how social change was reflected in their prevalence.

His later publications include *The Age of Unreason*.

Handy's philosophy is grounded in the belief that the organization can best be viewed as a social organism – a village – whereas much organizational theory still tends to assume organizations are, at heart, machines. Unlike most business writers, he has a keen ear for a handy metaphor, a sort of Dawkins of business.

TED TURNER: A BRAVE MAN

Media mogul, founder of CNN and philanthropist who donated $1 billion to create the United Nations Foundation, Ted Turner inherited his father's outdoor advertising business and expanded it to create a huge $10 billion media empire.

In 1976 Turner Broadcasting Systems (TBS) became the US's first superstation, using new satellite technology to carry its signal nationwide. In the same year he bought the Atlanta Braves baseball team.

No shrinking violet, he was nicknamed 'mouth of the south' and once challenged media rival Rupert Murdoch to a fistfight.

Educationally, Turner's father had hoped his son would go to Harvard, but he didn't make the grades. Instead he attended another Ivy League college, Brown, where he majored in Classics before switching to economics, only to be found with a girl in his room. This led to his eventual expulsion.

What makes Turner's relationship to the classics rather more poignant is his father's response to his son's academic choice.

The full letter is in the public domain because Turner later sent it to Brown as an act of defiance, only for them to publish it. The full 1,000-odd words are worth reading, but here is an excerpt:

———————

My dear son,

I am appalled, even horrified, that you have adopted
Classics as a major. As a matter of fact, I almost
puked on the way home today. ... I am a practical man,
and for the life of me I cannot possibly understand
why you should wish to speak Greek. With whom will
you communicate in Greek? ... I think you are rapidly
becoming a jackass and the sooner you get out of that
filthy atmosphere, the better it will suit me. ...
You are in the hands of the Philistines and, dammit,
I sent you there. I am sorry.

Devotedly,
Dad

———————

DAVID W. PACKARD: FROM PAST TO FUTURE

William Hewlett and David Packard founded their
eponymous company in 1938 in a garage in Palo Alto,
California. Fast-forward to 2000 and their heirs, espe-
cially Packard's son David W. Packard, were publicly
opposing the proposed $24 billion takeover of rival
Compaq by means of the David and Lucile Packard
Foundation, which held a significant 10.4% percent of
Hewlett-Packard's shares.

But rather than look to the future and technology
as his father did, the younger Packard turned to the
past and became a Classics professor. He developed

into a dedicated student of historical documents, publishing a book in 1974 on Minoan Linear A, one of the two scripts discovered by Sir Arthur Evans that remain undeciphered.

This second-generation philanthropist founded the Packard Humanities Institute (PHI) in 1987 and, amongst various projects, built the Monterey Bay Aquarium.

Most recently the PHI opened a $150 million facility in Santa Clarita, California, to house the UCLA film and TV archives. It announces that it is dedicated to the storage, conservation and study of "our audio-visual heritage".

COLIN DEXTER: NO RE-MORSE?

Oxford's most celebrated detective is Inspector Morse – a grump with a penchant for the Jaguar Mark 2, real ale, Glenfiddich whisky, Wagner and crosswords. In this way, he reflected many of his creator's own interests.

The author of the Morse books, Colin Dexter, also wrote a book called *Cracking Cryptic Crosswords*. Why not just call it *Morse Code*?

Inspector Morse was a big hit on ITV and ran from 1987 to 1993 and 1995 to 2000, with the title character played by John Thaw, and despite Thaw's death the Morse franchise has continued with a successful spin-off, *Lewis*, featuring his erstwhile sidekick, and a prequel, *Endeavour*.

Dexter had studied Classics at Christ's College, Cambridge, and was a former Classics teacher (Corby Grammar School, Loughborough Grammar School) and a Chief Examiner in Classics. In an interview with Strand Magazine he revealed:

———

One of the things I learned when I studied the Classics and taught them was *Initium est dimidium facti* – the beginning is half of the deed. I've never believed in writer's block because my own view about beginning to write is that you shouldn't think you're going to write the best first sentence or the best first paragraph. I used to think, I'm probably going to write the worst first sentence ever written. Once you've done that you're there, aren't you?

———

Dexter passed away at his home in Oxford on 21 March 2017.

SELECTED OTHER CLASSICISTS: I

If we widen the net to include those who studied Latin and/or Greek at (high) school, others come into view. We can start with Nick Owen, the veteran UK TV newsreader and presenter. Owen was one of the faces of UK's first breakfast television station, TV-am, in 1983 and later hosted *Good Morning with Anne and Nick* (alongside Anne Diamond) on the BBC. Prior to his career in journalism, he studied Classics at Leeds University.

Retired Chelsea, Manchester City and NYCFC and England football midfielder Frank Lampard took Latin GCSE at Brentwood School in Essex, achieving an A grade, an academic achievement that is rare among Premiership footballers. The closest some have got is through the medium of ink on skin rather than on papyrus or parchment.

On the subject of ink, former Manchester United and England footballer, the strangely-yet-to-be-knighted David Beckham, began his love of inking after the birth of his first child, Brooklyn, in 1999.

Beckham has tattoos in other languages, for example Sanskrit and Hebrew, but seems to have a special fascination with Latin. He continued his tattooing with the Roman numeral for seven (VII) – the number on his shirt for club and country in England, as well as fourth child Harper's middle name – on his inner arm. More Latin inkage followed, with *Ut Amem Ut Faveam* ("That I may love and cherish") on his inner left arm, and *Perfectio in Spiritu* on the inner right.

SELECTED OTHER CLASSICISTS: II

Eddie Izzard, the British comedian and actor, has toured and given shows in French, German and Spanish. It is said that he studied Latin at school.

Facebook founder Mark Zuckerberg studied Classics at Phillips Exeter Academy, New Hampshire, and listed Latin as one of the languages he spoke on his Harvard application. A bit of a closet classicist, he is known to quote lines from the *Aeneid* during Facebook product conferences and interviews, and now regards Latin as one of the keys to his success.

Another tech giant is Charles M. 'Chuck' Geschke, better known as one of the founders of graphics and software publishing behemoth, Adobe Systems. Before starting off as a research scientist at Xerox's Palo Alto Research Center (PARC), he studied classics and mathematics at Xavier University, Cincinnati. In a 2009 *Forbes* interview, he admitted that his ideal dinner guest would be Aristotle.

Back in the showbiz world, Vera Mindy Chokalingam, a.k.a. Mindy Kaling, is a writer and comedian who first came to prominence as Kelly Kapoor in the US version of *The Office*, on which she also acted as a writer and producer. She left that series to create and star in her own sitcom, *The Mindy Project*. Prior to that she studied at Dartmouth College, New Hampshire, where she started as a Latin major before taking up playwriting. A self-confessed Latin whiz, like Zuckerberg she seems to be specially keen on Virgil's *Aeneid*.

She is even known to tweet on the subject, employing a nice Latin insult to boot (*lupae filius* –

'son of a bitch') when the Superbowl stopped using Roman numerals.

Now let's go beyond classicists themselves and look at some of the abiding ways in which the Greek and Latin classics remain such a force for inspiration.

NO SEX, PLEASE, WE'RE ARISTOPHANIC COMEDY

If you tell someone "You're living in Cloudcuckooland" to criticize their unrealistic ambitions, you may be unaware that you are using a term invented by Greek comic writer Aristophanes in his play *The Birds* (414 BCE). It was also the name of the 1990 debut album by British band *The Lightning Seeds*.

Aristophanes' *Lysistrata*, originally performed in 411 BCE, is a bawdy Greek comedy in which the eponymous heroine gathers the women from the warring Athenian and Spartan sides in order to help end the Peloponnesian War by persuading them to deny their husbands sex. She encourages the older women to occupy the Acropolis in Athens where the treasury is held.

What makes *Lysistrata* so memorable for us nearly 2,500 years later is that its themes ring eternal: the desire for peace and harmony, the exercise of power, and the place of gender in politics. She is perhaps the first comic heroine in western literature, but we have to be careful not to be too anachronistic. In Greek comedy, as with tragedy, all the parts were played by men and in all likelihood the audience would have been laughing at rather than with Lysistrata ("A woman taking control? The very idea!").

But Lysistrata (literally 'she who dissolves or disbands armies') remains more than a metaphor because, like so many characters in classical Greek drama and comedy, she embodies universal human themes and truths, challenging us to look at ourselves through the prism of the past and the timeless.

STRIKE THREE – YOU'RE OUT...

The notion of a sex strike in modern times is more common than is thought.

In Colombia, it has been proposed several times to help end gang violence, leading to the use of the apt and elegant label '*La huelga de las piernas cruzadas*' ('the strike of crossed legs'). Other sex strikes have taken place in the Philippines, Sudan and Kenya.

Let's look at some examples of what activists refer to as 'Lysistratic non-action'.

The women of Naples, Italy, backed by the local authorities, pledged to refuse conjugal rights to their husbands, though in this case it was in the cause of preventing men from setting off illegal fireworks on New Year's Eve.

A local doctor put it with some diplomacy:

"The idea of no sex is not exactly popular and polls among local men have suggested they plan to make much greater efforts this year to prevent illegal fireworks being let off."

"Sex ban suggested for Belgian coalition negotiators," ran a BBC news headline in February 2011, when the Belgians had not managed to form a government

after 241 days of negotiations, because of traditional political fault lines between the Flemish, Dutch-speaking population and French-speaking Walloons.

"I call on the spouses of all negotiators to withhold sex until a deal is reached," said Socialist senator (and gynaecologist) Marleen Temmerman in an article for a Belgian newspaper. "Have no more sex until the new administration is posing on the steps of the Palace." Temmerman later hinted that her comments were meant as a joke, but the damage had been done. But, after 241 days, it's amazing that the Belgians could keep it up.

The last word should go to Christian Democrat senator Catherine Fonck for this observation:

"I do not want to take part in a sex strike. Politicians are not there to strike. On the contrary, politicians are there to arouse the country."

SPIKE LEE AND CHI-RAQ

Now for some cultural explorations that bring *Lysistrata* back into our lives and minds, constantly reminding us that sex and politics remain a potent cocktail.

First, Spike Lee.

The US filmmaker Spike Lee released *Chi-Raq* in 2015. A memorable film in many ways – not least for being the first movie funded by Amazon Studios – it was dogged by controversy, in no small part because locals (the film is set in Chicago) objected to what they felt was an inflammatory use of the name *Chi-Raq*.

This portmanteau term (Chicago + Iraq) – not to be confused with the French President from 1995 to 2007, Jacques Chirac – had been used by and of locals to describe the high levels of violent crime, especially black-on-black gun crime, with more Americans killed in the past 15 years in that city than in the Iraq and Afghanistan conflicts combined.

Described by various critics as a "blistering satire" of gang warfare in the US's third largest city, the film is classic Spike Lee, so it manages to be didactic (hectoring even), sexy, funny and musical, with characters speaking in verse.

Adapting the Aristophanic source material, it features gangs called Spartans and Trojans, a Greek chorus and Wesley Snipes as a Cyclops, with accompanying eye-patch. Lee translates the essence of Aristophanes to explore a different type of internal genocide, with Lysistrata's manifesto being translated into the succinct "No peace, no pussy."

Contemporary, if not always coherent, many felt it was Lee's best work in years.

CONSCIOUS OF 'UNCOUPLING'

Another adaptation of *Lysistrata* is the novel *Uncoupling* by Meg Wolitzer.

Wolitzer is an American novelist noted for *The Interestings*, an absorbing and astute story of compelling characters and shifting timelines. Six friends meet at summer art camp in the mid-1970s, proclaim themselves as 'The Interestings' and remain close for the next several decades. In 2016, it was turned into a TV movie.

This was Wolitzer's ninth novel, and in her eighth, *The Uncoupling* – which is set in suburban New Jersey – two events change the landscape and provide the thread for the story. New drama teacher Fran Heller arrives, and she announces that she will stage Aristophanes' *Lysistrata*.

In a departure from her previous work, Wolitzer introduces a touch of magical realism. A supernatural force or enchantment breezes into town, as a result of which the women just shut up shop (a hex on sex?). Unlike the original this is not a political decision; they simply stop feeling like sex.

It's sweet and it's touching but it's less overtly political than *Lysistrata*.

As with many adaptations, it asks us to look at our lives in a different way, but also invites us to reconsider the meaning of the original in a contemporary context.

ON THE ONE HAND, ON THE OTHER

Hellenophiles, or Greek students (more accurately, students of ancient Greek), will need no introduction to two small but perfectly formed particles, the quarks and leptons of classical grammarians.

Classical Greek authors frequently used 'μέν' and 'δέ' (pronounced 'men' and 'de') and they were a vital part of the Greek way of thinking and ordering. They are the matter and antimatter of Greek grammar, the skeleton on which are built antithetical clauses, opposition and revelation.

The Greeks were enthusiastic disciples of antithesis, alternatives and balance.

'μέν and δέ' work together to show weaker or stronger contrasts between thoughts, concepts, groups or sentences. As such they have been an invaluable part of the armoury of writers, speakers and orators from the sophists of Socrates' time all the way to today's politicians.

Insofar as they are translatable, the best way of explaining their sense is that together they mean 'on the one hand ... on the other', and they often work by establishing a proposition, only for the rug of 'but', 'however' or 'whereas' to be pulled from under it.

One of the favourite tropes of writing and thinking in Greek was the conceptualization of 'in word ... but in deed'.

This is a linguistic and conceptual way of making a number of statements or propositions, all of which hang on the contrast between appearance and reality:

- People said X was the case, but actually it was Y.
- At the time, X looked the like the explanation, but with time we can see it was Y.
- The speaker said X, but in fact meant Y.

BT AND AN '–OLOGY'

Logos in Greek is remarkably Protean, with meanings orbiting around a central core of 'language': it can mean anything from 'thought', 'speech', 'account' and 'meaning', to 'reason', 'proportion', 'study', 'principle', 'standard' or 'logic'.

This brings us to the British telecoms giant, the descriptively named British Telecom.

British Telecom (now BT) was associated with one of the most memorable commercials of the 1980s, created at the London office of JWT (J. Walter Thompson) by Richard Phillips.

The campaign featured a Jewish grandmother named Beattie (yes?) Bellman (got it now?), played by Maureen Lipman. The most famous ad in the series featured Beattie ringing her grandson to see how he had done in his exams. As she pores over the celebratory cake she has prepared in advance of his success, he tells her he has failed maths, English, physics, geography, German, woodwork and art. But, finally, and desperately, he reluctantly offers up that he did pass pottery ("Very useful," says Beattie. "People will always need plates.")...and sociology.

To which Beattie cheerfully responds:

"He gets an –ology and says he's failed. You get an –ology and you're a scientist."

The series of ads featured other notable actors of the era: Bernard Bresslaw (of *Carry On* film fame), Miriam Margolyes, a pre-*One Foot in the Grave* Richard Wilson, and Caroline Quentin as Beattie's daughter, Elaine.

While everyone then – and now – recalls Maureen Lipman's character and that dialogue, who can cite the end-line to that series of ads? It was in fact, "BT: It's You We Answer to."

BT AND AN '–OLOGY': THE SEQUEL

This corporate puffery, designed to rather awkwardly acknowledge the continued accountability that BT had to its customers, has not stood the test of chronological durability.

Which goes to show that often, advertising works best when it builds a character, a line of dialogue, an expression or a tone of voice rather than bombarding the audience with factual messages or corporate slogans. And often these details may be incidental.

The depth of feeling for the Beattie character and its cultural longevity was such that in 2014, then UKIP leader and Brexit cheerleader Nigel Farage could even cite it as a shared cultural totem for those of a certain age. He rather uncharitably blamed Maureen Lipman for encouraging too many young people to go university "to study poor-quality degrees and get an -ology".

Whatever one thinks of the political point being made, the fact that he can appeal to a cherished piece of shared cultural history says a lot for its potency.

This much-loved campaign ran until 1992, at which point the BT hierarchy decided on a change of direction.

Based on some insightful analysis, the company had come to the strategic judgement that it was not in the telephony, technology or even communications business: it was in the business of reciprocated confidences. A semiotic approach, this took the prescient view that the way to grow the business was by seeing the brand as enabling deeper human relationships through the sustenance of these small moments of exchanged confidences, especially among men, who still felt reluctant to engage in smalltalk on the phone.

The winning agency, Abbott Mead Vickers/BBDO, responded with one of the most enduring ideas of recent UK advertising history: "It's good to talk," fronted by Cockney hard man (but also star of Richard Williams's *Who Framed Roger Rabbit?*) Bob Hoskins. Hoskins had a direct appeal to men in particular, both encouraging them to open up on the phone and demonstrating that it wasn't a heavy financial cost either.

The "It's good to talk" campaign ran for five years from 1994 and analysts estimated it brought in something approaching £5 billion in revenue. Its residual adstock (to use a technical term) is such that a 2008 poll voted it one of the ten most commonly quoted ad slogans.

ECCE HOMO, THEN AND NOW

The Latin expression *Ecce homo* ('Behold the man') is said to have been uttered by Pontius Pilate, according to the Vulgate, the 4th century Latin version of the Bible largely prepared by Saint Jerome, which became the official version according to the Catholic Church.

Vulgate comes from the Latin *vulgus* and the word retains a shadowy presence in the word 'mob'. Dating back to the 1680s, it was a shortening of *mobile vulgus* – the fickle or excitable common people. Later in the US, especially when capitalized, it became synonymous with the Mafia. If you wish to pursue this further, I suggest you investigate the Mob Museum in Las Vegas, the National Museum of Organized Crime and Law Enforcement. Offering to "bring Mob stories to life so completely, you'll feel like you're part of them," and including an exhibition of the Mob's Greatest Hits and Nevada's first gas chamber, what's not to like or take the kids to?

The words of Pilate are found in John 16:5, and are pronounced as Christ is presented before his crucifixion.

Probably translated from the Greek, this scene is a key component of the Passion and Life of Christ in art: depictions include those of Titian, Bosch, Dürer and Caravaggio, among many others.

ECCE MEME

Ecce Homo is also used as the title of a representation in art of Christ crowned with thorns. Its natural home may also be considered as being in the Fail Room (Chapter 3), but we'll look at it here.

The painting in question was a 19th century Spanish fresco painted by Elías García Martínez. It was donated to the Centro de Estudios Borjanos in Borja, Spain, by the painter's granddaughter, and was on the walls of the Santuario di Misericordia, where it was deteriorating significantly. In 2012, a local octogenarian and amateur art restorer, Cecilia Giménez, took it upon herself to carry out an (allegedly) unsanctioned restoration, but the result was not considered a miracle; many described it as looking like a "blurry potato" or "a monkey".

The Spanish media dubbed it *Ecce Mono* ("Behold the monkey") or the "Potato Jesus". It found its way onto the face of the Mona Lisa, the Madonna and Child and The Last Supper, was the subject of a *Saturday Night Live* sketch with Kate McKinnon as a rather too Italian-sounding Giménez being interviewed by Seth Meyers, and even gained a Twitter handle (@FrescoJesus: "once a handsome fresco, now a hedgehog").

And those were the kinder assessments.

HOW MUCH LONGER?

We can all think of some Latin expressions that are now so deeply embedded in our language that we may have even forgotten their origin (*ad hoc*, *bona fide*, *et cetera*).

Some Latin expressions have surprisingly longer afterlives than others.

The inauguration of President Trump in 2017 brought one to prominence, after a picture was tweeted by @whitmanthesloth to the Cambridge Classics Professor, Mary Beard. She had already written a post in 2012 on her *A Don's Life* blog for the *Times Literary Supplement* (*TLS*) website talking about the history of this saying.

The placard shown in the picture bore a modified version of the Latin expression in question (substituting *Trumpolina* for the original *Catilina*):

Quousque tandem abutere, Trumpolina, patientia nostra?

Soon after this, the British Labour party lost the vote in the institutionally safe seat of Copeland, following the resignation of sitting Labour MP Jamie Reed. Conservative victor Trudy Harrison ensured that this was the first time a governing party had made a gain in a by-election since 1982. In response, former Chancellor George Osborne tweeted: "How much longer is the Labour party going to put up with its utterly useless, shambolic and frankly embarrassing leadership?"

Literally translated, the *Quousque* expression means: "How much longer will you abuse our patience?" Its continuing relevance may stem from its applicability to many manifestations of political or economic discontent.

The words come from the first of four speeches made by Marcus Tullius Cicero in 63 BCE. Cicero, a noted lawyer, politician, philosopher and orator, made a series of speeches in an attempt to prove to the Roman Senate that an aristocrat-turned-demagogue by the name of Lucius Sergius Catilina – commonly called Catiline – was plotting an insurrection against the Republic. The four speeches Cicero delivered helped convince the Senate to pass a *senatus consultum ultimum* – effectively the imposition of martial law – and drive Catiline and his fellow conspirators from Rome.

So popular was the saying that at least since the 18th century, *Quousque* was often used as dummy text for typesetting, alongside –*lorem ipsum*, which we met in Chapter 6.

Quousque still turns up in all sorts of places.

Other political uses have included a grievance against the mayor of Venice; a protest in October 2016 against the former speaker of the lower house of the Brazilian Congress, Eduardo Cunha, who was arrested in connection with a major corruption scandal; a lament about French politics; the title of an Italian book on *Forgotten Crimes of World War II* by Francesco D'Aurial; a satirical representation of Silvio Berlusconi online; at least two Twitter handles; and a blogspot.

The American online retailer Café Press sells a surprisingly broad range of *Quousque* merchandise: T-shirts, mugs, even a clock.

O TEMPORA!

Later on, in the opening paragraph of the same speech of Cicero against Catiline, we find another expression beloved of all schoolboys studying their Latin, namely, *O tempora, o mores!* (It also occurs in the fourth book of Cicero's second oration against Verres.)

Meaning literally "Oh the times, oh the customs!" it is almost endlessly flexible as an exclamation of woeful despondency at present-day trends, habits or corruption; a nostalgic (or even reactionary) lamentation that 'Things ain't what they used to be'; or a sense that 'Everything is going to hell in a handcart,' a failsafe cry of despair at the state of … whatever. (This usage is not to be confused with "O tempura, o mores!", a phrase I am prone to utter when the batter on my Japanese deep-fried vegetables fails to meet expected levels of perfection.)

O tempora has had a less roller-coaster history than *quousque*, but has been the title of a poem by Edgar Allen Poe and a joke by English musical comedians and gentle satirists Flanders and Swann in their 1963 musical revue *At the Drop of Another Hat*: they parodied the British press, translating the phrase as "O *Times*, o *Daily Mirror!*"

CRUZ CONTROL

US Republican senator Ted Cruz is no stranger to either of these Ciceronian allusions and has been by no means the first politician to invoke Greek or Roman references for contemporary political purposes.

Senator Cruz may have tried to assume some of the mantle of Cicero, a defender of the old order against an opponent he claimed was an upstart insurrectionist.

Ted Cruz veiled himself in Cicero's toga to decry an overreaching, imperialistic and unconstitutional leader (namely, in his eyes, Barack Obama). In a speech in February 2015, he channelled his inner Cicero and described the then-president as a "lawless imperator" (the Roman term for commander of the *imperium*).

At the time of writing, the most recent citation of this time is probably Imperator Furiosa, the character played by Charlize Theron in *Mad Max: Fury Road*, though when referring to a woman the correct term is *Imperatrix*.

But earlier, in November 2014, Cruz made his Cicero-worship and the forced parallel between Catiline and Obama even more explicit. He took a large chunk of the first *In Catilinam* ("Against Catilina") speech and modified it for his own political ends, starting with "When, President Obama, do you mean to cease abusing our patience?" and modifying *O tempora, o mores!* into "shame for the age and its lost principles".

Classics professor Jesse Weiner, writing in *The Atlantic*, argued that Cruz's rhetoric was inflammatory and deeply problematic, as well as inaccurate.

But whatever one believes about the parallel, it shows the continued vitality of Cicero's words.

ASTERIX: THE GALL OF THE MAN

While still talking Rome, let's also look at everyone's favourite diminutive Gallic resistance fighter.

Since 1959, Asterix has been the pint-sized hero standing up against the mighty Roman invaders, after Julius Caesar carried out a campaign from 58 to 50 BCE against Gaul. Asterix's village is unnamed but is said to be modelled on Erquy in Brittany, northwest France.

Created by René Goscinny and Albert Uderzo, the comics have been translated into 100 languages, adapted into movies and even inspired a dedicated theme park.

In the 17th book, *The Mansions of the Gods*, Julius Caesar tries once again to put down the Gallic rebellion, this time by cutting down the trees around their village and building in its place a Roman colony in the form of an apartment complex, called The Mansion of the Gods, a project to be supervised by the architect known in English as Squareonthehypotenuse.

To continue the campaign of non-violent irritation, Asterix arranges for the stridently grating bard, Cacofonix, to move into one of the apartments in the mansion in an attempt to terrify the occupants into leaving.

The occupants are at their wits' end and are heard (via speech bubbles) exclaiming, "The gods are angry!"; "The building's collapsing!"; "Start packing tomorrow – we're off." But in a knowing display of their Cicero, the writers also have the Romans saying *Quousque tandem? Quousque tandem?*

In this context, the meaning is something like: "Please stop! No more! We've had enough!"

HELL IN A HANDCART?

As we saw above with "O tempora, O mores", another exclamation that seems to be gaining in prevalence in these uncertain times is 'going to hell in a handcart'.

Let us explore for a moment the origin of this increasingly popular idiom, which now seems to have displaced 'going to the dogs'.

'Going to the dogs' itself lacks a clear origin. One source suggests an origin in ancient China where dogs were not permitted within the walls of cities. So, any stray dogs that roamed the areas outside the city walls lived off the rubbish thrown out of the city by its inhabitants. More outlying proposals are that it may be derived from 18th/19th century England, as – largely speaking – horsemeat wasn't considered suitable for human consumption, so old and knackered horses were most likely to be sent 'to the dogs'.

'Going to hell in a handcart' was used for example by former British prime minister David Cameron in 2011, when arguing that the recent riots reinforced his belief that a sizeable amount of money should be spent on so-called 'troubled families':

"The point is, this will save a fortune. More importantly, early intervention of this kind would also save a lot of lives that otherwise would go to hell in handcart."

Elsewhere, the *Daily Telegraph*'s assistant editor and financial writer Jeremy Warner advised against blaming an absence of credit for all the financial woes:

"We may be going to hell in a handcart, but it has little to do with absent credit."

In the US, the more commonly used form is 'hand-basket', 'handbag' or even, oddly enough, 'Harley'. But *Wikipedia* hides beneath the catch-all of "an expression dating back to the 19th century of unclear origin".

Our old friend alliteration has a great deal to do with it, no doubt.

However, the idea of the vehicle of choice to the Underworld being a wheelbarrow or cart does have some support.

In St Mary's Church in Fairford, Gloucestershire, there is a stained-glass window depicting a woman being wheeled in a barrow by a blue devil. This was installed before 1517, so the idea is at least 500 years old.

CICERO THE GUIDE

Before we leave the Roman orator Marcus Tullius Cicero, we may note that 'cicerone' is an old term for a guide: someone who conducts visitors and sightseers to museums, galleries and the like, and explains matters of archaeological, antiquarian, historic or artistic interest. In Italian, *fare da cicerone* means to show someone around or act as a guide.

The term is commonly considered to be taken from our old friend M. Tullius Cicero, in honour of his all-round learning and eloquence.

It is also the name of a publisher of guidebooks for walkers, based in Milnthorpe, in England's Lake District; the title of a Beer Certification Programme to train "expert beer sommeliers"; the name of someone at the US National Institute of Standards and Technology, who with colleagues introduced in 2004 the world's first broadband-coherent anti-Stokes Raman scattering microscope; and it is the name of the manual for understanding NASA's Fermi Gamma-Ray Space Telescope, "the tools that will enable you to derive astrophysical information from the lists of photons detected by Fermi's two instruments".

THE SUGABABES PARADOX

As avid excavators of the cultural zeitgeist, many of us are used to the modern philosopher-kings such as Julian Baggini and Alain de Botton trying their damnedest to bridge the gap between philosophy and life as lived by the rest of us. Try as they can, Zeno's paradox or the story of Epimenides (the Cretan who asserted that all Cretans are liars) just don't make much of a dent in the post-truth world of overcommunication and hyperchoice.

But hark: the fact that the English girl band Sugababes have philosophically ceased to be the Sugababes has unexpectedly brought this arcane conundrum to a broader audience, opening up philosophical shockwaves that might even exceed the boundaries of Twitter.

The Sugababes were formed by the manager of the band All Saints, when the three founding members were 13 or 14 years old. When the last of the three original members quit the band and was replaced, the question was: was this band still the Sugababes?

Others, especially those in the business of teaching recalcitrant philosophy students, will now have the opportunity to use their new-found media-savviness to try and "Push the Button" for their charges. Or even, heaven forefend, "Get Sexy."

Many cultures have their own example of this phenomenon highlighting the question of "When does X cease to be X?" The Americans have Washington's axe, and the French Jeannot's knife.

The BBC recently discovered this philosophical dilemma after the three star presenters of its driving programme, *Top Gear* – Jeremy Clarkson, Richard Hammond and James May – quit and effectively took their format (and characters) to Amazon, as *The Grand Tour*. The BBC replaced the three principals, but most of the audience concluded that *Top Gear* was no longer authentically *Top Gear*.

TAKE ME TO THE SAME, RIVER?

But if you didn't study Greek, you may be unaware of what is known in the trade as the Ship of Theseus, a philosophical thought experiment about identity and persistence, which is not dissimilar to the questions raised by Heraclitus about whether we can ever step in the same river.

The legend was first reported by Greek-turned-Roman-citizen, the 1st century CE biographer and essayist Plutarch.

This is one of a number of philosophical paradoxes used to explore issues such as essence and identity.

What does it mean to be the Sugababes? Can the new band have the same identity if the constituent parts are completely different? If Keisha, Mutya and Siobhán (the founding band members) formed a new band, would they be the true and only Sugababes?

Is this really about structure, shape and relationship, emotion, memory and history?

Is it true that in these cases the criteria for identity fail us?

Of course, these days, with broader issues of intellectual property (IP) and brand identity, these academic issues are no place for philosophical fainthearts. Some IP lawyers deal with these issues every day and need public discussion of this like a hole in the head.

So, maybe we can offer our thanks to the Sugababes, past, present and potential, for legitimizing debate of some troubling thoughts about the persistence of identity.

14. THE SCREENING ROOM

Where we take a look at a generation of 'Mad Men' from the UK who became the leading lights of Hollywood.

THE BRITISH ARE COMING...

The first generation of movie magnates who started off on the small screen all had roots in the London advertising scene of the 1960s.

Ridley (now Sir Ridley) Scott set up Ridley Scott Associates (RSA) in 1968 with his brother Tony.

They would go on to work with some of the greatest ad industry giants in London, such as Alan Parker and Hugh Hudson who worked at the Collett Dickenson Pearce advertising agency (CDP), one of the creative hubs at the heart of the London agency world that was the beating heart of the London creative scene during the revolutionary 1960s and beyond.

It was also the home of another copywriter, one Charles Saatchi, who would go on to make quite a name for himself in advertising and politics but not in banking. (In 1987, at the peak of the Saatchi and

Saatchi global dominion, the brothers made a bid to buy Britain's fourth-largest bank, the Midland. The bid failed, and the brothers were accused of hubris.)

Hudson created a series of ads for Benson & Hedges cigarettes, including the 'Swimming Pool Lizards' cinema spot in 1978, as well as the British Airways 'Face' ad, first aired in 1989 but a fixture globally for another ten years. This at the same time as he was building a career on the silver screen with *Chariots of Fire*, which gave the British film industry one of its regular fillips – and the belief that it might be more sustainable than ever seems to be the case.

Famously, the actor and screenwriter Colin Welland, when accepting the Academy Award for best original screenplay in 1982, announced "The British are coming." Apart from the hint at Anglo-American relations from the mid-18th century, it would prove to be an optimistic war cry for British moviemakers and cinemagoers bemoaning the chronic lack of investment in the UK film industry.

PARKER, WELL DONE

Alan (now Sir Alan) Parker himself moved from copywriting at CDP advertising agency to directing ads through his own company.

Always a natural storyteller with a gift for the comic touch, he moved on to writing and directing *Bugsy Malone* and, in a radical shift of tone, *Midnight Express*. He will always be held in fond regard, too, for *The Commitments* and *Evita*.

Ridley Scott gained fame for directing the Hovis bread ad known as 'Boy on Bike', shot on Gold Hill, Shaftesbury, Dorset and featuring a brass-band version of Dvořák's *Symphony No. 9*, which regularly features at the top of the most loved commercials in UK history.

Perhaps Scott's most enduring advertising legacy will be the 1984 Apple ad, created by Chiat/Day and taking its inspiration from George Orwell's *Nineteen Eighty-Four*. It was aired only twice: famously in Superbowl XVIII on 22 January 1984 (its only national airing), but it had been broadcast initially on 31 December 1983 so it could qualify for advertising awards.

One small detail: Big Brother is played by David Graham, an English character actor and voice-over artist, whom many of us will automatically recognize as being the voice of several characters from the puppet (sorry, Supermarionation) series *Thunderbirds*, a highlight of 1964-66. He notably supplied the voices of Brains and Lady Penelope's trusted chauffeur, Parker (no relation to Sir Alan, if only because he is a puppet).

Graham reprised the role of Parker in the modern, CGI-based 2015 reboot, *Thunderbirds Are Go*, at the age of 91.

END OF THE LYNE?

In the same British wave was Adrian Lyne, another alumnus of the CDP advertising agency, who started in the mailroom at J. Walter Thompson (JWT) in London before making ads for Brutus Jeans among others. Brutus was founded by the Freedman brothers at the ages of 17 and 18 respectively.

The jingle "I put my Brutus jeans on," written and performed by David Dundas, was then released as "Jeans On" and reached number three in the UK singles chart in 1977; it was even recorded in a French version.

After making his big screen debut in 1980 with *Foxes*, Lyne garnered attention by developing his bravura visual style for *Flashdance* in 1983. He then moved into more controversial terrain with *9½ weeks* in 1986 and the massive blockbusters *Fatal Attraction* in 1987 and *Indecent Proposal* in 1993.

Among those who trod the same path, we could also add Lindsay Anderson, Stephen Frears, Karel Reisz, Richard Loncraine, Ken Russell, Tony Scott and Peter Greenaway.

SURFING UK...

Tick followed tock followed tick followed
tock followed tick...

In November 2009, *The Independent* newspaper named the Guinness "Surfer" ad amongst the greatest advertising of all time, and in 2002 it was voted the "Best Ad of All Time" in a poll conducted by Channel 4 and the *Sunday Times*. It was directed by Jonathan Glazer and aired in 1999.

The inspiration came from *Moby-Dick*, combining pulsating beats with the art of 19th century English painter and book illustrator Walter Crane, specifically "Neptune's Horses"; it featured horses galloping through the surf as a Polynesian surfer attempts to ride an enormous wave.

Equally memorable and pioneering is Glazer's work on the Sony Bravia "Paint" ad, created by the Fallon agency and the much-anticipated successor to the startling and charming "Balls" commercial which used 250,000 real balls on the real streets of San Francisco to create an exuberant riot of colour.

Set to a classical soundtrack (Rossini's *Thieving Magpie* overture), a spectrum of paint is cascaded all over a drab-looking housing estate in a balletic firework display.

Some 70,000 litres (15,000 gallons) of paint were used and it needed over 200 people to make the ad. Other relevant information: it required 58 single bottle bombs, 33 sextuple air cluster bombs, 2 triple-hung cluster bombs, 268 mortars, 33 triple mortars, 22 double mortars, 330 metres (360 yards) of steel pipe and 57 km (35 miles) of copper wire.

The high-rise flats in Toryglen, Scotland, were finally destroyed by a controlled explosion in January 2007.

OTHER DIRECTORS ARE AVAILABLE

A selection of other directors at ease in the world of commercials might encompass:

Spike Lee: take, for instance his 1991 Nike Air Jordan ad, featuring Lee himself and Jordan, but most jarringly Little Richard as Aladdin's genie, whose turn is worth 30 seconds of anyone's time.

Spike Jonze, who was born Adam Spiegel, but received his nickname in honour of the leader of Spike Jones and his City Slickers, an arranger of satirical versions of big band classics such as "Cocktails for Two", a huge hit in the 1940s and an inspiration for the likes of The Goons, Bonzo Dog Doo-Dah Band (in the UK) and "Weird Al" Jankovic in the US.

Jonze started off directing music videos for Fatboy Slim ("Rockafeller Skank" and "Praise You").

Then there was the award-winning video for "Weapon of Choice", filmed in the lobby of the then Marriott Hotel in Los Angeles in December 2000, featuring actor Christopher Walken, who had previously trained as a dancer before his acting career. It featured Walken dancing and flying around in the empty hotel in time to the music.

Add to this his work on "It's Oh So Quiet" for Björk, "Da Funk" for Daft Punk, not forgetting

"The Suburbs" for Arcade Fire, for whom he also directed the live performance of "Afterlife" from the *Reflektor* album, at the 2013 YouTube music awards, featuring the actress Greta Gerwig.

Finally, Michel Gondry similarly emerged from the advertising and music video world, and like Jonze got one of his biggest breaks working alongside Björk on "Human Behaviour" in 1993.

At about the same time he made the Levi's "Drugstore" ad, set in the US in the 1920s or 1930s but with a techno beat, followed by a spot for Smirnoff "Smarienberg", a dazzling high-octane series of minimovie set-pieces.

OVER 'ERE, SON, ON ME 'EAD!

This was a line from the "Hamlet" ad, one in the memorable and successful campaign from the mid-1980s for the British beer brand Carling Black Label (now known more snappily as "Carling").

It knowingly played on a bit of football language that would be known to its young, sport-loving and beer-drinking audience.

After a rather dull and combative semifinal of the Champions League between two of England's minnows (due disclosure: I am a Manchester United fan), Liverpool and Chelsea, Jorge Valdano, coach and the former general manager of Real Madrid, let rip in the Spanish paper *Marca*:

"Chelsea and Liverpool are the clearest, most exaggerated example of the way football is going: very intense, very collective, very tactical, very physical, and very direct," he said. "But, a short pass? Noooo. A feint? Noooo. A change of pace? Noooo. A one-two? A nutmeg? A backheel? Don't be ridiculous. None of that. The extreme control and seriousness with which both teams played the semifinal neutralized any creative licence, any moments of exquisite skill."

As if to demonstrate his own artistic finesse in an industry often known for its banality and lack of "exquisite skill", he made his point about the passion of the game and the fans' (in this case from Anfield, home of Liverpool) overwhelming their ability to discern genuine talent and skill.

"Football is made up of subjective feeling, of suggestion – and, in that, Anfield is unbeatable. Put a shit hanging from a stick in the middle of this passionate, crazy stadium and there are people who will tell you it's a work of art. It's not: it's a shit hanging from a stick."

Less colourfully, Valdano put the blame squarely on the two coaches of the teams, but what is most relevant to the argument here is that he accused them of failing the beauty of the game because of their "desire to have everything under control".

THE USEFULNESS OF USELESSNESS

Finally, let us end with another great piece of writing, another great title. "On the Usefulness of Useless Knowledge" was a paper penned in 1939 by Abraham Flexner, the founding Secretary General of the Institute for Advanced Study in Princeton. Reprinted in 2017, his fluid prose argues in favour of enquiry unfettered by short-termism and pragmatic utilitarian objectives, which he saw as a threat in the 1930s and which (I would argue) remain stubbornly entrenched in the modern age.

Flexner believed in abstract knowledge for its own sake, in creating a space for nurturing "curiosity, freedom and imagination".

At the time, he could point to the invention of electromagnetism, lasers and X-rays as proof of his theory.

In today's prevailing mood towards accountability and applied research, of increasing compartmentalization and the echo-chamber effect, we need to bring back the joy of learning, to encourage all forms of combinatorial creativity and cross-pollination.

In our final leg of the tour, the Classics and Arts Room, we have:

- Witnessed a bevy of Borises and orators from Cicero to Ted Cruz;
- Had our fill of Handy and Hiddleston;
- Observed the parenting skills of Ted Turner's father;
- Stopped off at Oxford to visit Morse;
- Explored the modern-day relevance of a 2,000-year-old sex strike.

EXIT:
BEFORE YOU LEAVE...

IV

EXIT...

Before you leave the Inspiratorium, we crave a moment of your time.

We hope you will have picked up some useful thoughts and connections and that your magpie, unconscious System 1 will be voraciously incubating and creating new improbable free associations now and in the future.

These will stir themselves, bubble vigorously and stimulate unanticipated and fortuitous thoughts that will find a welcome asylum when you least expect it.

But to outline a few pieces of System 2 consciously directed output, we can suggest that the way to breed a brain, a company and a culture of inspiration would be to take some of the lessons of serendipitous discovery on display here.

Let us imagine instead a world of countries-hyphen-nations, if you like, where hyperlinked wandering and wondering is the norm, where the Inspiratorium is the blueprint for lifelong learning, where playfulness, fun and the joy of learning are not only condoned but encouraged, where education is not sturdily segregated from entertainment and fun, and conventions are not revered as gods, and where no one says "leveraging synergies" – or if they do, it is punishable with a remedial spell in a brutal correctional facility run by economists, accountants and people who work in procurement.

What would such a world look like? On what principles would it be run? Would it still have performance targets and impact assessments?

For all the 'upskilling', there would be joyous discovery and paths that lead to as yet unknown destinations. Righteous certainty would be outlawed and a Socratically informed creative doubt would be fostered across boundaries.

PRINCIPLES FOR LIVING WITHIN AND WITHOUT THE INSPIRATORIUM

We could start by ensuring that a modern understanding of human behaviour, its biases and prejudices is a part of the curriculum as soon as practically possible. If we want to understand the issues facing our nations, cultures and indeed our species, we need to be fully equipped with an understanding of how we reach decisions and the biases that often impede us from coming to the optimal decision: the new thinking collected under the heading of "behavioural economics" is the best place to start.

If, first as children and then later as consumers and citizens, we become familiar with the workings of our mind – how it can mislead us, how much of what we think is happening now is merely echoes of decisions-long-made, the power of context, emotions and the need to conform – we will surely be better equipped to buy, to vote, to parent, to learn and to act. Any attempt at introducing critical thinking within the educational system to prepare the citizens of the future will be hampered unless accompanied by such an understanding of the software that evolution has equipped us with: not just its crowning glories, but the bugs that are part and parcel of the system.

Finally, some last thoughts to take with you as you leave the Inspiratorium:

- Use the Inspiratorium as a 'Collide-a-scope' that allows unconnected thoughts to collide into new visions and insights.
- Try to be less of a One Big Idea hedgehog and aim for the wily versatility of the fox.
- In order to let your unconscious System 1 run riot with ideas, make sure you stand back and 'JOOTS' (jump out of the system).
- Remember to let the connections and links froth and bubble in the most convenient incubator – be it bed, bath or bus.
- Look for juxtaposition, peripeteia and the unexpected 'haha!' jolt of surprise: you'll find these most when you seek out external serendipitous influences (ESIs) and the joy of serendipity, rather than via linear or sequential processes.
- Be an oblique outsider: from wandering comes wondering. And this at a time when diversity and inclusiveness are on everyone's lips, and critics and the public are lauding a film about

a mute cleaner falling in love with an amphibious alien, which in writer-director Guillermo del Toro's words is about "embracing the other".

- Like Charlie Kaufman, be an anomaly-seer, a genre-hopping Protean: this will, in Ronald Burt's words, "put you at risk of having good ideas".
- Encourage and endorse failure and error. Stay foolish and naïve. Notice the negligible. Break in order to reveal.
- Search for harpoons. Love language in all its playfulness and deceptiveness.
- Acknowledge your constraints: as Anaïs Nin said, "We don't see things as they are. We see things as we are."

I can only hope that your journey into the Inspiratorium has given you a sense of these horizons, both at the conscious or unconscious level.

– THE END –

NOTES AND ACKNOWLEDGMENTS

ACKNOWLEDGMENTS

Thanks to Martin, Sara and Liz for the constant nudging, support and patience in the face of, well, me.

As ever, a big shout out (if only to embarrass them) to Josh, Zach and Saskia, and to all those who have contributed Earl Grey tea and occasional donations of confectionery.

Above all to Egg, for pretty much everything else.

NOTES: INTERLUDE ANSWERS

I)   BLEND IT LIKE BECKHAM

1. Güggle,
2. The i-Kia,
3. Scottish Windows,
4. Von Haagen-Daz
5. Clear Chanel no. 5

II)   SPOILER ALERTS

a) "You maniacs! You blew it up! Ah, damn you! God damn you all to hell!": The ending of the original *Planet of the Apes*

b) Kevin Costner was the spy all along: *No Way Out*

c) The Verbal Kint revelation: *The Usual Suspects*

d) Malcolm Crowe's shocking realization: Bruce Willis's anagnorisis in *The Sixth Sense*

e) Who is Tyler Durden? But we don't talk about it, except about the Pixies' "Where is My Mind?": *Fight Club*

f) Nicole Kidman, Christopher Eccleston and their two children: Gothic horror *The Others*

g) Gwyneth Paltrow's head in a box (no, not a meal solution): *Se7en*

h) Residents of a 19th-century commune aren't what they seem: Shyamalan's *The Village*

i) Two rival magicians in 19th century London (double twist – and David Bowie): Christopher Nolan's *The Prestige*

j) Leonardo di Caprio investigates a disappearance at a hospital for the criminally insane: *Shutter Island*

k) Dutch film (remade in US) with the protagonist buried alive (Kiefer Sutherland in the US version): *The Vanishing*

l) Dorothy has a bad dream: Really?

m) Two people on the Starship *Avalon*: *Passengers*

n) Tim Robbins as a traumatized Vietnam war veteran finds out that his postwar life isn't what he believes it to be: *Jacob's Ladder,* directed by Adrian Lyne

o) 1955 French film: corpse in bathtub: *Les Diaboliques*

p) Keira Knightley and James McAvoy don't actually get together at the end: *Atonement*

q) A Nobel Prize-winning mathematician has imaginary friends: Russell Crowe as John Nash in *A Beautiful Mind*

r) 1953 Vincent Price horror: *House of Wax*

s) Edward Woodward, Christopher Lee 1973: *The Wicker Man*

t) Dil isn't who Stephen Rea thought: *The Crying Game*

u) Second Charlton Heston appearance where he discovers the secret of a processed food: *Soylent Green*

v) The main character dies a third of the way through the movie: amongst others, *Psycho*

w) A six foot rabbit named Frank: *Donnie Darko*

III) PALINDROMES

1. The most famous Scandinavian band: Abba
2. One of their biggest hits, from 1975: "SOS"
3. The name of an album recorded by Black Sabbath and Miles Davis (separately): *Live Evil*
4. Another famous Scandinavian Band, Norwegian specifically: Aha
5. Walter O'Reilly's nickname in MASH: Radar
6. Dictionary definition: "made into, or treated as, a god": Deified
7. A one-man canoe: Kayak
8. Kevin Kline's character in *A Fish Called Wanda*: Otto
9. The main character in *Holes*: Stanley Yelnats
10. "My brother's keeper's" mother: Eve.

AN INTRODUCTION TO ANTHONY TASGAL

Tas is a man of many lanyards.

He runs his own training company and is a course director for the Chartered Institute of Marketing, the Market Research Society and the Civil Service College, teaching courses on storytelling, behavioural economics, and insightment, among others, in the UK, US, China, Australia, Sweden and UAE.

He is also a long-term ad agency strategist, an associate lecturer at London College of Communications, Bucks New University, Nottingham Trent and Beijing Normal Universities, and regularly speaks at international conferences.

His first book, *The Storytelling Book*, is an award-winning guide to using storytelling techniques to improve presentations and communication.

Sharing knowledge since 1993

- 1993   Madrid
- 2008   Mexico DF and Monterrey
- 2010   London
- 2011   New York and Buenos Aires
- 2012   Bogotá
- 2014   Shanghai